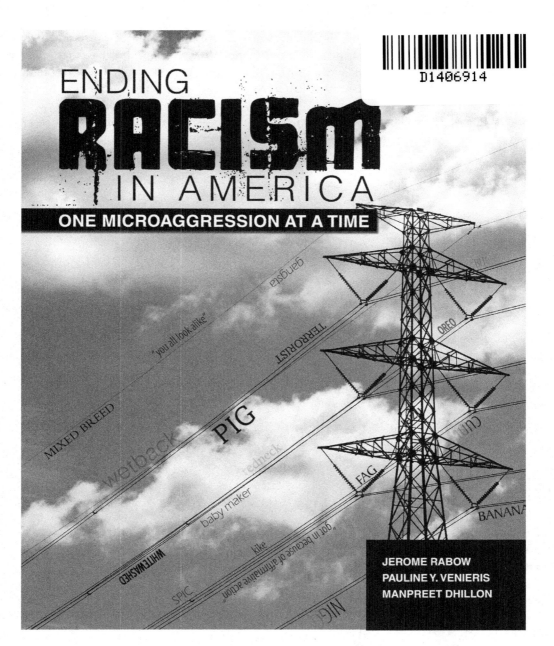

ENDING RACISM IN AMERICA
ONE MICROAGGRESSION AT A TIME

JEROME RABOW
PAULINE Y. VENIERIS
MANPREET DHILLON

With the Assistance of Heidi Joya, Yvette Meza-Vega, Jennifer Moore, Sophie Nazerian, Katya E. Rodriguez
Foreword by David Lopez

Kendall Hunt
publishing company

This book is dedicated to the thousands of students who have trusted us with their fears and their hopes that these stories will lead to personal and collective healing. All of you have shown us that America can move toward its ideals of freedom and equality. May all children, students, and citizens throughout the country come to understand and believe that RACISM need not be endemic to American life.

A portion of all royalties will be given to a scholarship fund for deserving students at the University of California, Los Angeles & California State University, Northridge.

Cover image © Shutterstock, Inc.

www.kendallhunt.com
Send all inquiries to:
4050 Westmark Drive
Dubuque, IA 52004-1840

Copyright © 2014 by Kendall Hunt Publishing Company

ISBN 978-1-4652-3703-3

Printed in the United States of America
10 9 8 7 6 5 4 3 2 1

Contents

FOREWORD

By David Lopez

As I write these lines not only is a Black man president of the United States but, if polls are to be believed, a likely Republican nominee who will challenge him in next year's election is also Black. Yes, the Republican primary race has seen a series of flame outs at the top, and Herman Cain will surely be replaced by a White man within a week or two. For that matter, Barak Obama himself may well be replaced as president by a White man next year. Still, only a few years ago, who would have thought? One can say that the increased political prominence of a few African Americans does not equal the "declining significance of race" in American society. Racial economic inequality and judicial inequity are unquestionably still with us, impacting day-to-day lives and dimming the prospects of Black and Brown youth. But, debilitating as these injustices are, might it be that they are only unfortunate remnants of earlier times, and that Obama and Cain represent, or at least presage a declining significance of racial prejudice and discrimination in everyday social life, a decline that itself will gradually dissolve economic and social inequalities? Many scholars of race in America contend that continuing racial inequality is due largely to inherited class factors, not to racial identity and interpersonal discrimination. Others acknowledge that prejudice and discrimination are still with us, but that they do little actual harm, and that the real forces holding down non-White Americans are intrinsic to their very own cultures, family, and community structures. Jerome Rabow, Pauline Venieris, and Manpreet Dhillon have little patience for such arguments and, while they do not deny the handicaps of economic racial inequality, their interest lies elsewhere: in the pain that Americans inflict on each other on the basis of perceived racial and ethnic differences…and on the pain that they inflict on themselves.

"Ending Racism: Students Speak of Pain, Hope, and Change" is firmly allied with the tradition of Feagin (2000), Bonilla-Silva (2006), and others who emphasize the continuing reality and consequentiality of racism in America, including how it has become more subtle and embedded in seemingly universalistic ideas dear to contemporary liberals. But Rabow, Venieris, and Dhillon's emphasis is unique: They focus on the personal, bravely going beyond the structural and demographic levels so beloved in American sociology. Where others might see only the random comments of benighted individuals—an insecure White young woman here, an old-time baseball manager there—they see a troubling pattern: the continuing exercise of verbal racial abuse to enforce inequality and feelings of inferiority. Rabow, Venieris, and Dhillon leave to others the detailed elucidation of how inequality is reinforced by verbal abuse; it is the pain and suffering themselves, and their effects on the inner lives and psyches of individuals that most concerns him. They want to document and elucidate the pain and suffering, but above all they want to help its victims overcome it. Pain but, more importantly, Hope. To this end they adopt the metaphor of learning how to paint, specifically how Whites learn to paint everything good and normal in one color, their own, and in so doing set an unachievable standard for non-Whites. They take us along a path of learning...from early learning in families, through learning from schools and other institutions, on through learning how to paint inferiority as deficient and the opposite of Whiteness and how we learn to see individuals of another race only in racial terms, not in the content of their individual characters. The painting metaphor is helpful but the real backbone and life of the book is in the stories that are its core, stories drawn from years of teaching and talking to students of all races, backgrounds, and initial inclinations. The progression of stories, told in the students' own words, allows Rabow, Venieris, and Dhillon to take us through the stages of how racism is embedded by families and schools, and practiced in everyday life. But in the last chapters the stories also take us through the dilemma that multiracialism poses to dominants and subordinates alike, and to individual struggles to toss the white paint away, and create new ways of thinking about and treating others. Like all that preceded it, these hopeful and courageous voices come from students in Rabow, Venieris, and Dhillon's classes over the years, classes that defied academic political correctness and asked students to examine themselves, not just sociology articles full of numbers. In so doing, they are telling three stories...about racism in America, about his students, and about the unique and cherished courses that he has taught to those students.

Chapter Two begins with a nod to one of the most hard-hitting songs in American musical theater: "You've Got to Be Carefully Taught." Those of a certain age will recall that it was sung by Lt. Joe Cable, the Philadelphia gentleman whose character does not live long enough to challenge the racism that he was so carefully taught. It is left to Nellie Forbush, *South Pacific's* cock-eyed optimist from Little Rock, Arkansas, to be the one who defies and transcends her upbringing. In fact, America may very well have largely left behind the axe handle racism of Little Rock. It is the more gentlemanly ways of Philadelphia racism that we still have in abundance, and have such trouble seeing, much less overcoming. "Ending Racism: Pain, Hope, and Change, Students Speak" shows how a university teacher, his chief facilitator, and his students in southern California have understood and fought against the gentlemanly racism of our time, and challenges the rest of us to do the same.

David Lopez
Los Angeles, February 2012

A REVIEW

Listen here to hard messages from youthful voices of color, most on the pain of daily racist oppression, yet many on countering strategies used to survive and succeed. Listen to hard messages from youthful whites recounting much racist behavior, yet also how some have unlearned and countered racism. A book of a different tack, this one not only offers youthful voices of oppression, pain, and heroism, but also provides many concrete exercises and experiments for effective anti-oppression teaching and learning.

Joe R. Feagin, Ella C. McFadden Professor of Liberal Arts Texas A & M University and Past-President, American Sociological Association

PREFACE

In the books that preceded this, *Voices of Pain and Voices of Hope* (2002, 2004, 2006, Kendall Hunt), I have documented the ways in which racism is embedded in the minds and hearts of the students that I teach at the University of California, Los Angeles and California State University, Northridge. In teaching students it was clear that students of color had very little faith and trust in their White counterparts (Conley, Rabinowitz, & Rabow, 2010). It was also apparent that White students often felt that racism had ended, that affirmative action was reverse racism, and that privilege was nonexistent in America simply because they themselves had worked hard to get where they were. For the students, these were some of the major resistances to understanding their own role in perpetuating racism. These resistances were addressed, in part, through reading about the microaggressions that students experienced in their everyday lives. Through class dialogue and readings, the White students were able to understand their privilege and their participation in racist institutions. They overcame their resistance and slowly began to see that their intentions were less important than their behavior. With that recognition came an understanding of the racist ideology of White supremacy and its practice. In reading about the racism that students of color felt towards other ethnic or racial groups, they began to see how their internalized oppression was an imitation of White oppression. The disparagement and hostility of these students toward other students of color functioned in the context of White supremacy. The multiracial students served as a challenge to the simplistic thinking of "only four racial categories." Multiracial students also revealed stories of exclusion and provide some of the most painful stories of the book. After starting the fourth edition of "Voices of Pain and Voices of Hope," I slowly began to feel that I wanted a book that race and ethnic relations professors can use to guide them in transforming the prejudice, stereotypes, and discrimination of their own students. I want to encourage professors to think about ways in which students can leave their classes not only with knowledge of the different theories and empirical consequences of racism, but also with the belief that they could, if they choose to, become anti-racist. My research with Pauline (Yeghnazar) Venieris (2009) demonstrated that my students made such significant shifts and left with an anti-racist outlook. It is our hope that educators will benefit from exercises and suggestions that accompany each chapter. They have proved to be potent ways for students to become aware of the ways in which racism is planted within individuals at the moment of birth till the moment of death. The tress of racism are planted by parents, teachers, peers, police, sales people, and is encountered on a more or less daily basis for men and women of color. This teaching seeks to uproot the everyday racist beliefs deeply embedded within ourselves and within others. The exercises help your students dig into these roots and allow them to process and understand these microaggressions as racist. Prior to these class experiences such microaggressions were responded to as "jokes." Another way to play down racist comments is to describe the perpetrator as "ignorant" or "lacking in education." Such responses do not challenge the speakers' beliefs and often allows the person to continue using microaggressions. By reinterpretation and renaming these microaggressions as racist, they will be capable of speaking out against them. While such "speaking up" and "speaking out" may annoy or even anger the perpetrators of the microaggressions, our students quickly learn how good it feels to speak up and speak out.

The process of transforming students is long and complicated. To begin this process we establish that the class will be highly interactive and deeply personal. We assert that their fellow students will serve as sources of knowledge. We emphasize that their fellow students bring their own set of "truths" or multiple realities into the classroom. And we affirm that these realities can be modified. This book will help professors achieve these goals. Transformation can begin on the first day of class. While there are other ways to begin the transformation this is what we do. Two or more students, of a different gender and race, and who have taken the class and know the goals of the class, are chosen to facilitate the very first class activity. They walk into class and without my presence indicate that Professor Rabow will be unable to teach this class and that they will be responsible for the conduct of the class. They proceed to spend about five minutes on the required books, assignments, and attendance. I then enter the classroom and we begin discussing their feelings about seeing young women of a different race in charge of the classroom. This brings identity issues to the forefront. Students express how it feels to have a younger person, a female, and a non-White professor teach the class. Identity then is established as a way we look at the world. (One of the interesting side notes is the disappointment that my African American students felt when they realize I am not African American myself since the name Jerome is a name that stereotypically "belongs" to Black males.)

There are of course other outstanding books that emphasize teaching social justice. Our book does not touch issues of classism, gender oppression, homophobia, or sexism. Although those topics are brought into the classroom, they are not the stories that are portrayed in this book. We include gender and homophobic exercises because we feel it is impossible to teach racism without dealing with the issues of sexism and homophobia. As Steinem (2008) says, "The reality is that racism and sexism are both profound and pervasive throughout our society."

This book has been greatly aided by the careful editing, rewriting, and challenges from Heidi Joya, Yvette Meza-Vega, Jennifer Moore, Sophie Nazerian, and Katya E. Rodriguez. Their sensitivity and acuteness will not be obviously apparent to the reader, but they are present in this manuscript. The manuscript in its final form was shepherded by Heidi Joya, Yvette Meza-Vega, and Jennifer Moore.

Over the years, I have taught this class with some students who have taken on the role of chief facilitator. Their sensitivity, keen intelligence, and identity difference have made the teaching more exciting and more rewarding for my students and me. These people include Azin Amahdi, Jeimee Estrada, Heidi Joya, Ian Mullins, Jennifer Odum, Jennifer Moore, Donna Rahimian, Janet Ruiz, Katya Rodriguez, Nancy Rodriguez, and Tricia Taylor. They are individuals who I am proud to know and are all involved in the struggle to make America more decent. I am very pleased to have been part of their education.

All of us who teach recognize the importance of a department or institution that supports and believes in the work we do. I am most grateful for the support of Professor Jennifer Wilson, Assistant Vice Provost for Honors at UCLA, and Professor Herman Debose, Chair of the Sociology Department at CSUN, for allowing me to teach the classes I love. The colleagues who sustain my spirits include Robert Emerson, Michael Goldstein, and David Lopez.

CHAPTER 1

The Realities of Racism

"Love is listening." —Paul Tillich

*"It takes two to speak the truth—one to
speak and another to hear."*
—Henry David Thoreau (1817–1862, American
author, poet, abolitionist, and tax resister)

When first glancing at this book, you
may feel that there is not much to
possibly learn about racism. Un-
doubtedly, you already have some degree
of awareness that racism exists and you may
have even experienced it firsthand. This
awareness doesn't necessarily extend to a
deep understanding of the ways in which
racism affects you directly and indirectly.
Consequently, the experiences you have
had with racism or the knowledge you have
about it may not have been put into a context that allows you to understand where the
racism you experience or perpetuate comes
from. After reading this book, you will not
only be able to recognize how racism operates in your daily life but you will also be

able to place these observations and experiences in the larger context of American society and its institutions. We hope that this recognition and understanding will also open the door for action on your part.

You probably already condemn the White Supremacist racism of the KKK and other hate groups. This condemnation recognizes that racism is evil. However, this awareness of the evil nature of racism can actually work against a deeper understanding of racism's pervasiveness and immediacy. The awareness is conscious and feelings of disdain can be easily verbalized. No one would argue that physically harming someone else or depriving them of basic rights is just. It is your conscious awareness that may lead you to ignore the unconscious biases, prejudices, and racist thoughts that exist in all of us. You probably understand that racism operates in job selection, promotions, housing, and bank loans. It is more difficult to discern the racism that surrounds you in your daily life. This includes the institution you attend, the classes you are taking, the social events that make up your college life, and the classmates that are reading this book along with you. Therefore, rather than focus on the racism that is "out there," this book focuses on the racism that may subtly dominate your daily social, intellectual, and emotional life.

One of the major ways to achieve an understanding of the multiple dimensions of racism that operate in your life is to have honest discussions about this topic. These discussions rarely occur among families, educators, religious leaders, peer groups, or on campuses (Chesler, 1981; Chesler & Peet, 2002). The facilitation of such conversations usually reveals that students are eager to talk and discuss these matters but have been "educated" to shut down about this subject. Portrayed as a very "hot topic" in the media, talking about racism openly can be difficult for students who are eager to speak honestly, but afraid to be perceived as "racist" or "ignorant." Many students were never encouraged to talk about it openly with others or to confront the issue of racism. Not speaking about racism in an honest and open forum with others guarantees that racism continues unabated.

Another factor preventing honest discussions of racism is the belief that an "intense dislike of an entire race must pervade the U.S. for racism to exist" (Hacker, 1998). Because intense dislike of any race is not a pervasive phenomenon, many believe that racism is no longer a reality. We may not have massive burnings of crosses or lynchings, but racism is not dead. Though James Byrd and Matthew Shepherd may seem like the isolated and random acts of a few "crazies," for many people, these dramatic acts symbolize something more all-encompassing.[1]

1 James Byrd was an African American murdered by three White men in Jasper, Texas, in 1998. The three men dragged Byrd behind a pickup truck for about 2 miles. Byrd was killed and his torso, minus his head and arm, was left in front of Jasper's Black cemetery. Byrd's lynching-by-dragging gave impetus to passage of a Texas hate crimes law. Matthew Shephard was a 21-year-old student at the University of Wyoming who was tortured and murdered near Laramie, Wyoming, in October 1998. He was attacked because he was homosexual. Two men tortured and tied him to a fence in a remote, rural area, leaving him to die in freezing temperatures. There is a documentary (*The Laramie Project*) and a movie (*The Matthew Shepard Story*) that details the events. These two hate crimes led to the federal October 22, 2009, Matthew Shepard and James Byrd, Jr. Hate Crimes Prevention Act, commonly known as the Matthew Shepard Act (CNN, 1998a) (CNN, 1998b) (Pershing, 2009).

Derald Wing Sue (2010), a professor at Columbia University, has asserted that racism cannot be dismantled until individuals accept that they themselves carry prejudices. Only when we are able to see our racism, name it, and understand how it affects us and those around us, will we be able to oppose it. This goal requires honest dialogue about racism, which this book serves to stimulate. Providing models of student behavior to stimulate change is a second goal. This book should not paralyze. Rather it should empower your abilities to combat racism. We provide models of student transformation and some of the steps involved in becoming an anti-racist (a person who engages and questions long-held assumptions and prejudices when racism occurs). Because students we teach have changed, we are confident that students reading this book can change as well.

TODAY'S RACISM

The college students' voices you will be reading are taken from classroom discussions, journals, and web-posts. We cannot ignore that institutionalized or structural racism has a sweeping effect on the landscape of American society. Structural or institutional racism affects all students at a personal level. Institutional racism was once open and pernicious. It was once common for Whites to openly express racist attitudes and beliefs in order to defend segregation and the inferiority of Black and Brown Americans. This old-fashioned racism, called Jim Crow racism, seems to have disappeared. A more insidious, but equally powerful, form of racism has replaced it. This new form of racism is subtle and disguised, but still embedded in the policies and structures of institutions and in the beliefs and actions of many Americans. Even individuals who believe in equality and democratic ideals may embrace this new racism. Sociologist Eduardo Bonilla-Silva (2006), of Duke University, has described this as "Color Blind Racism." He discusses the four salient "frames" of this modern form of racism. These frames include abstract liberalism, naturalization, cultural racism, and minimization of racism.[2] These four frames work together to prevent individuals from believing that racism is present, prevalent, and embedded in all our institutions. Color Blind Racism prevents a serious examination of race relations as racial realities are ignored, diminished, and passed over.

The belief that there is a biological basis for distinguishing races prevents racism from being evaluated as a real and serious problem. This biological determinism, with the White race being superior genetically or intellectually, and the social and economical differences between races being the result of immutable, inherited, and inborn distinctions, is **false** (Desmond & Emirbayer, 2010). Biological determinism has been used to

---

2 Abstract liberalists would say, "I don't believe in affirmative action because it gives minority groups preferential treatment." Naturalization allows individuals to explain segregation as natural because "people like to be around other people who are of the same race." Cultural racism suggests that the low level of Latinos in college occurs because "Latinos don't put much emphasis on education." Minimization of racism relies on statements such as "there is way less racism now than there was in the past."

justify injustices and to naturalize inequalities. As recently as 1994, Herrnstein and Murray attempted to establish this idea in "The Bell Curve." They concluded that Whites had higher IQ levels than Blacks, and for the most part, attributed these differences to genetics. However, in reviewing their reasoning, statisticians discovered that Herrnstein and Murray demonstrated their findings in a way that obscured their analyses and hid results that contradicted their central claims regarding racial difference in intelligence levels (Jacoby & Glauberman, 1995). The widespread scientific consensus concluded that "The Bell Curve" was deeply flawed work (Fisher et al., 1996).

In reality, biological differences between racial groups do not exist. A scientific examination of DNA strands reveals that humans share 99.9% of the same genes with other human beings and there is 8.6 times more variation within traditionally defined racial groups than between them (Desmond & Emirbayer, 2010). Thus the variability that makes a Black person different from another Black person is greater than the variability between Blacks and Asians. Race has no biological grounding, but rather is a social construction based on social, historical, and political processes.

Racism also persists because of a new ideology that is exemplified by Whites who say such things as "stop acting like victims," "stop playing the race card," or "if minorities could stop doing this or that then we could all get along." Personal comments like these constitute the body of this book and are called *microaggressions*. The term was created in 1970 and is defined as "a subtle, stunning, often automatic and non-verbal exchange, which is a 'putdown'" (Pierce, Carew, Pierce-Gonzalez, & Willis, 1978, p. 66). Solorzano, Ceja, and Yosso (2000) describe microaggressions as "subtle insults (verbal, nonverbal, and/or visual) directed toward people of color, often automatically or unconsciously" (p. 60). They are insulting, demeaning, and belittling, even if not consciously meant to be so. Our book enhances Solorzano et al.'s research, which focused exclusively on African Americans, by including all races, ethnicities, and religions that experience microaggressions. Our daily interactions, which often include these microaggressions, are not innocent. They are detrimental as they erode the psychological and spiritual energy of the recipients, and continue to create or perpetuate inequities. They are injurious because the recipient spends time and energy wondering about the remark and whether in fact the speaker has racist intentions. More often than not, the speaker is unaware and unconscious of the severity, implications, or impact of their comments. This book will make the reader aware that unconscious or unintentional microaggressions should not be dismissed or ignored.

The personally debilitating consequences of microaggressions are the other face of institutional racism which has been well documented in scientific research. These effects include significant treatment differences between Whites and people of color in income, net worth, education, housing opportunities, public places, loan offers, car leases, houses, and interest rates. Not surprisingly, harassment when driving is now so well known that most people recognize the acronym "DWB" as referring to "Driving While Black or Brown." When it comes to the justice system there are differences in rates of arrest, sentencing, incarceration, and the death penalty. Yes, we have made progress in race relations, but we should not confuse that progress with the current realities of racism.

The progress and entrenchment of racism is illustrated by the utterances of public figures that make racist comments, but can no longer walk away without paying a price. Ted Koppel, a 42-year veteran of *ABC News*, asked Al Campanis, an executive who helped build successful Los Angeles Dodger teams, why African American managers and general managers were virtually nonexistent in the sport. Campanis answered by stating, "It's just that they may not have some of the necessities to be, let's say, a field manager, or, perhaps, a general manager." When Koppel objected, Campanis responded, "I know that they have wanted to manage, and many of them haven't managed. But they are outstanding athletes, very God-gifted and wonderful people … they are gifted with great musculature (sic) and various other things. They are fleet of foot and this is why there are a number of black ballplayers in the major leagues" (Johnson, 2007). He was fired after this comment.

Michael Richards played the wacky Cosmo Kramer on the hit TV show *Seinfeld*, and in 2006 was performing onstage at the Laugh Factory in West Hollywood. When being heckled by African American males in the audience, he responded by screaming: "Fifty years ago we'd have you upside down with a f***ing fork up your ass. You can talk, you can talk, you're brave now mother f**ker. Throw his ass out. He's a nigger! He's a nigger! He's a nigger! A nigger, look, there's a nigger!" (TMZ, 2006).

Mel Gibson, a major Hollywood personality, referred to one of his domestic workers as a "wetback" during a secretly recorded rant at former girlfriend, Oksana Grigorieva (TMZ, 2010).

Haley Barbour, former Mississippi governor and former head of the Republican National Committee, made this statement when asked about what life was like for Black people in Mississippi during the 1960s: "I just don't remember it as being that bad." Barbour also defended the White Citizens Council, which used their leadership positions in civic and political organizations to engage in discriminatory practices aimed at non-Whites and those who supported non-Whites (Ferguson, 2010).

Laura Schlessinger, a talk show celebrity, responded to a call from an African American woman who felt that some of her White husband's comments were racist by saying that she was being "too sensitive." Schlessinger added:

> …without giving much thought, a lot of blacks voted for Obama simply 'cause he was half-black. Didn't matter what he was gonna do in office,

it was a black thing. You gotta know that. That's not a surprise. Not everything that somebody says -- we had friends over the other day; we got about 35 people here -- the guys who were gonna start playing basketball. I was going to go out and play basketball. My bodyguard and my dear friend is a black man. And I said, 'White men can't jump; I want you on my team.' That was racist? That was funny. (Holden, 2010)

Clearly, celebrities are not the only carriers of racism. In 2011, a White female UCLA student uploaded a video on YouTube railing against her fellow Asian classmates. She complains about their manners, their language, and the ways in which her fellow students are treated by other family members. She states:

> The problem is these hordes of Asian people that UCLA accepts into our school every single year, which is fine. But if you're going to come to UCLA then use American manners… so it used to really bug me but it doesn't bother me anymore the fact that all the Asian people that live in all the apartments around me—their moms and their brothers and their sisters and their grandmas and their grandpas and their cousins and everybody that they know that they've brought along from Asia with them—comes here on the weekends to do their laundry, buy their groceries, and cook their food for the week. It's seriously, without fail. You will always see old Asian people running around this apartment complex every weekend. That's what they do. They don't teach their kids to fend for themselves. You know what they don't also teach them, is their manners.

Similar to the public personalities who had to resign or withdraw from their positions, this student withdrew from the university.

When celebrities and public figures express these sentiments aloud, they are denounced and may lose their jobs, as was the case with Laura Schlessinger. While we applaud the public outrage, the efforts to suppress the public expression of racist comments do not lead to open discussions of the racism that is still flourishing today in the form of microaggressions and interpersonal slurs. They may actually work to just warn people about expressing their racist and personal views to the wrong audiences rather than inviting people to think about the validity and impact of their racist thoughts and ideas. We believe that this last frontier of racism might prove to be more difficult to transform than the legal structures that have supported racism. Our experiences in the classroom have confirmed this belief. Our experiences with teaching White students and students of color are that, generally, White students have difficulty recognizing the reality of racism and the ways in which they are implicated in it directly and indirectly. We have also found that students of color feel that they have exhausted their energy trying to convince

White students of their reality. As a result they enter our classes feeling that there can be no understanding or dialogue. Whites have given up because they believe that racism is perpetuated by "dwelling on the issues." Students of color have given up believing that White students can understand or want to change.

THREE METAPHORS OF RACISM

A metaphor is a way of understanding and experiencing one kind of event in terms of another. Different scholars have used metaphors to portray the extensiveness and pervasiveness of racism. These metaphors illustrate the omnipresence of racism in America. There are three scholars for whom the realities of racism and oppression still exist. Professor Beverly Tatum (1997), a psychologist and president of Spelman College, in Georgia, uses a metaphor to illustrate the omnipresence of racism:

> I sometimes visualize the ongoing cycle of racism as a moving walkway at the airport. Active racist behavior is equivalent to walking fast on the conveyor belt. The person engaged in active racist behavior has identified with the ideology of White supremacy and is moving with it. Passive racist behavior is equivalent to standing still on the walkway. No overt effort is being made, but the conveyor belt moves the bystanders along to the same destination as those who are actively walking. Some of the bystanders may feel the motion of the conveyor belt, see the active racists ahead of them, and choose to turn around, unwilling to go to the same destination as the White supremacists. But unless they are walking actively in the opposite direction at a speed faster than the conveyor belt—unless they are actively antiracist—they will find themselves carried along with the others.

A social psychologist, Raphael Ezekiel (1995), uses another metaphor to explain the daily doses of racism that we all witness:

> Racism is a way of perceiving the world and a way of thinking. To a certain degree, it is part of everyone who lives in a racist society. Imagine growing up next to a cement factory, and imagine the cement dust inevitably becoming a part of your body. As we grow up within a society that is saturated with White racism, year after year we pass through interactions in which White racist conceptions are an unspoken subtext. We make lives in institutions in which this is true. We cannot live from day to day without absorbing a certain amount of White racism into our thoughts.

(We similarly absorb homophobia and sexism.) It is foolish to say, "I am not racist." Part of one's mind (if one is White and perhaps if one is a person of color) has necessarily absorbed racist ways of thinking. It is important to discover the subtle ways our culture's racism has affected our thinking: to identify those habits of thought and learn how to keep them from influencing us. We can get tripped up by ideas we don't allow ourselves to acknowledge.

Sociologist Joe Feagin (2000) is more specific and concrete about our racial oppression. Feagin suggests by implication that we are all racist—we all have racist feelings and we all engage in racist behaviors:

In the United States racism is structured into the rhythms of everyday life. It is lived, concrete, advantageous for Whites, and painful for those who are not White. Even a person's birth and parents are shaped by racism, since mate selection is limited by racist pressures against interracial marriage. Where one lives is often determined by the racist practices of landlords, bankers, and others in the real estate profession. The clothes one wears and what one has to eat are affected by access to resources that varies by position in the racist hierarchy. When one goes off to school, her or his education is shaped by contemporary racism—from the composition of the student body to the character of the curriculum. Where one goes to church is often shaped by racism, and it is likely that racism affects who one's political representatives are. Even getting sick, dying and being buried may be influenced by racism. Every part of the life cycle, and most aspects of one's life, is shaped by the racism that is integral to the foundation of the United States.

INTRODUCTION TO THE PAINTBRUSH

We, like others, will use a metaphor to describe the ways in which students learn and practice racism. The metaphor involves a painter, a paintbrush, and buckets of white paint. We select this metaphor because it denotes action on the part of the painter. This is an active metaphor in that it requires people to administer the paint. The administration of this paint can be through looks or words. In America, this broad paintbrush moves over and through the lives of children of color. The brush is very wide, always dipped in white, and almost no one can avoid its touch. Some believe that the paint is benign, but it is not. The paint is corrosive, leaving scars and memories of pain. The white paintbrush is applied differently to children at different ages, and various people do the painting, but the messages are the same. The messages, as microaggressions, are caustic, critical, and condescending. "Your hair is too curly!" "Your eyes have a weird shape!" "Your eyes are not blue or green and they are ugly!" "You are ugly!" "You have an accent!" "You dress funny!" "Your features are too broad!" "You have a funny name and it is too difficult to pronounce!" "You are dirty!" "You are too dark!" All of these sentences, or painting efforts, have a common meaning: "You are not like me, and I don't like you. Since you're not like me, you make me uncomfortable, and because I'm normal and you're not, I'll tell you what I don't like about you." Children of color who are born in the United States and children of color who immigrate to our country are painted and scarred with the strokes of white paint delivered by parents, teachers, friends, and classmates, as well as by books, magazines, and television. Children of color, having been painted so often, begin to paint themselves and others.

The paintbrush is wielded by dominants. When we refer to dominants, we mean a group that has not only the power to differentiate itself from "others," but also the privilege to see its difference as superior. Dominants have a group identity and collective interests. The work they do to maintain their interests often results in prejudice against those who are not members of the dominant group. Dominants and subordinates have existed since the first collectives on earth. Moreover, dominants and subordinates have a relationship to each other (Miller, 1998). The relationship can be temporary as in playgroups or permanent as in institutionalized slavery.

The one dominant group that will be discussed in this book is White Americans. There are certainly other dominants such as males, heterosexuals, able-bodied people, and Christians.[3] Whites are the people who, through no fault or effort of their own, belong to the normative race in the United States. Whiteness frequently brings unearned privilege and advantage (McIntosh, 1998). Some White people understand how Whiteness brings privilege, but many White people are often unable to see the benefits that accompany their skin color. They may not even think they have a skin color. They are merely "white," "normal," or "non-ethnic." The failure to see themselves as a race blends in with their inability to see how their color grants them certain honors and allowances. White privilege and racism are linked inextricably. White privilege depends on the perpetuation of racism (Rothenberg, 1998a). Additionally, since dominants believe they are superior, there is no need to have extensive knowledge of subordinates. Individuals in dominant groups only have to look at themselves, and people like them, to gain identity and knowledge of the world.

Most White people, when they look at themselves, do not see race and racism because their race is normal and racism is not part of their world. Dominants know very little

---

3 A survey of efforts in higher education to increase diversity has been made by Hurtado, Milem, Clayton-Pedersen, and Allen (1999). A survey of the views of White students on affirmative action has been completed by Chesler and Peet (2002). Further details for both studies can be found in the reference section at the end of the book.

if anything about subordinates. Subordinates, on the other hand, know dominants very well. They notice them immediately because their survival, achievement, and accomplishment often depends on dominants' recognition. Subordinates cannot avoid hearing evaluations from Whites or having their differences with dominants valued as "less than." In America, this message comes directly and indirectly from many sources and eventually subordinates may begin to internalize the views that dominants accept as true. Dominants are not born with a brush in hand, but at a young age they acquire one and quickly learn how to use it. The brush is made up of stereotypes, prejudices, philosophies, beliefs, and ideas in which "White" and all of the features, qualities, beliefs, values, and norms that go with it are the standard against which all others are judged. Dominants use the brush to paint those who do not meet these standards, and thus a series of interpersonal and personal dynamics are put into motion with painful consequences. The political and social consequences of these acts are the perpetuation of racism.

Dominants, the wielders of the brush, learn a philosophy about their rightful place in the world. Many dominants exert great effort to justify their prejudices, which in turn supports their interests and goals. Much of the history of dominants in the United States is extremely malevolent. It is a history of poisoning and discarding cultures and peoples because they were perceived as different and thus dangerous (Takaki, 1993, 1998). While our pernicious and racist history needs to be told and remembered, this book is not about those stories. Instead, it is a book about today's racism and prejudice. It is a book about the more invidious and subtle sides to racism revealed by our students. It is racism in which statements like "God Bless You" and "Have a Nice Day" are prefaced by a refusal to rent an apartment or to accept a check.

There is a legacy of racism that exists and is enacted daily in the United States and it touches all our lives. Racism is a daily fact of life in our families, schools, playgrounds, corporations, smaller businesses, and universities. Though many dominants do not intentionally discriminate and do not mean to be prejudiced, the White paintbrush creates a world in which dominants are the standard by which all others are evaluated. Those who are different are painted as deviant and somehow inferior. These prejudices are used as justification for exploitation but much of the power of the brush lies not in its use as a deliberate weapon of domination, but in much subtler uses as a marker of what is "normal" and right.

Dominants learn at an early age that people of color are different. They learn that these "different" people must prove themselves in order to be seen as "normal." Often, they learn that subordinates are not worth knowing at all. Subordinates are often not even seen or noticed. When subordinates are noticed, they may be seen as esoteric, strange, overemotional, funny, lazy, stupid, sick, dangerous, or un-American. Further, dominants do not learn about subordinates from subordinates themselves, but rather from other dominants. Dominants are instructed about their exclusivity by their parents, friends, classmates, books, magazines, and television. They learn to teach themselves and each other.

To practice superiority, dominants use the brush to seek out difference and to ensure that subordinates learn about themselves from the perspective of the powerful. Because dominants have power, they can use the paintbrush to make all kinds of strokes. The brush wielders can label groups as inferior. They can suggest and command social roles appropriate for subordinates.

The paintbrush is wielded when dominants can benefit economically, politically, and socially by exploiting their difference and using their power to paint subordinates as undeserving, unmotivated, less rational, less civilized, less intelligent, dangerous, and even subhuman. A prime example of this is American slavery. Other examples are what dominants did to Native Americans, Chinese laborers, and to Japanese Americans during World War II. This domination and painting of the other as "less" occurred with all the European efforts of colonization; the missions established in North, Central, and South America; and in the Bracero program developed by our government to import and exploit migrant Mexican workers. We exclusively focus on race and racism, but race is only one pattern of domination and subordination. It is this same pattern of domination that can be observed today as corporations deny benefits to homosexual partners because their unions are deemed "unnatural." It happens every time a woman is denied a leadership position because she might be "too emotional" to handle the pressure. It occurs in every collective in which there is an uneven distribution of power.

Prisons, universities, corporations, and families are all collectives in which dominants have views about what is right and fair. Not surprisingly, these views are usually at odds with many of the views of subordinates. For the readers who feel that they have never been dominant, think about your younger siblings or cousins. Think about your view of them—their faults, their lesser value, and their lesser worth. For readers who feel they have never been a subordinate, think about your parents and the ways in which they have found fault with you and sought to criticize and correct your behavior—behavior that in your view was completely justifiable and responsible.

Dominant groups have their paintbrushes ready to provide and impose morality, philosophy, standards of beauty, and even scientific "truths" that justify their own and subordinates' rightful places and positions in the world. When parents (dominants) and children (subordinates) are involved, we assume the inequalities will be somewhat temporary. Under temporary inequality, differences can enhance each party. Children can gain wisdom and guidance. Parents can learn patience and acceptance. Furthermore, as children grow, they may, given the context and family situation, be able to gain an equal position with their parents. As parents age, the children themselves may become dominants with the allowance to exercise judgment and power. As we shall see, the inequality between Whites as dominants and people of color as subordinates in the United States has not been ephemeral. The United States was created as a country with permanent inequality. The struggle to change that inequality continues. These inequalities and differences do not enhance or enrich each party. Rather, structures, beliefs, and values are developed to sustain these group disparities.

In the United States, wielders of the paintbrush often believe they are supporting equality. Most Americans do not believe in slavery and do not believe they are racists. Most dominants do not believe that they possess a paintbrush. Those who do know about the brush are likely to believe that the strokes delivered by themselves and others are harmless or even helpful. Dominants often refuse to accept the relevance and reality that race has for subordinates. Yet, "it is not the White supremacists, Ku Klux Klan members, or Skinheads, for example, who pose the greatest threat to people of color, but instead well-intentioned people, who are strongly motivated by egalitarian values, believe in their own morality, and experience themselves as fair-minded and decent people who would never consciously discriminate" (Sue, 2010, p. xv). While dominants may not be concerned about race and racism, for subordinates, race "… is the only relevant factor defining their existence" (Cose, 1993, p. 28).

INTRODUCTION TO STUDENTS' VOICES

"Never doubt that a small group of thoughtful, committed people can change the world. Indeed, it is the only thing that ever has." — Margaret Mead

The legacy of what our country has done to Native Americans, African Americans, Asian Americans, and Central and South Americans is an ugly, violent, land-stealing, people-murdering history that has been supported by laws and legislation. These laws have also been supported with a culture of hatred that justifies treatment of Native Americans as uncivilized savages, of African Americans as subhuman and violent, of Asians as sneaky and untrustworthy, and Central and South Americans as violent breeders, and most recently of Middle Easterners as terrorists and anti-Christians. Although the laws that allowed racist behavior have ended, the hostile, cruel, and negative sentiments regarding people of color remains. The legacy of privilege and the superiority of Whiteness remain. The expression of those ideas is what this book addresses.

The people you will read about are all students. The experiences in this book are based on college students from UCLA—a highly diverse, public university, two state universities—CSUN and CSUCI, and one private university—USC. Most of the students were raised in California and one might assume that these students would have been exposed to and learned to appreciate diversity, as California has one of the most diverse populations in the entire world. Indeed, no race or ethnic group constitutes a majority in the state of California. Furthermore, the reader should not believe that the experiences of the students that you will be reading about occur only in California's educational institutions. Another book (Seltzer & Johnson, 2009) uses students' experiences with racism from 11 other universities outside of California. Their experiences echo the voices that you will hear in this volume. Racism seems to be the experience of almost every single student we have known; it is constantly in their hearts and minds.[4]

In this book, the reader will see how race is a salient fact of life for college students of color. Although we have no slave owners or internment camps, and though slave wages have been replaced by minimum wages, anti-Black, anti-Asian, anti-immigrant, anti-Middle Eastern, anti-Semitic, anti-Latino, and anti-gay remarks are often acceptable. The reader will see that the brush strokes delivered by dominants do not come from members of the Klan, skinheads, or Aryan groups. Peers, teachers, parents, and professors deliver them. They are delivered by people who believe in fairness, in God, and in the United States. They are people who go to church, a mosque, or a temple, and who pay their taxes. They are honest people—but they are racists. And their actions are not harmless. These brushstrokes are delivered by dominants to subordinates and from subordinates to other subordinates. It's important to note that the latter form of racism, though painful and important, lacks the power that accompanies the racism from dominants. Painting by dominants does not enrich the differences between us. As these strokes scar and hurt individuals, they also undermine the sense of justice and fairness that Americans believe should be their right. There is a legacy of racism in this country and the brushstrokes are delivered in that context and because of that legacy.

This racism has enormous consequences for the recipient. The costs in physical and mental health are well documented (Feagin & McKinney, 2003). The costs to those who benefit from oppression are also real but less pernicious. As readers of this text will discover, depending on the situation, they themselves can be a member of both the targeted and advantaged groups. This personal aspect of the book is to help you, the reader, discover that you are not alone. It is not only students of color who the reader will be able to identify with; we have also found that our White student readers are able to echo experiences similar to the White students whose voices appear in this book. Thus, while institutionalized racism in America is pervasive, we do not focus on this embedded

4 Diversity on college campuses is no guarantee that students will get to know each other and reduce stereotypes and acts of racism. Students will come to campus with a sense of privilege and will reenact that privilege in everyday life without recognizing it as such. See Shamus Rahman Khan. (2011). *Privilege: Educating the New Adolescent Elite*. Princeton, NJ: Princeton University Press. Diversity in communities is also no guarantee of increased positive attitudes across races. In Los Angeles, one of the most diverse cities in America, race relations are not influenced by the demographic mix. See Mara A. Cohen-Marks and Jim Faught. (2011, Spring). The perceptions of race relations in contexts of ethnic diversity and change. *Sociological Perspectives, Journal of the Pacific Sociological Association*, 53(1).

societal racism, but rather on how these material and structural oppressions play out in the lives of college students. In this book we focus on interpersonal racism. These are the everyday microaggressions—the experiences, practices, and interactions between oppressors and oppressed and between oppressed and oppressed.

We hope that your personal engagement with the voices of our students will allow you to make sense of your experiences and the choices you make when you experience racism. We hope that your understanding of your personal problems and experiences with racism will not be dismissed as rare encounters, but rather can be transformed into an awareness of institutional racism. Although the racism you will be reading about is interpersonal, we do not want you to believe that the problem of racism lies only within individuals and not within institutions. Individuals can perform racist acts, but they can also fight against the structures that continue to promote racism, and against a culture that advances the privileges of Whiteness so that it permeates the individual, interpersonal level. It is toward this end that our book is aimed. We must learn, be aware, and understand racism so that we can work against it. It is this consciousness that by beginning with ourselves at the individual level, we can turn this into a public issue that can change institutions.

MOVING FORWARD

Many students breathe in the dust of racism without necessarily being conscious of it. For others who are aware of the dust and poison, it is a daily attack on their health, well-being, and worth. Racism and prejudice are alive and flourishing. These students experienced prejudice, racism, anti-Semitism, sexism, xenophobia, Islamophobia, and homophobia. Its extent and pervasiveness can be debated, but it must be called what it is. In most cases it was ignorance and in other cases it was, and is, evil racism. Racism touches all of us daily. The students you will hear from have experienced enormous hurt and pain. The words that you will read come from students' hearts and these memories can be hurtful, embarrassing, and shameful. They are presented to you with the hope that there can be a bridge between them and you, between you and them. If you can connect to and remember their words, you will have taken a step toward them as they have opened up and taken a step toward you. Their words can instill a sense of hope and create a sense of the hunger that we all have to be more human and more connected to each other. Though they were our students, they are your brothers, your sisters, your cousins, your neighbors, your fellow citizens, and your children. We must not continue to fail them.

"If you find in your heart to care for somebody else, you will have succeeded."
—Maya Angelou

CHAPTER 2

Introducing the Paintbrush:

Learning to Paint from Family and Peers

"A people that values its privileges above its principles soon loses both."
—Dwight D. Eisenhower
(Thirty-fourth president of the United States of America, 1953–1961; commanding general in World War II; supreme commander of troops invading France on D-Day, 1944; president of Columbia University)

How do dominants learn to paint? Where does the desire or even the need to paint arise? We are not born with the desire to paint. Infants and toddlers treat each other equally regardless of race. Indeed, early childhood may be the only time in our lives when we are truly colorblind. Yet, racism is pervasive. Research suggests that infants as young as 6 months respond differently to pictures of White and Black people. Other research (Van Ausdale & Feagin, 2001) indicates that by the age of 3, children develop a sense of "outsiders," people who are different from themselves;

and because of societal influence, they may target those "outsiders" for prejudicial behavior (Sleek, 1997). At some point, children of all colors begin to learn to paint by participating in a cultural system that provides them with categories for classifying objects and people. All societies and groups determine which differences are important for distinguishing one group from another. In the United States, a person's skin color is a marker for categorizing people because it is considered important. By the age of 7, about 90% of children are aware of racial categories and have begun to act like the adults of their culture (Hirschfeld, 1996).

This chapter illustrates how children and young adults learn to paint from their families and peers, and reveals how minority children learn to paint themselves. In Chapter Three, we demonstrate how the other major institutions in society provide painting lessons. To begin, we have provided you with a visual (Table 2) that organizes the stories you will read about in this chapter. We have broken down the racial compositions of those teaching others to paint, those learning to paint, and those being painted.

TABLE 2

The Teachers, Learners, and Targets of Racism

Teachers		Learners		Targets	
Parents	10	African Americans	2	African Americans	14
Peers	14	Asian Americans	10	Asians	10
Other family members	9	Latinos (as)	3	Latinos(as)	7
		Middle Easterners	6	Middle Easterners	2
		Whites	12	Whites	2
Total	33	Total	33	Total	35

LEARNING TO PAINT FROM ONE'S FAMILY

We learn about the world and ourselves from our family members. They help establish our identities and our belief systems. Familial bonds shape our interests, values, goals, and our very connections to each other and the world around us. They also teach us about shame, guilt, oppression, hate, and racism. Children's impressionable nature and the influential role adults serve in children's lives leads to our contention that racism is initially learned in the bosom of the family.

The understanding that racism is learned in the family is musically illustrated in the American musical written by Rodgers and Hammerstein in 1949, *South Pacific*. One song in this musical work, entitled "You've Got to Be Carefully Taught," created great controversy in some sectors of American society. One Georgia legislator tried to ban the musical, stating that the ideas of interracial love were inspired by Moscow (Most, 2000). You can hear the song by going to http://www.youtube.com/watch?v=nHKzn8aHyXg&feature=related.

Family instructions for *who* to paint and *how* to paint provide the canvas for future painters. Although instructions in painting will continue as children grow, we believe that the family can be a major influence for and against racism. Specifically, family members can instill the belief that being White is synonymous with privilege and therefore entitles one to paint. Of course they can do the opposite, by having friends who are different, by inviting their children's classmates to parties and sleepovers, and by engaging in actions that are consistent with their beliefs in social justice. In this first excerpt, a White female describes her father's attempt to teach her the strokes of racism:

> I was a junior in high school and I had a friend who was Black. I never paid any attention to this fact but as soon as he started to like me I found out something about my father that I didn't like. The boy's name was M and he called me one day. My dad answered the phone and gave it to me. I talked to him for about 20 minutes and when I got off the phone my father started asking me who he was. I told him because I thought he was just being a protective father. When I described him as being Black, I thought my dad was going to faint. He had this weird look on his face and it scared me. I thought I had done something wrong but I couldn't understand what it was. He told me that he didn't think it was a good idea for him to continue calling and he told me he didn't want me to hang out with him anymore. I was very confused and upset. I asked my mom why he said this to me and she explained that he didn't believe in interracial relationships. (White, female)

In the following example, a White female is taught to be comfortable with the word "nigger." She learns it from her sister and receives support in its use from her father and stepmother:

> When I was about nine years old my step-sister told me that all Black people were called niggers. My dad and step-mom lived in a very rural area in the South and I was visiting them. I remember one day my dad, step-mom, step-sister and I were driving to a restaurant and my step-sister pointed to a Black man on the street and said "Mama, listen . . .

Michelle, who's that man on the street? What's he called?" Then I hesitantly said "He's a nigger." My step-mom and dad started laughing. They said "Did Amanda teach you that?" They thought it was really funny, but I knew it was probably wrong. (White, female)

The South is not the only place in America where painting instructions are given. In the following example, a White male visiting the Midwest describes his grandfather's instructions:

I visited my grandparents in the Midwest when I was in the third grade and gained exposure to explicit racism. My grandpa referred to an African American as a "jigaboo," one of the first times I can remember hearing a derogatory name for a minority. I heard this term before, but I had never heard "nigger" used. I respected my grandpa and therefore did not question his racial views. Hearing my grandpa talk to me about "jigaboos" and how they were not welcome in his house gave me my first notion of White superiority . . . I had been attending a Christian church since I was a baby and considered myself a moral person. I knew that I should be a moral person, but also had been implanted with the conflicting notion that Whites are superior. I wanted to treat all humans with compassion yet my grandpa was a respectable man . . . how could I look badly upon his views? I was in a racial dilemma. I had realized that people look different and I didn't know how to act upon this fact. I played with many friends of racial minorities at school but never questioned what my grandpa told me. (White, male)

A White female who grew up in the Northwest describes her grandmother's racist beliefs and teachings:

As for racism, I have never had much experience with it other than from my family. My grandma is very racist. She lives in Oregon and when we visit her, I sometimes feel uncomfortable. She still refers to African Americans as "niggers" and I feel that this word is wrong. Maybe I even feel it is dirty. I never use that word and don't even like to repeat it. She is very forward and believes in the "Southern Ways." That is, in the South, most people are very racial. They do not believe that they are equals to African Americans. They believe that they are superior to them. My grandma still carries on the stereotype of "slave boy." I hate it when she talks that way but I could never disrespect her by telling her she is wrong. I just quiver inside and try to ignore it. (White, female)

A White male, growing up in the Northeast, recalls lessons learned from his parents when he was 12 years old. The message is clear: being White means being "good." People of color don't behave well, he is told, and when his conduct is less than exemplary, he is "no better than them":

> The summer before I was to enter the seventh grade, we moved from our racially mixed neighborhood. Up until then, I had gone to school with African Americans, Puerto Ricans, Native Americans, and Asians. I had a hard time making friends at my new school. Everyone was White. I was the new kid and I got picked on a lot. As a teenager, I fell in with a gang and got into some trouble. I remember sitting in the driveway in my dad's car with him one time when he was really angry at me. He said, "Jesus Christ! What's the matter with you? Don't you know how hard your mother and I have had to work to get you kids out of the old neighborhood, away from the niggers and spics? And still, you're no better than them, for Christ's sake!" (White, male)

A White woman analyzes the origins of her racism toward Asians. The student describes the paintbrush her mother gave her. The brush would be used to paint Asians as cheap and less deserving of equal treatment:

> When I think about where some of my racism toward Asians could have started, I recall the things my parents taught me in regards to "Orientals," as they were called in those days. My parents owned a business that I often worked in to secure spending money. When an Asian would walk in, my mother would make derogatory remarks about how "tight" they were (with money) and how they were notorious for asking for discounts. She therefore did not greet or treat them in the same manner as other customers. She would be more apt to ignore them and try to avoid spending too much time with them. This left a lasting impression on me, and I began to make similar attributions when working at the shop. The stereotype became internalized. (White, female)

In a telling example of cross-generation racism, a White female describes how she learned to view African Americans through the teachings of various painters in her family. She recalls that her grandfather and father were the main instructors of racism:

> When I first learned about race I see the innocent little girl I once was who was so unaffected by racism or divisions and I wish I could be her now. All her stereotypes I've inadvertently picked up, internalized, all the racism covering over my once pure heart. When I was a little older

I remember my grandparents espousing racial epithets and phrases like, "Why would you want to watch a show with a bunch of niggers in it?" when referring to the TV show *The Jeffersons*. Or they would say things like, "Look at all those Blacks on TV now." Saying this in front of a child is so inappropriate; it makes me so angry now that I didn't fight back more. I'd say something to the effect of, "Oh grandpa, that is not nice or that is stupid and racist." . . . I was about 12 or 13 [at the time]. My father would say a lot of things about Black people being lazy and not wanting to work. Therefore, he wasn't going to support them. (White, female)

Another female student recalls learning about racism at the young age of 6 from family members. Her father and brothers instructed her that she was not to socialize with an African American boy in her class:

I was six years old and there was a little Black boy in my class whom I adored; I had my first crush on him. I told some people on the bus on the way home one day after he had gotten off and they made fun of me for it. I don't recall who made fun of me but I remember my older brothers telling me that I couldn't like a Black boy, as if something was wrong with me. I remember being confused and feeling a sense of shame. At that point it dawned on me that something must be wrong with me for liking him. I don't recall what if or what my parents said, if anything, although later my father made his thought on the matter clear. He would not approve of my ever dating, much less marrying, a Black man. Since growing older I've challenged him on these thoughts and his rationalization now is that the world is a hard enough place without being in a biracial relationship and if we had kids how difficult that would be for them. Of course, I don't buy his bigoted excuses and we have had many heated debates about these issues. (White, female)

Though one might hope that all minorities who have been victims of racism would unite to fight against it, this is not always the case. Unfortunately, solidarity and unity among different students of color is rare. The discrimination received by one racial minority often leads to acts of discrimination and racism toward another racial minority. It is as if each group needs to assert its position of dominance on the hierarchical ladder, which is achieved through labeling and stigmatizing anyone who is different. Why would minorities hurt or have prejudice against other minorities? Growing up in the United States means we are all painters. No one escapes. Minorities also breathe the air of racism. We all play in the buckets of White racist paint and emerge knowing how to paint. So it is not surprising that minorities treat other people of color the same way that dominants treat them. However, a major difference between dominant versus subordinate racism is power. When dominants treat subordinates as lesser, there are norms and traditions that support this treatment. When subordinates treat other subordinates as lesser, there is little institutional power to enforce that difference. Subordinate on subordinate racism can be understood as occurring within a frame of dominants' racism toward subordinates. It is imitative of dominants' treatment of subordinates.

In the next three examples, three children of color, a Chicana, an Indian American, and a Filipino male, describe the instructions they receive for painting from their families. Sometimes the instructions direct the child to paint particular minority groups. A Chicana recalls the racist views her father instilled in her. Her father taught her to fear African American males simply based on their color:

> I can honestly reveal that depending on how a Black man "looks" I fear them. I know this is racist but the more I think about it, actually I fear any man that has a certain "look." I know that it is not a whole race of people that does wrong, it is that person as an individual. It is unfair and detrimental to classify and damn their whole race for what one person has done. And I am conscious that sometimes I think this way. I learned at home how to be a racist because my father always had this deep hatred for anyone other than Mexican. He had a sinister loathing for Blacks. I was told to never have Black friends and to stay away from them because, according to him, they were inherently evil and lazy and would get me in trouble. An early childhood experience with a Black woman who befriended me caused my father to be physically violent. He beat me for associating with her. This was when I was in preschool, and incidentally was the catalyst for the reinforcing of his views on me. (Chicana, female)

Similarly, an Indian American female recounts how she developed racist feelings toward Asians. Her mother painted all Asians as the same and labeled them as Orientals.[1] The student tried to correct her mother's use of the derogatory term, but her mother was unwilling to accept her daughter's attempt to change the canvas:

> My racist attitudes about Asians come from my home. My mother always calls Asians "Orientals." I just found out, last year, that this is not the correct term. Oriental is used for furniture and food, not people. When I told this to my mother, she said "oh" and did not think twice when she called them Oriental again. I do not know if she forgot or if she is overlooking them as people with feelings. I also began to realize how I am sometimes like my mother. I often ask people of color questions like

---

1 Beginning in the late 1960s and early 1970s, Asian American activists rejected the term "Oriental" because it "connotes images of the passive, the exotic, and the foreign" (Lee, 1996, p. 44). The label "Oriental" makes it easier for the Western mind to treat Asians like the "other." See Said's (1978) book *Orientalism*.

"Where are you from?" and when they answer "San Diego," I ask again. In this class, I realized that the girl is from San Diego and not from Korea because she was not born there. Up to this point, I never really realized what an idiotic question I was asking and that I looked like an idiot to others I interacted with. Even worse, I realized how many people I must have offended with questions such as these. (Indian American, female)

In the following excerpt, a Filipino male describes the powerful influence that his father had upon him. His father taught him to be suspicious of Filipinos:

Throughout high school, I often painted myself as "White" and not Asian to be accepted in my White peer group and to make myself an "exception" to "normal" Filipinos. I often made a big deal of my racial make-up, highlighting the fact that I was 7/8 Filipino and 1/8 White because my great-grandfather was White. Often I also argued that I was literally "White inside" in order to distance myself from Filipinos and to assimilate into the White culture. Because of my good grades, I felt that I had more in common with the honors students, who in my community were predominantly White. Because of "high academic status," I looked down (elitism) on "stupid-gangsta Filipinos" who wore baggy pants—a blanket and narrow view of them as a group. I participated in racial jokes that specifically ridiculed the Asians in order to disconnect myself from the gangster Filipinos. Where did all of this self-distancing come from? I think that I learned to feel "different" and "special" because of my father. As a young child, he often warned me to be suspicious of Filipinos because he said they were like crabs: if one were to succeed and make it out of the bucket (my father), the others would enviously pull him down. Though he has many friends, he makes sure that we remember that they weren't educated like him. (Filipino, male)

In the next excerpt, a second-grade Iranian girl learns about her parents' racial attitudes. Her parents were quite comfortable with her friend sleeping over, until they discovered that the friend was Latina. The student knew that her parents' behavior was unjust. She lied to her friend, even though she felt embarrassed and knew she was being rude:

When I was seven years old and in the second grade, I invited my friend to come over and spend the night. I had told my parents that she was coming over for the entire day and that she was also going to sleep over, but I never mentioned that she was a Latina because it had no meaning for me. When she came over to our house they didn't really say anything about her being a different ethnicity from us, but when it was getting close to bed time they said that she could not sleep over anymore. I asked them why but they basically ignored my question; I figured out the answer when they asked me why I did not tell them that she was Latina. I replied that I did not think it mattered or that I needed to tell them. This put me in the position of having to lie to my friend and tell her that my family and I were going to go somewhere that night so she would have to go home. I was so embarrassed to lie to her and it made me feel as if I was rude because I had already said that it was okay for her to spend the night with me. I felt like it was not right for my parents to bar her from spending the night because she was not Iranian like us. Their point of view was very different from mine. I still remained this girl's friend and I didn't think of her any differently, but I also did not want her to come over again because I was embarrassed of the way my parents treated her. (Iranian American, female)

The hypocrisy of these Iranian American parents is duplicated by a White parent in the following story. At the age of 17, a young man finds out that his close friend's father has feelings that he never knew existed. In order to maintain his friendship with his close friend, he never reveals how he felt upon hearing his friend's father use the phrase "fucking wetbacks":

When I was 17 years old I had a White friend named Brandon. He was always a very cool guy when it came to the way he treated me. One day I went to his house and we were hanging out in his bedroom when I asked if I could use his restroom. When I was walking to the restroom I passed by his father in the living room watching the news. There must have been some kind of segment about minorities or something because I overheard him say "fucking wetbacks." This seemed very strange to me because just a few minutes ago this man had shaken my hand and was being very nice to me. This was the first time that I realized how two-faced and cowardly racists can be. I realized that people can be nice to your face and hate you behind your back. This made me feel sad but I never said anything because I liked my friend so much. (Mexican American, male)

You don't have to be born in America to learn racist attitudes. Newly arrived immigrants learn these attitudes very quickly. What is remarkable is that immigrants, despite their own persecution and struggles, express beliefs that are prejudicial. In the following example, a 6-year-old is instructed by her Armenian grandfather. The grandparent, while able to say something about not judging African Americans, instills his view about the superiority of White people. She, like other children her age, is innocent in wanting to know whether that person who looks different is similar to the people that she knows—as "kind" and "normal." She has no reason to believe her grandfather is spreading misinformation and disseminates this new knowledge to her peers:

> I recall my astonishment when I first saw a Black man on TV when I was six years old. I asked my grandfather about the Black man and specifically asked why he was so dark and whether he was "normal" and "kind," like us. My grandfather explained to me that the Black man was a "nigger" and that there were a lot of "niggers" in Africa and America, and that the Americans oppressed them. He told me that some "niggers" were gentle and kind, but some of them were aggressive and angry. He also told me that "niggers" would be offended and would get angry if I directly addressed them in that way. He told me that I was White and that white people are generally smarter than black people. After we were done talking I ran outside to meet my friends and tell them about the new information I had just learned from my grandfather. (Armenian, female)

In this next excerpt, White parents instruct their 8-year-old son to have nothing to do with his classmate. The parents are very explicit about why their White son should not play and hang out with an Asian female student:

> When I was around the third grade, eight years old, I started to have a crush on a boy in my class. He was my best friend. He was handsome and tall, with big brown eyes and light-brown hair. He looked nothing like the boys I grew up with in my home country. He reminded me of my favorite actor, John Travolta. We would play with each other every day. We played tetherball, we ran around the school playing tag, and we often studied together. We spent most of our time during the lunch hours. I started to like him so much that I decided to tell him. That afternoon, after school, I called him to ask him about a homework assignment. I then said bluntly, "I like you!" He paused and laughed and played it off. It hurt so much because it was actually my first time I had liked a boy. The next day, I was determined that I was going to ask him if he wanted to be my boyfriend. His answer to my question was so sharp and it felt like a knife had rammed into my heart. He said, "I just like you as a friend. You're funny, but you're not my type." TYPE? We were eight years old!!! I asked him why and he said, "I like girls like me." I could not understand him. He then said, "My parents told me that I shouldn't hang out with you too much because you're not like us. You're different. You don't look like me. See? I have big eyes and my skin is lighter." I was so enraged. His parents, including him, were prejudging me strictly based on my appearance. They wanted me to be like them. He told me that if I had bigger eyes and

I had lighter skin he would like me. He said, "maybe my parents will let you be my friend if you had made your skin whiter and your hair lighter." The next day after school, I went home and tried to rub my skin off with a towel. I felt so ridiculous and stupid. But I guess I must have really liked him because no matter how much I knew this would not help, I was still trying my hardest to make my skin lighter. (Asian, female)

Parents of color are often concerned with protecting their children from racist attitudes and behavior. In the following excerpt, a Chinese parent seeks to protect her son from her White neighbor's racism. The mother did not want to frighten her child, and so did not fully disclose what she knew about her neighbors. At a young age, the child was confused. Later, upon learning the truth about what this neighbor had done to his family, he became frightened:

Throughout my early childhood, my mother would never let me play with my White neighbor, who was a year older than I was. I was always angered that my mother would tell me that it was not safe to play with him. It was not until I was older, perhaps in middle school, that my mother told me that the parents of my neighbor friend were racists. She then told me a story about when my family first moved into our predominantly White neighborhood. After we moved into the newly constructed tract, my parents were unable to immediately landscape the property, due to other logistical commitments. Apparently, my mother received harsh looks from our neighbor and was told that my family needed to landscape the property because it was an eyesore. Eventually, my mother received a note that was comprised of cutouts from a newspaper, akin to the quintessential ransom note as popularized by the media. The note was harsh in demeanor and accused my family of being financially unable to afford residing in our neighborhood. Being the only Asian family on the street—it was clear we were not welcome. Although culpability was never firmly established, my parents always suspected the note was constructed by the mother of my neighbor. At this point, I was able to understand that my mother was protecting me when she refused to let me play with my neighbor. Unfortunately, I began to fear my neighbors and I was also afraid to go outside. (Chinese American, male)

This next selection involves two lessons learned in kindergarten. The first lesson involves a mother teaching her son about Japanese hatred toward Chinese people. The second involves discovering that his mother had racist attitudes toward Japanese people. The student had a 7-year-old brother who was not promoted to the next grade level by his Japanese teacher. Instead of trying to find out what would be necessary for her son to move forward, the mother teaches her son about the atrocities the Japanese committed in China and attributes this "evil" to the teacher responsible for failing her son:

> When I was in kindergarten my brother was in the second grade and had a teacher of Japanese descent named Ms. T. My mom came back one day after having a meeting with Ms. T about how my brother may have to repeat the second grade because his reading and pronunciation skills were not up to par. My mom was really upset and began telling us about how all Japanese people were evil and racist against Chinese people because of the atrocities they committed during WWII—she said she was going to complain to the administration and get the teacher fired. I guess this is when I first realized that some people dislike other people on such an arbitrary basis and that some people did not like Chinese people. I remember that I began to avoid people who I knew were Japanese because I was afraid that they would not like me. (Taiwanese American, male)

Sometimes parents provide indirect lessons in painting. They may be unable or unwilling to openly discuss racial issues with their children. Consider this example taken from a class discussion. A Black student recalls overhearing a White mother explaining race to her child. The child asked, "Mommy, why is that man so dark?" The mother responded "God probably decided to leave him in the oven a little bit longer but we shouldn't make him feel bad." After my student reported the story to his classmates, two other students of color also indicated that they had heard identical comments from White parents to their children. Helms (1992) cites this example and describes similar comments that children make to parents:

> *"Mommy, look at the chocolate man. Can I bite him?"*
> *"Why is that man so dirty?"*

Parents are often embarrassed by their child's innocent questions. Children learn that race is a sensitive issue that makes many adults uncomfortable and that they should not talk about it. Children learn that being White is favored by God. Families can provide painting lessons which may be continued from one generation to the next.

Unfortunately, most adults do not have the understanding of how to talk to their children about race. Professor Beverly Tatum illustrates how she insightfully handled a comment about difference made by her son. She had set some eggs out on the kitchen counter. Some of the eggs were brown and some of the eggs were white. Her son commented on the fact that the eggs were not all the same color. "Yes," she said, "they do have different shells. But look at this!" She cracked open a white egg. "See, they are different on the outside, but the same on the inside. People are the same way. They look different on the

ENDING RACISM IN AMERICA

outside, but they are the same on the inside" (Tatum, 1997). Though some families do teach their children to understand, welcome, or appreciate skin difference, such teachings are rare. This opening section has argued that many White adults harbor racist images and stereotypes and practice racial discrimination in their daily lives. Children are exposed to this reality and their activities often reproduce what they observe and understand. Thus, racism is not an abstract concept; it is learned in concrete, real ongoing relationships. Van Ausdale and Feagin (2001) argue that the experiences of childhood create the foundation for adults' social lives. Feagin's work is quite important as it documents how children learn racial slurs even when parents do not use racial epithets in the home, further establishing the idea that racism can be preconscious and unconscious.

LEARNING TO PAINT FROM PEERS AND INTIMATES

Family members are not the only teachers of racism. As our young students entered school and began encountering peers, they discovered a powerful new paint brush. This is the paintbrush brandished by their peers. Peer groups are as powerful, or more so, than families in promoting racism. Van Ausdale and Feagin (2001) note that "the friendship and peer relationships that children develop in their earliest years can generate or reinforce stereotype or intolerance based on racial and ethnic origins" (p. 126). The peer group teaches its applicant the rules for participation and full acceptance. Therefore, it is not surprising that many of the students reported learning racial stereotypes and prejudices from their social cliques. This was achieved through a combination of both subtle and explicit messages.

Like the family, the peer group can instill the superiority of one group over another. The peer group empowers those who perpetuate the values of the group and rewards those who remain loyal. This goal must be accomplished for the peer group to successfully exist, and is often achieved at the expense of others. Both White and non-White children learn to label and ostracize the "other" in the confines of their own social group.

In this first example of peer painting, a Jewish male is scolded by his father for repeating racist jokes. He is unable, however, to stop this behavior in front of his peers; he merely hides it from his father. He gains a feeling of satisfaction from retelling derogatory jokes to his friends about African Americans, Latinos/as, Asians, and non-Jews. He is able to repeat derogatory jokes in spite of the lessons he has been taught in Hebrew school and by his father:

> When I was 12 my cousins felt that it was okay to start telling me racist
> jokes. Most of these jokes were about Blacks. They told me jokes about

Blacks being stupid, having big lips, being criminals, and having large penises. There were jokes about Latinos having large families, having beat-up cars, and being criminals. There were jokes about Asians having slanted eyes, flat faces, driving "rice rockets" and having small penises. There were also jokes about Goys (non-Jews) being stupid and putting too much mayonnaise on their sandwiches. I don't know why, but I found these things funny. I began to see myself as a Jew and a White person who was above everybody else in society. Everything I had learned in Hebrew school told me that everybody was created equally, but the opinions of my cousins meant more to me. I began retelling these jokes to my friends. My friends found these jokes funny as well and I enjoyed the feeling I got from the laughter I was able to create through these jokes. I never saw this as being something bad until I told one of these jokes in front of my father. He went crazy, he yelled at me so loud that I cried. He told me that I should never tell racist jokes. I did not stop telling the jokes, however, I just never told them in front of my father again. (Jewish American, male)

White peers taught a 6-year-old Korean child that her physical characteristics are deficient. They first treat her like a "China doll" and give instructions about what she would have to do to belong. They suggest that she needs to change her skin and hair color. A belief in their superiority is exemplified in their idea that their round-shaped eyes allow them to see more clearly than their Korean peer and her slanted eyes:

I had just come to the United States and the first school I had attended had very few students of color. My brother and I made up the only two Asians in the school; there was one African American, and one Hispanic. This was San Dimas, CA in 1982. The first set of friends I had were White girls from middle-class families. We were only six-years-old and though I did not understand them, we communicated using our hand motions and our facial gestures. They would talk amongst themselves, but I did not understand. It took me about six months to fully understand the English language. Though my pronunciations were not perfect, I understood most all of the language used by my peers. The girls would approach me and touch my hair and feel my skin and make facial gestures. They looked confused and looked in awe. They would say, "You have darker skin than us, you have such dark, straight hair, and you have such small eyes." They looked astonished, like I was some antique China doll. They were confused at what they were seeing. They did not know how to respond to my features, and I did not know how to respond to their words. They would also ask me, "Do you take showers, do you see clearly through those eyes of yours, and does your hair wash out from that color?" They would also say, "When you go home today, try to scrape it off, maybe it will come off, and maybe if you wash your hair, it wouldn't be so dark."

They were so cruel even though I believe they did not mean to be. I ran into the restroom and looked at myself in the mirror. I was darker, I had black hair, and my eyes were half the size of theirs. They would often say "Chinese, Japanese, Cantonese," while they were squinting their eyes with their fingers.

I went home that day and watched an episode of the *Brady Bunch* on television. I saw that Jan Brady put lemons on her face to get rid of freckles. I ran to my mother and asked for lemons. She thought I wanted to make lemonade, so we went to the store and I bought a bag of lemons. The moment I got home, I ran into the restroom and locked myself in. I could not imagine the reaction from my mother if she had known what I was doing. I started to get scared and nervous. I quickly peeled all of the lemons using a plastic knife and started applying it onto my skin and hair. I thought this would make me lighter and make my hair lighter as well.

The next morning when I woke up from bed, I ran straight to the mirror. Unfortunately, I found the same person I had seen the day before. I saw the dark skin, the dark hair and the slanted eyes. For weeks, I had irritated skin. I was miserable. I was not only dark but scratching myself everywhere. However, through all this, I was the best smelling kid in the whole class. (Korean, female)

In this next example, a young Argentinean-Italian female learns that her hair is unacceptable. It is unattractive and does not conform to the models of beauty that her young peers already uphold. She is made to feel ugly. She will not be invited to future sleepovers and she will feel left out for a very long time:

When I was nine years old, I lived in North Hollywood and attended a private parochial school. I was invited to my first all-girls sleepover party and was incredibly excited. There were at least a dozen of my classmates there, and everything started off very normal for a sleepover: dancing in pajamas, eating pizza and popcorn, making crank calls, etc. I was having so much fun until one of the girls pulls out her older sister's *TEEN Magazine*. After reading everyone's horoscopes, the girl who brought the magazine displayed to everyone a four page spread on the latest hairstyles, complete with "step-by-step-do-it-yourself-easy" directions for each style. This fascinated all the girls, who then all wanted to French braid or tease someone's hair, sparking the idea that there was to be a beauty pageant complete with "hair, makeup & Polaroids" that night. So to participate in this contest, I released the ponytail that always held my hair back. I could be beautiful, right? Well, when one of the girls tried to comb my hair with a fine-tooth comb, it literally got stuck. Unlike all the other girls in the sleepover, my hair was not straight, long, and blonde with bangs. I inherited brownish-black, super curly hair from my father's side, the Argentine-Italian side. My younger sister was lucky enough to inherit my mom's straight hair. The girl that attempted to style my hair quickly gave up, and tried to recruit another girl to take her place as the stylist. She tried putting water and hairspray, and it still would not hold in the braids or crimps that they were trying to accomplish. As disappointed as I was that my hair wasn't cooperating, the comments that the girls made regarding the ordeal bothered me more: "I've never seen hair like yours before," "Are you the only one in your family that turned out like this?" "Doesn't it ever get straight?" "What are we gonna do to her hair? The magazine has no styles for frizzy hair." After three girls tried styling my hair in vain, they then smeared pink makeup on my face and gave me heavy clip-on earrings to make me pretty for the contest. The end result was a Polaroid with me in bright makeup, a single clip-on earring (because those things hurt), and my puffy, frizzy hair, stiff with starchy Aquanet hairspray and topped off with a small, half-attempted braid dangling in front of my forehead. Needless to say, I didn't win the pageant.

Never before had I felt so ugly, so left-out. I began to hate my hair as if it was a curse for something I did wrong. After the pageant was over, I got a hold of the magazine. Not one model with naturally curly hair, not one model with dark skin, not one model that looked at all like me. The models looked like older versions of the girls in the sleepover: blue-eyed, green-eyed, straight-teethed, straight blonde hair, and the occasional freckle on someone's nose. This was beautiful. This was "perfectly put-together." Was there anything I could do to make my hair straight, like the White girls at my school? I kept thinking about this as I fell asleep that night, not knowing at the time that this was the last sleepover I was ever invited to by that group of girls. (Bicultural, female)

In the next selection, a young African American describes how she grew up without intimate experiences with White children. She goes to a camp where only 3 of the 120 children there are of color. Her initial feelings of excitement and satisfaction are drastically altered when she signs up for a hair and makeup activity. Like the young woman in the previous story, she is made to feel ashamed and different. Other girls have no inhibitions about asking insulting questions and invading her personal space by pulling her hair "to see if it's real":

> Until the age of ten I had grown up and only played with Black and Hispanic children. The only reason I knew children of other races existed was due to the television shows I watched like *Sesame Street, Reading Rainbow, The Cosby Show* and other kids' shows. I went away to summer camp for two weeks and I didn't know anyone. It was a culture shock because there were only two other black girls (making a total of three) out of 120 campers. I actually adjusted very well within the camp environment; my cabin mates and I got along great and I thought "Hey, these girls are just like me (these white and Asian girls)."

> One day I signed up for hair and make-up as my daily activity. I went to the workshop and the two female counselors that were leading it were White. They separated us into two groups; one working on hair and one working on make-up. I was sitting on the hair side. There were two girls in front of me so I waited with excitement; I couldn't wait to get some tips about hair and make-up from these two counselors who I thought were just great. When the counselor that was doing hair noticed that I was next, she told the other counselor, "Maybe we should switch." The counselor working with make-up looked at me and said "No way." I saw them continue to look at me and I began to feel sad and ashamed. I knew that they were looking at me and I realized that they had no idea what to do with my braids.

> I was happy to be saved from further embarrassment because we ran out of time before my turn came up. The rest of the week I had a heightened awareness of my ethnicity. I was constantly being reminded that I was Black through the activities that we did while at camp. The other girls in my cabin wanted to tan and they told me that I did not have to worry about having color in my skin. Even though they told me that they admired my dark skin, it didn't make me feel any better because I felt so different. My braids were also an issue with other girls at the camp. Curiosity does not give another person the right to invade your personal space but that is what was happening. One of my cabin mates wanted to know if my hair was real so she pulled my braids really hard. I told her to stop and she did, but I didn't appreciate the fact that it had happened.

> At the time I do not think I was able to realize the effect this experience had on me but looking back now, as an adult, I can see how these people's

actions shaped the way I view race and especially the way I perceive myself. (African American, female)

In the next example, a Filipino male describes how his participation with and acceptance by his peers would mean belittling others, even at the expense of other Asians:

> I am very ashamed to talk about it now, but my friends and I used to come up with names for people. We had this inside joke of speaking backwards, so that no one else would understand. I can't believe we used to do this, but whenever we would see an Asian that was really "Fresh off the Boat" we would call him or her a "dekcaj pin" which meant, in a roundabout way, "jacked nip." (Filipino, male)

Another Filipino male analyzes his negative views toward Latinos. This student, in part, attributes his racism to hearing his peer group's derogatory stereotypes about Latinos as dirty and uneducated. These early stereotypes influenced his view that Mexican American students on the UCLA campus were there only because of affirmative action:

> It is hard for me to admit this, and I feel shitty for thinking this way, but prior to taking this class I used to look at some Mexicans and say they got in here because of affirmative action. But from this class, I can honestly say that I am looking at people now on a personal level. I used to believe that I could figure out a person just by knowing their ethnicity. It's funny, but this very act that I did, I hate in other people when they do it to me. My friends in Napa forced their negative views of Mexicans onto me. Mexicans were the field workers who picked the grapes. They were looked upon as uneducated and dirty. What changed my views was my self-realization. The hatred I felt so long while growing up and being looked upon as different, I was in turn doing it to another ethnicity. So now I try to look at everyone equally and in an unbiased way. (Filipino, male)

This student acknowledges that some of his racism toward Latinos arises from the prejudices and discrimination he suffered growing up as a minority. Stigmatizing another minority allowed him to feel empowered. This student was able to begin to question the prejudicial practices of his peer group and to decide for himself that he did not want to align with their message of hate.

In college, there are few organizations that maintain a more powerful hold on shaping the ideals of students than the Greek system. Though minority groups have their own fraternities and sororities, the Greek system tends to remain an exclusive club of White privilege. As exclusive clubs, they are potential breeding grounds for prejudice and oppression. Indeed, within the confines of some fraternity and sorority houses lies shockingly raw racism. In this first example, a White male describes the ongoing, omnipresent racism in his fraternity:

> I had asked why his fish tank was so dirty, and his roommate replied to me by saying, "Oh don't worry, I'm probably going to have some Mexican come and clean it up. It will be funny to watch, and I won't even pay him much." Two minutes later, I heard one of S's friends call him a "Jew bastard" for not sharing his dessert with him. I could not believe my ears. Possibly the worst thing about the whole situation was the fact that there was one Latino male in the whole house and he heard what these guys were saying. He didn't say a word, but he definitely wasn't laughing. This type of shit happens all the time. The fraternity single-handedly slammed almost every single race there was except their own. I heard "smelly nip," "lazy porch monkey," and even "wetback," in the short time I was there. (White, male)

In this second example a White female has been afraid to disclose the fact that she is in a sorority house. She is ashamed of the practices of her house and the entire Greek system, which she knows to support privilege and exclusivity. She would like to confront what she sees and hates about racism, but she is also afraid of losing her privileges:

> For the past five weeks, I have basically hidden the fact that I'm a part of the Greek system. Well, I am more than a part of it, I hold a high position in my house. The fact that I have hidden this part of my identity says quite a bit. It shames me to be part of this discriminating organization in mixed company (yet another manifestation of my dominant mentality—ignoring the problem; it's not real if you don't talk about it). As much as I've tried to defend and prove that my house is different, I have found it harder and harder to do so. There is only one black sorority member in the entire system and a handful of Latinas. Although there are quite a few Asians, as a whole, Pan-Hellenic (comprised of sororities with houses) is around 80–90% White. Yet, as much as I am disturbed by our various practices and exclusive membership, I cannot imagine deactivating (which leaves me with a heavy sense of guilt that I cover up by believing anyone could join though I know in my heart it's not true). My feelings about belonging to this organization are very much tied to my feelings about being White. Both of these facets of my identity have undeniable advantages, which I am afraid to lose; they have become a part of my life. It terrifies me that I would probably be miserable if I woke up tomorrow

without these advantages. It seems to be a complex situation—individually, I win because I gain an edge and maintain it, yet morally, I lose as I perpetuate and propagate what I hate about this world. (White, female)

One of the earliest critics of Greek organizations, Alfred M. Lee, wrote in *Fraternities without Brotherhoods* (1955) that fraternities represent a basic threat to democracy in the United States. Almost 50 years later, Feagin, Vera, and Imani (1996) write that "white fraternities can play a negative role on race relations on campus, there have been homecoming floats with racist themes, staging racist skits, and parties with racist themes are not uncommon." There is a paradox facing students of color on college campuses who join predominantly White sororities and fraternities. Students of color who join "White" sororities and fraternities cannot be "authentic." In our discussions with students of color who have joined Pan-Hellenic sororities and fraternities, they continually express wanting to be themselves ("I am a student of color"), but feel pressured to fit into the White version of how students of color should act ("I can't be a student of color"). Students of color face the insurmountable problem of being "authentic" (Hughey, 2010). Their white sisters and brothers set the stage for the paradox by sending the contradictory message of "I want you to be White, but I know you can't be." This dilemma is illustrated in the next excerpt:

> Not just the White guys, but lots of folks, didn't matter, Black, a Korean guy…I don't know what to do when it happens…it's not like it happens every time, but it happens enough. They always try to make me drink the craziest stuff. Someone got some grain alcohol, and they always want me to drink that stuff until I'm really sick. I mean, I like to drink, especially with my fraternity brothers, but I don't want to get crazy…So they say "He's got that Latin blood…yeah, your blood will just burn that [expletive] liquor right out of your system."…I feel like, when we drink, like I'm a mascot. They say I've got a "Mexicano stomach"…I told you before my folks are from Puerto Rico…they stand around and cheer, making that dumb [expletive] stereotype "yayayaya" call like they do on TV… So, it's not racial, it's not just the White guys, its everyone. They are just assholes sometimes. That's just life. (Hughey, 2010, p. 671)

Hughey (2010) also describes how one Asian woman in a Pan-Hellenic sorority is told not to hang out with the other Asians. Two Asian women hanging out together and not being seen with their White sisters was worrisome. This would make it appear as if the White women in the sorority were excluding the Asian women and that their sorority encouraged racial segregation.

The racist practices of sororities and fraternities can lead students of color to develop their own fraternal organizations. In the following example, a Latina student refers to the exclusionary practices of "White" sororities, describes her initial ambivalence about joining a sorority and her subsequent feelings of acceptance and sisterhood that developed within a sorority that catered to Latina students. She argues for the virtue and benefits of students of color having their "own":

My sorority is non-exclusionary and we do have a few women of other races such as White, Egyptian, Middle-Eastern, and Bi-racial. But, by the nature of the sorority we do mostly attract Latinas. I often hear criticisms from my sister and others that I am excluding myself by choosing to be part of a sorority that is racially-based. The class discussions made me further contemplate the reasons why I joined my sorority and the overall reasons why minorities create separate groups for themselves. I honestly do feel that groups and organizations that cater to minorities such as African-American fraternities or Latina-based sororities are necessary because of the exclusionary nature of "main-stream" organizations. It is similar to the concept of affirmative action in implementing policies that help diversify schools that have historically served only Whites. The majority of elite and private universities are populated by a majority of White students. My sorority was first founded in New Jersey in 1975, during a time where there was an influx of Latinos in colleges and universities. During this time there were no organizations that catered to the Latino student's needs. And so my founding mothers created an organization based on academic achievement and success. This was a support group for them to continue on in their education and battle social injustices together. As I mentioned in class, many of the Panhellenic sororities are obviously catering to a certain population when they charge thousands in dues just to live in a mansion-like house. I have nothing against those who can afford such luxuries, but there is obviously a population of students who are not able to acquire these resources because of finances. This is why my sorority limits the financial burden we place on sisters by reducing quarterly dues, and by not owning a house, because doing so means we have to pay more. When I think back to why I joined my sorority, I remember at first being wary of Latina sororities because I thought they would think I wasn't "Latina" enough and I was also disillusioned of the whole sorority concept because of bad experiences from the past. However, I decided to give it a chance, and when I attended my first meeting I just remember feeling extremely welcomed and "at home." This was my place on campus where I could be myself and feel like people truly accepted me for who I was, not by the way I looked. I decided to stay and pledge my sorority because of the real sisterhood I witnessed between the older sisters and because of the high aspirations they all had. Before coming to UCLA, I never pictured myself going on to graduate school. I didn't have anybody in my family to look up to who had done so. After joining my sorority and seeing women who LOOKED LIKE ME, who came from similar backgrounds, and who went through the same struggles I did as a Latina, accomplishing such amazing things like going on to Medical school, Law School, Masters programs, and the Peace Corps, I was inspired to accomplish more for myself. I can honestly say for all of my sisters, higher education beyond the undergraduate level isn't even a question. What keeps us united is our aspirations and passion for social justice. It is not like we sit around at meetings talking in Spanish, we came together as a group to motivate and inspire each other to dream big, and to give back to our communities by equally inspiring them to break barriers and aspire for more.

And so to those critics who say minorities are excluding themselves by forming their own groups, I argue that we are not because there is a necessity for the disenfranchised to empower themselves by working together. When you have been excluded from a system for so long you need a support group to lift you up and remind you of your worth and capabilities. Specifically, for my organization I want to say that we really are non-exclusionary. Any young women, regardless of ethnic background or economic capital, is welcomed with open arms into our organization as long as they display passion for academics, social justice, community service, and convey a commitment to the organization itself. Any one of my sisters will tell you that we are all about self-transformation, personal growth, and empowerment of the universal woman. (Bi-racial, Latina, UCLA)

Subordinates who challenge the norms that their peers hold about cross-race contact learn quickly that peer group norms are powerful. In the next example, an African American male was able to stand up to his peers. He describes the tension that was set in motion when he acted against the beliefs of his peer group by dating a White woman. Specifically, this student recalls how he learned to stand up for what he believed in even if his peers disapproved:

I dated a White girl in high school, and although none of the Black women at school wanted to date me, they were very upset that I was dating a White girl. They constantly made racial comments about her and me, and even talked poorly about me to my younger sister (who was in the ninth grade). After speaking with my father about dating someone outside of my own race, he reminded me that in God's eyes, everyone is the same color. Soon after, I decided that I did not have to be Black enough for them. I just had to be myself and stand up for what I believed in. (African American, male)

In another example of subordinates being painted by other subordinates, an Asian female remembers how her own Asian peer group shunned her when she went to a dance with a White boy. She eventually learns to move beyond the anger and shame she felt from the label "White-washed" imposed by her peers:

> I cannot relate to some Asians who feel that they can only relate to other Asians. I feel like those people are closed-minded and have a false sense of pride in their Asian heritage. Many of them don't know the first thing about the native land or culture. As a freshman in high school, I went to a dance with a White guy and since that day, the label "White washed" stuck on me, no matter how many Asian friends I hung out with. I struggled with this label, feeling anger, shame, disgust. Then I got over it. I thought, what do they know about me? I gained enough confidence to look past it and even not to hate the labelers. (Asian, female)

In the following excerpt, a Filipina woman describes the conflict she endures after she refuses to accept the prejudice that she overhears. She fights against the stereotypes her own peer group maintains for Iranian people:

> I can recall playing the role of the ally when I was with a friend one time and we were just talking in the Kerckhoff patio (UCLA). Now in that patio, most of the people there are Iranian. I guess they just tend to congregate there. Well, my friend proceeds to tell me the same things or "complaints" I've heard many people say before about them like "They're too loud and obnoxious" and that they always sit in the patio. People at my work at the Kerckhoff Coffeehouse always complain about them. To me, sometimes they get on my nerves because they can be really obnoxious, but I try not to play it up or else I'll be just like my friends and people at work and I don't want to be. So, my point is that I think it's really kind of jacked how so many people complain about them. Also, now people think that just because I always defend the people they make fun of or complain about, that I am calling them racist or that I'm just some uptight person who can never hear or listen or be exposed to anything remotely bad. That, actually, is tough to deal with. (Filipina, female)

The power of the peer group is captured in the above excerpt. This student has rebelled against the stereotypes her friends inflict on Iranian people. Her courage to fight racism is not met with open arms. Instead, she is criticized for speaking out against the group's collective mindset. She is made to feel that she is naïve and cannot handle the mature and raw content of her co-workers' conversations.

Some readers might believe that on the sports fields and in the gyms of America, the playing fields have been leveled. The following selections suggest the powerful privilege that White males still exert over America's supposedly "level playing fields." In this first passage, a White student admits his own resentment and discomfort about his behavior when a subordinate had the talent and audacity to outperform his White peers. In recalling this experience, the student was prompted to reflect and examine his racism. He struggles to understand why he let his peers continually foul a Black teammate:

> It's now three weeks into the course and I remember a distant high school memory. When he arrived on campus he was about 115 lbs and 5′7 inches tall. He was a small kid, but he could play some serious basketball. From the first day of practice, I knew, aside from his exemplary basketball skills, that he would stand out from within and from without. First of all, he was a freshman and a tiny one at that. Second of all, he dressed completely different from the rest of us. To add to the list, he was obnoxious and made a habit of "talking trash"; a regular event on most basketball teams and in most games, but not at my high school, not from a bunch of "clean-cut" White kids. Lastly and seemingly most important, he was Black. Not only was he the first Black basketball player at my high school in over a decade, he was among only 10–15 African American students in the entire school. For many of my teammates and I, he was instantly foreign in almost every way.

> At first we were very proud to have someone of his talent come to our school, but as time passed and practice began, things started to unravel. I soon came to realize that he was going to take my starting position, a feeling I had yet to experience in my life. I was upset until he physically humbled me on the court just about every day in practice. So I learned to accept the fact that he was a better basketball player than me. But it didn't stop there. He was extremely cocky and his personality was very . . . Black. He sagged his shorts, pointed in your face after a good shot, and made fun of us when we weren't as graceful as he with the basketball. He listened to a different type of music; he was loud and overly confident. As days went by and the differences between us began to display themselves, we decided to put an end to it.

> We ostracized him at school, but more glaring in my memory is that we systematically made sure that every time he went to the hoop he received

a foul. This started out in a minor way, but every time he bounced off the floor and talked trash, the fouls became harder. After about a week, he had had enough and he reached his breaking point. On that particular night, he must have been fouled about 20 times by various teammates. And finally, he started to cry. Here he was, the smallest, youngest, and best player on our team, completely alone, too abused to raise his usual psychological front and bearing his soul for all of us to see. He muttered a few words through his tears, he made a desperate plea for an explanation and I specifically remember him saying the following words, "Why are you doing this to me? I want to be your teammate, but I can't take this anymore."

At the time, I felt bad, as any human with feelings would, but I never really examined either of our actions. We instantly became very good friends, but that night still kind of haunts me. I remember not actually partaking in the physical abuse. I wasn't doing the fouling and I wasn't actually asking my teammates to do this, but I didn't stop it. In fact, if it had worked, I would have been the beneficiary of the starting position I had quickly lost. So I let it happen. Today in class I openly tried to find out why. I think I was so used to having the advantage in life. I didn't respect where he was coming from and I didn't know how to react to someone so different from myself. (White, male)

California has one of the highest rates of intermarriage in America. Campuses that are diverse include couples that are dating and deeply committed to each other. Despite the intimacy that emerges in a romantic relationship, race continues to divide couples. It is a subject that is often ignored or when discussed, can lead to fights regarding the validity of subordinates' experiences. Sometimes public events stimulate discussion between intimate partners that makes it very clear that the person you love is living in a different reality. Reactions to current events such as the murder of Matthew Shepard in 1998[2] and Hurricane Katrina (Dyson, 2005) can set up fault lines in America—not only between couples, but between families and communities, as well.

In this first example, the ripples of 9/11 begin entering the world of a Sri-Lankan female and her African American boyfriend of a year and a half. Her boyfriend cannot believe that his girlfriend is opposed to the Al-Qaeda attacks. He refuses to recognize the possibility of a Muslim who is extremely upset by the attacks on America. He cannot accept her grief about the possibility that she herself may have lost friends in the Twin Tower attacks. Ironically, he is an individual who himself has known prejudice and persecution

---

2 Matthew Shepard was murdered in 1998. The movie *The Matthew Shepard Story* (2002) describes the way in which this gay student was tied to a pole and left to freeze to death. *The Laramie Project* (2002) describes the deep divisions in the community over his murder.

and who now is turning on his own girlfriend. Even her religious practices, which he had never commented upon before during their relationship, are belittled and insulted. This young man is unable to comprehend that not all Muslims support terrorist attacks in honor of their religion. The young woman also predicts the rise of future anti-Muslim behavior:

> September 13th, 2001 will forever remain engraved in my mind. The unfortunate events that occurred a few days before were the topic of the conversation with my boyfriend, who I had been with for about a year and a half. I was overwhelmed by sorrow given that I had friends and relatives, who lived in the area surrounding the World Trade Center, who were still unaccounted for. After speaking about the matter for a while, my boyfriend asked me how I felt about the attacks. I responded by reiterating that I was horrified and extremely empathic to the families of the victims; emotions that paralleled those of most individuals in the country. My boyfriend DID NOT SEEM quite satisfied OR CONVINCED by my response—his contention being that since I was Muslim, much like the terrorists who flew the airplanes into the Twin Towers, I must identify with their cause. I defended my position quite vehemently and he conceded. However, he went on to question what my parents thought apropos of the attacks. He was quite adamant in his belief about my parents. He said that he could understand that I might not condone the actions of the terrorists because I was partially raised in the United States. He was, however, quite sure that my conservative Muslim parents were in support of the terrorist cells in some form or manner. Once again, I repeated that they were stunned and horrified by the harrowing event. However, he questioned as to what they "really" thought about the attacks as if to suggest that we support the acts in silence for fear of reprisal from the U.S. government. I was enraged that my African-American boyfriend, who was quite active in fighting racism and prejudice in the African American community, would be so incredibly ignorant as to associate the acts committed by the terrorists to my spiritual beliefs. UNFORTUNATELY, that conversation served as a microcosm of the gamut of events that would occur in the months to come. Suffice to say, my relationship did not last for long—not only was he quite firm in his belief that Muslims around the country endorsed the terrorists, he would also make derogatory comments such as referring to the Friday prayer at the mosque as the "weekly meeting for terrorists." This experience made me feel uneasy about who I am not because I had taken part in an atrocious act but merely because I had chosen to adhere to Islam. (Sri-Lankan, female)

In this second example, a young woman of Armenian background describes the ongoing arguments with her Mexican boyfriend. She continually sees him as responsible for what happens with the police, his job search, and family issues, while he deeply feels that she does not understand what racism has done and is doing to him. Her transformation in understanding came about fortuitously. Their 3-year relationship never gets past the issue of race:

> We had one of our biggest fights when D. wasn't invited to my brother's wedding. He was furious and convinced that he was being left out because he was Mexican. I told him that his race has nothing to do with it and that I was getting annoyed at him always bringing race into every topic we discussed. "My family, especially my brother, don't want you coming because they think you don't treat me well," I said. "Well if I wasn't Mexican I think they would like me a lot more, even if I didn't treat you amazingly all the time," he responded. I didn't believe that my family disliked him because he was Mexican. The truth, which I could not even admit to myself at the time, was that, because he would be only one of two Mexicans invited to the entire wedding, I was uncomfortable having him there—not because we fought and often disagreed, not because he wasn't always great to me, but because he was Mexican. We never resolved the differences that we both deeply believed in. We fought over many issues after this, including things like speeding tickets, and his long search for a job, and even following family functions. In the long run, not being able to understand where he was coming from, and maybe not even wanting to deal with my own racism that lay so deeply buried, was a major factor in our breakup. (Armenian, female)

In this chapter there were different messages and lessons of "truths about racism." The instructors or teachers believed that what they were saying was true and wanted the listeners to learn those lessons. The family and peer groups are the most proximal collectives that influence children. These journal excerpts and web-posts illustrate the pain and trauma that may accompany painting from family and peers. Names, behavior, jokes, and questions can all leave a legacy of pain, suspicion, mistrust, anger, and rage. An example of lessons in hatred, discrimination, and racism is illustrated in the song "National Brotherhood Week," written by Tom Lehrer. He mocks our tendency to practice principals of respect and democracy for only 1 week a year. Many feel that our national holidays that honor Cesar Chavez and Martin Luther King Jr., as well as Black History and National Hispanic Heritage months are artificial. When we celebrate all Americans, all year round, we will not have songs that point out our hypocrisy. Black history and Latino history are American history. We encourage our students to listen to the song at http://www.youtube.com/watch?v=OAOwYDlEQXo.

All of these student stories contain lessons that are taught by families and peers on the subject of race. Unfortunately, the lessons learned are about demeaning and distancing others rather than about inclusion and acceptance. A summary of the lessons conveyed in the preceding stories is presented below. Other lessons on race exist! We are sure that our readers can provide their professors and classmates with their own lessons and we invite them to send these lessons to us at jrabow@soc.ucla.edu.

RACIST MESSAGES FROM FAMILY MEMBERS AND PEERS

African Americans

- African Americans are inferior to Whites.
- African Americans are lazy.
- African American men are violent.
- African Americans cannot act equal to Whites.
- Do not date African Americans.
- African American women are not beautiful.
- White women are more physically beautiful than African American women.

Latino/Latinas

- All Mexicans are illegal immigrants.
- Mexicans only work menial labor.
- Mexican Americans are inferior to Whites.
- Latino/a children are disgusting.
- All Latinos are Mexicans.

Asian Americans

- Asian Americans are cheap.
- Asian Americans are not true Americans.
- Japanese Americans harbor hate for Chinese Americans.
- Filipino Americans are gangsters.

Middle-Eastern

- Middle Eastern Americans are dangerous.
- Persian Americans are loud and obnoxious.

Muslims

- All Muslims are terrorists.

Non-Whites

- Minorities should only date other minorities.
- Minorities who act White and associate with Whites are superior to other minorities.
- African Americans, Latinos, and Asian Americans look weird.
- White skin is preferable to dark skin.
- Non-White hair is ugly hair.
- Non-Whites are okay to taunt.
- Minorities are too sensitive about discrimination.

Anti-racist Talk

- Speaking out against racism means you are overly sensitive.

STEREOTYPE EXERCISE

This exercise will allow instructors to expose some of the pernicious stereotypes that students bring to class. You have the option of doing it, but if you do it, it must be done with enough time so that the results can be processed and discussed. It is also very important that students work quickly and anonymously.

Instructors:

Ask your students to write down the first three words that come to their mind upon seeing the categories that appear on the hand-out at the end of these instructions. The size and composition of the class affects the type and number of categories that are chosen. You should delete any identities from the table below that don't exist in your class or add some identities that are not provided in the first page. Latinos may prefer Salvadorian, Guatemalan, Cuban, or Puerto Rican. A general category should be used if there are only a few students in that category. "Asian" can be used with only a few Asian students in the class, but can be further broken down into "Chinese," "Korean," "Vietnamese," and other categories. It is best to use the identity groups that exist in the class. In that way, students can see the stereotypes that exist for their classmates. You can include as many categories as are represented in the class; for instance, deaf became a category when I was teaching at Northridge. The response sheets are anonymous. After the papers are handed in, have someone put all the responses under the different racial and ethnic categories on the board so all can see. You can do this more rapidly by having five or six students work at the board. It is important to stress the anonymous nature of this survey with the idea that it is only by being honest that we can begin to look at covert racism, which is buttressed by stereotypes.

When the sheets of paper are collected and the responses to the categories are written on the board, students in the class immediately become aware that their fellow students have stereotypes about them. This is often shocking and very hurtful. Even positive stereotypes may cause harm. The "stereotypes wall" is visual evidence that can debunk students' initial resistance to the idea that we are all racists. Because your students are in college, the exercise illustrates that education is not a guarantee for reduced prejudice. What is even more remarkable is that out of all the stereotypes that are posted, there are very few that members of any particular group have not heard. In the processing of this exercise, students are asked to recall specific times that they were called any of these names. This is a powerful exercise for it not only makes racism palpable for the students in class, but it also makes racism as close as the student right next to them.

Students:

We are providing you with 16 identity names. Please respond with the first three words or phrases that come to your mind when you read each identity name. This exercise is anonymous. Please be as honest as possible. Do not discuss it with your fellow students. It would be better for the class if you do not compare notes. Again, write down the first three words that come to your mind for each category. Please do not take offense if your own identity has been left out. If you would like to have your identity on this page, please indicate this to the instructor. There is room at the back of the page.

Biracial Male 1. _____ 2. _____ 3. _____	**Biracial Female** 1. _____ 2. _____ 3. _____	**Multi-Cultural Female** 1. _____ 2. _____ 3. _____
Middle Eastern Male 1. _____ 2. _____ 3. _____	**Middle Eastern Female** 1. _____ 2. _____ 3. _____	**Multi-Cultural Male** 1. _____ 2. _____ 3. _____
Gay Male 1. _____ 2. _____ 3. _____	**White Male** 1. _____ 2. _____ 3. _____	
Asian American Male 1. _____ 2. _____ 3. _____	**Asian American Female** 1. _____ 2. _____ 3. _____	
White Female 1. _____ 2. _____ 3. _____	**African American Female** 1. _____ 2. _____ 3. _____	
Latina 1. _____ 2. _____ 3. _____	**Lesbian** 1. _____ 2. _____ 3. _____	
African American Male 1. _____ 2. _____ 3. _____	**Latino** 1. _____ 2. _____ 3. _____	

CHAPTER 3

Learning to Paint: Institutional Settings

"Where justice is denied, where poverty is enforced, where ignorance prevails, and where any one class is made to feel that society is an organized conspiracy to oppress, rob and degrade them, neither persons nor property will be safe."[1]

—Frederick Douglass, 1886
(1817–1895, prominent abolitionist speaker, author, and publisher)

Though a great deal of painting is learned from families and peers, there are others in our society who are instrumental in teaching us how to become painters. These painters reside in all institutions and look for subjects to teach their racist practices. In the journals we surveyed, we found five institutional settings that provided instructions on how to paint. The norms that govern these institutions will not be documented in this book. Rather, we offer the reader examples

---

1 Speech delivered April 16, 1886, in memory of the abolition of slavery in the District of Columbia.

that occur within our everyday institutions—specifically, schools, media, law enforcement, workplaces, and public settings.

Table 2 describes the four institutional representatives who act as teachers and who instruct 36 students from six ethnic and racial groups. The targets of their instruction include ALL major ethnic and racial groups.

TABLE 2

The Teachers, Learners, and Targets of Racism

Teachers		Learners		Targets	
Media	10	African Americans	11	African Americans	14
Peers	10	Asian Americans	9	Asians	9
Police	5	Bi Ethnics	1	Latinos(as)	8
Teachers/Superiors	11	Latinos (as)	9	Middle Easterners	3
		Middle Easterners	2	Whites	1
		Whites	4		
Total	36	Total	33	Total	35

SCHOOL

The school environment serves many functions as children develop. Schools teach children educational skills, independence, socialization with peers, and numerous other skills that will follow them through life. Yet, it is in schools that children learn about racism. Often, teachers, counselors, psychologists, social workers, and administrators have not confronted their own stereotypes and prejudices and they teach racism to their students. These lessons from school personnel reinforce the racism that they have learned from family members. Elementary schools are breeding grounds for teaching children to become painters, and colleges throughout the United States are places where the seed of racism bare bitter fruit.

Teachers have the opportunity, ability, and authority to shape the minds of their students. Though it is our hope that most educators use their tremendous power and influence in the classroom to dispel myths, stereotypes, and prejudices involving race, this is not always the case. Instead, teachers are often the painters of racism; they can hold impressionable minds hostage to their damaging ideologies. Teachers instruct White students that it is acceptable to paint. As recipients of the painting, students of color often learn that they deserve to be painted because they are different.

Painting or racism takes a toll on the self-esteem and performance of students of color. For example, standardized testing serves to perpetuate the myth that students of color are academically inferior to White students. White students, on average, have better scores than students of color. What is the possible explanation for this difference in academic performance? A false myth of genetic inferiority is easily alleged. A more plausible explanation is that schools do not prepare students of color to succeed academically, but ensure that White students succeed. Claude M. Steele (1997) has discovered one major reason for this discrepancy. He found that scores of non-White students varied depending on how the test was presented. When presented as an intelligence test, students of color did worse. When presented as a general skills test, their scores were equal to those of White students. White students' scores did not vary by how the test was presented. Steele's work demonstrates that lower test scores are caused by the ingrained beliefs and stereotypes of lower achievement that students of color carry.

These findings suggest that many students of color may perform lower than average on important tests like the SAT, LSAT, and GRE because they believe they are academically inferior to White students. The importance of these findings is immeasurable. Steele's research highlights the harrowing, life-changing effects that painting has on the self-worth, career, opportunities, and performance of students.

In addition to the testing situation that Steele describes are other key dimensions of schooling that perpetuate racism. We will describe these experiences within three categories: (1) elementary to the ninth grade, (2) high school, and (3) college.

ELEMENTARY

In our first example, an African American woman discusses an early experience with racism. She had always been in honors classes. She was selected with three other students of color as being incapable of continuing on in honors classes. If it were not for her mother, this teacher's racism would have been academically consequential for this young woman, as well as leaving her with a strong sense of injustice:

> I had always been in honors classes as far as I can remember. So when it came to my placement in a seventh-grade chemistry class, honors was the automatic choice. Well, my teacher felt differently. At the time I did not see it, but she systematically picked out all the blacks (two) and Latinos (one) in the class and said we could not be in her class because we did not

pass the test to qualify. The other kids just went to the regular classes. I would have too if not for my mother. I brought home a letter explaining my placement but my mother would not have it. The next day, she came to school with me and had a meeting with my counselor. She demanded to see the test that said I did not qualify for the honors class. I was embarrassed because my mother was making a scene. She asked to see the test scores and apparently I scored very high. She then asked for my teacher to join the meeting so that they could go over my test scores. My mother said that when she showed her the test, the teacher's face turned bright red and she made up the excuse that maybe she got me mixed up with another person. My mother said that she asked her "How many Ijeoma Audrey Ekwunifes are enrolled on this campus?" and the teacher was dumbfounded. (African American, female)

Unfortunately, as our next selection reveals, racism can start as early as kindergarten. A teacher mistakenly believes that one of her students can only speak Spanish. She believes that Latinas can only pronounce the letters of the alphabet in Spanish. The student is made to feel confused and different. This was such a powerful experience that she never told anyone about it until college:

A week after I started kindergarten I remember the teacher saying that she was going to call out names and wanted the students whose names were called to sit at a round table with the teaching assistant. She didn't explain why she was doing this and I could tell some of us were confused. We didn't know if it was good or bad. The teacher started calling out names and then I heard mine so I went to sit with the assistant at the round table. After the teacher was done calling out names the assistant took out a deck of cards with the letters of the alphabet on them. She began to speak to us in Spanish and told us she was going to test us to see how many letters of the alphabet we knew.

At this point I was really confused and I wondered what was going on. I panicked because I only knew my alphabet in English and not in Spanish. When it was my turn I told the assistant that I didn't know the alphabet in Spanish. She asked me to try anyway and to do the best that I could. I was only able to say a few letters. After I was done she sent me back to sit on the rug with some of the other students. At the time I didn't understand that this incident was about my race but what it did do was make me feel different from everyone else. I don't think I ever told anyone else what happened. (Mexican American, female)

In the next excerpt a Latina student comments about a White teacher's stereotyping of an Asian student. The teacher cannot believe that the student has studied hard. She discredits the student's efforts because of her belief that Asians are the "model minority." The student acknowledges that she held the same stereotypes as the teacher:

> In fourth or fifth grade, I can remember a teacher responding to an Asian boy based on his race. It was not just a one-time thing but a constant stream of comments about his mathematical ability. I guess he had problems with the math content, which went against the stereotype she had of Asian students. One time when passing back the test she told him that "he must not have tried his best because you guys always get A's." The poor kid mumbled something quietly about studying really hard for the test, but the teacher did not hear him. Another time the teacher commented to the same boy that "Sara got a better grade than you and she is not even Oriental." I did not say anything when this happened because at that point of my life I totally had the same stereotype of Asians and their math ability. (Latina, female)

Another student recalls how her elementary school teacher taught her that as an Asian, she could not be an American. For this painter, being American was equated with being White:

> I remember asking my teacher when I was in elementary school if I was White. I wanted to draw myself using the white crayon. But my teacher said that White people were Americans. So my question was: "What's an American?" To that my teacher replied, "They have white skin, they speak English, and they were born here." To a little kid, the underside of my arms and my stomach certainly looked white to me. Plus, I was born here, and I also spoke English. But I couldn't understand why I wasn't considered White. My teacher told me I was Yellow and I should use the yellow crayon. I drew myself with the yellow crayon, but my skin didn't match the yellow crayon. To this day, I don't think I've ever found a shade that matches my skin color. (Asian, female)

Another Asian female recalls how she internalized the message that she was stupid in kindergarten because she spoke little English. Moreover, her teacher instilled in her the image of White beauty:

> When I entered kindergarten, I spoke virtually no English (although I understood it to a large degree). But because I spoke no English, other kids and some teachers treated me like I was stupid. As a child, I wanted so badly NOT to be Asian. I wanted to look like the people on televi-

sion and speak perfect English. The only role model I saw for myself on television was Wonder Woman, who with her dark hair, I imagined, was part Asian. A strong, but similar kind of prejudice against myself came in the form of a doll. I wanted so bad to have blond hair and blue eyes like Barbie. And it was always painfully obvious to me that I couldn't be without major expense. My friends from school in Irvine were all White with light-colored hair and blue or green eyes. I remember when the teacher would make comments about how some girls had pretty eyes and golden curls were always the prettiest. My mother always reminded me that I would "always have yellow skin." But I couldn't do anything about it, unless I took it to the point of totally reconstructing my face and body. Regardless, as a child, you don't have much choice (though nowadays, with plastic surgery, almost anything is possible). When I was ten, I talked about getting blue contacts, dying my hair, and getting breast implants and artificial legs because I hated my Asian features. I don't know when I grew out of this, but this was a childhood fantasy of mine. I hated myself so much that when one of my aunts bought me an Asian doll that looked like me for my birthday, I threw it away the next day. (Chinese, female)

Teachers are not the only painters on school grounds. As stated previously, the peer group is extremely potent in influencing its members, particularly when young. Painful and damaging messages are often transmitted to those who appear different from the clique. Also, since children have not learned the more manipulative and subtle skills involved in political correctness, their racism is usually uncensored, raw, and extremely cruel. In the following excerpt, a Latina student recalls her fourth-grade experience with the racism inflicted by her peers in the classroom. Her peers gave her a bar of soap to wash off her less-than-White skin color:

In elementary school, I was an ugly little thing, or at least, I thought I was. I was tall for my age, too skinny, and I had big, puffy hair. It wasn't that I was teased about it; it was more that the boys did not like me. It made it even worse that my sister and cousin were in the same school, and they were considered to be the prettiest girls around. The worst part about me, I thought, was my skin color. This is exactly how my classmates felt about me. One day, in the fourth grade, someone placed a little box in front of my desk. I looked into it and saw a bar of soap and a bottle of water. There was a note that said something like, "go wash yourself and scrub that dirt off." I felt really bad and wished that I could be as light as my cousin C. She always got all the attention because she had blonde hair and light eyes. Being dark in my school, or even in my neighborhood, taught me that I was ugly and that no one would ever like me. (Latina, female)

In the next example an Iranian-Jewish female recalls hearing a joke about her ethnic identity that seems normal to her fellow White counterparts, but that has a different meaning for her:

> When I was 13, I had an experience sitting in Homeroom waiting for the teacher to take roll. Our seats were positioned in groups of four facing each other. Sitting diagonally from me was this White boy who asked our table, "How do you know if you are Persian?" He answered before any of us could respond: "When you have a uni-brow and you are hairier than a monkey." The teacher was out of hearing shot, and I never told her what happened; I didn't want to be the class "tattle-tail." The other people sitting at our group desks laughed it off and moved on without thinking any more of the joke. (Iranian-Jewish, female)

In this next example an African American woman recalls the uncomfortable classroom atmosphere she was subjected to whenever her class discussed slavery. The repetitiveness of this classroom experience develops an anticipatory response of how to deal with the topic of slavery:

> It was around third grade that I began to get stares when the topic of slavery came up. At first I didn't know why I was being stared at. Was it because of what I was wearing? Was something on my face or in my teeth? It wasn't until I was older and my parents told me about my slavery ancestry that it began to get very uncomfortable. I felt like I was being singled out. I felt like I was part of an experiment. I felt like I was sitting there and people were waiting for my reaction to hearing about these negative things. They were waiting to see how I would react to someone being beaten or pictures of hangings. Eventually, I knew this would happen when we talked about slavery, so I would make sure that my face didn't show a reaction during these times in hopes that my classmates would stop staring at me. (African American, female)

The feelings expressed by this student have now been brought to the screen in *Freedom Writers*. In this movie scene, a White teacher requests that the only African American student in his honors class provide the Black perspective on *The Color Purple*:

> She responds, "Do I have a stamp on my forehead that says 'The National Spokesperson for the Plight of Black People'…How the hell should I know the black perspective of *The Color Purple*?"

The actress in the movie and the student in class express the deep frustration and anger when they are called upon to speak for their entire race.

In the next excerpt, an African American male discusses how prejudice occurred in the confines of his school. He recalls first learning about racism in third grade when a peer called him a derogatory name:

> I first learned of racism outside my home. I learned it because I had to deal with it as an everyday struggle. It became particularly prevalent when I was in the third grade, and my friend called me a "nigger." Being called a "nigger" was the equivalent of stabbing me in the heart. Here I am, playing with this kid, whom I consider a friend and equal, and he has the audacity to call me a "nigger"! I did not know exactly what the word meant but I knew it was degrading. No one should ever dare to call a Black person a "nigger." Those days of oppression should be over. I was only nine years old, but my blood was boiling and my temperature was rising because this kid was prejudiced. (African American, male)

HIGH SCHOOL

This next passage, taken from an African American high school student, reveals how her self-esteem is destroyed when she is told that she should go to college to become a nurse rather than to be a doctor, like her mother:

> In high school a guidance counselor told me that instead of going to college to become a doctor, I would probably be more comfortable becoming a nurse. She said things like "medical school is costly and highly selective" and that "they only select the best people." I was so angry. How dare she think me poor and stupid when I knew I was black, cute and smart! All my classes were advanced placement classes. I was in every club and on every sport team and I got straight A's. My mom was a doctor and I had always wanted to be like her. Now this woman was telling me that I was not good enough. She took my power and my energy away in just a few moments and all that I had worked for seemed irrelevant. (African American, female)

In the following excerpt we learn how a high school counselor treats a Latina, who is eager to turn over a new leaf and start college life. The counselor evaluates her as a student who cannot possibly succeed. The counselor not only misperceives her ethnicity but also can't believe that this student does not wish to get married and have babies immediately after high school:

I finally built enough courage to speak to my high school counselor about college. That week, I had overheard a couple of seniors discussing community college. They assured me that high school transcripts are not given to the college; it would be a new beginning. Thus, I made an appointment with my counselor to share the revelation that I had experienced of dedicating myself to attending community college. I anticipated that he would be excited and encourage me to pursue my academic dreams.

When I arrived at his office, he was buried in a newspaper and refused to look up. He assumed that a teacher had sent me to his office for disrupting the class. After I assured him this was not the case, he proceeded to remind me that I should be in class and not wasting time. "I want to go to college," I blurted out.

He finally put down his newspaper and stared at me for a few minutes. I held my breath and awaited his response. Strangely, a smile began to form. Finally, I thought, I have made him happy and excited about my future. But then he covered his mouth after letting out a slight chuckle. "You know Ms. M," he said. "You are not qualified to go to a four-year university straight out of high school. This school provides information to serious students about college and I think you know you are not one of them." He reached into his desk, pulled out my transcript, and plopped it in front of me.

"Now, let me ask you, do you know of any university that accepts students who have wasted four years accumulating C's and D's?" He proceeded, "Let me remind you that you need to focus on graduating. And besides, aren't you Mexican?"

"No!" I snapped. "I'm from Chile."

"Oh," he replied. "Isn't that the same thing? I mean, isn't it part of the Hispanic culture for females to get married and have children as soon as you turn eighteen?"

For a moment, I couldn't quite understand what he was (and was not) saying. I knew some Mexican young women who had children, but I also knew White, African American, and Asian young women who had children as well. I looked deeper into his cold face. My face began to get hot and tears formed in my eyes. I bravely swallowed my tears and said, "Look, I didn't come here to discuss my culture with you. I would like to receive more information on community college."

He took a deep breath and sat quietly for a moment. Finally he said, "Ms. M, I'm glad that you are thinking about your future. I'm going to be brutally honest with you because it is obvious that no one else is providing you with direction. You will remain trapped in the unmotivated life that you lead and the people you surround yourself with forever. I am certain that you are going to get yourself pregnant within years after you graduate."

"How could you say that to me? You don't even know who I am!"

I stormed out of his office and ran to the furthest part of campus. I cried out all the confusion and hurt and recognized that I had been looking at myself through the eyes of those who despised my skin. And so I began the lifelong journey of finding comfort with people with my own skin. (Latina, female)

In the next excerpt, an African American woman discusses her experiences with racism in her diverse high school. When students of color congregate they are seen as a threat:

At my ethnically diverse public high school, our principal—an old White man—made a rule that students couldn't walk together in groups larger than three because more than three of us together was intimidating. He reasoned that if large groups of us (I think I remember the words "hoodlums" or "thugs" being used) invoked fear in him, then certainly some of the smaller or more timid students would be scared of us, and the school should be an environment where everyone felt safe.

While it was never overtly said, large segments of the student body were people of color. When students were released from class, large visible groups of Filipino, Samoan, Black, Latino, Asian, and White students would congregate in their chosen home bases on campus. The White students on campus seldom had to feel the burn of the pepper spray the authorities commonly sprayed to break up a fight. Nicer areas of the city didn't have anything like our version of discipline. Once this new rule was implemented, though it seemed ludicrous to me—a well-behaved 14-year-old—I quickly found out that the new rule wasn't a joke.

Sitting with my predominantly Black crowd of friends in our usual hangout having lunch, we quickly made a group larger than three. The police didn't bother us at first, as many students crowded together in their usual hangouts; there were only so many places to eat. Whenever we stood up to walk somewhere in a group of more than three, an officer would quickly approach us with their pepper spray drawn, and would tell us to spread immediately. After an officer threatened my friends and I with pepper spray (a group of four petite Black girls) as if we were criminals, I decided to avoid walking anywhere anymore.

But the threats were inescapable. The next day, the moment the bell signaled the end of lunch, the police again came to where we were sitting comfortably and threatened us with their pepper spray drawn and ready to shoot. "Disperse," they said. We quickly grabbed our backpacks and ran to class. At the same time, I saw a group of Latino students being assaulted in the same fashion. (African-American, female)

Can you imagine White students being told they cannot sit or congregate together in groups larger than three? An explanation of why Black students congregate together is offered by Beverly Tatum (1997) in her wonderful book, *Why Are All the Black Kids Sitting Together in the Cafeteria? and Other Conversations about Race*. In high school, it is a normal developmental process for adolescents to begin thinking about and negotiating their identities. For White youth, their explorations involve choosing majors and occupations, dating and meeting friends, as well as trying out different types of clothing, music, and other preferences. While this process also occurs for students of color, their identity development is unique as it also involves their examining their racial and ethnic identities. It would be quite rare for a White student to ask, wonder, or deeply think about the kind of White person they want to be when they grow up. For Black and Brown students, however, this question is extremely salient. For the young men and women of color, issues of dress, patterns of speech, music, and whom they hang out with at school are also paramount. They sit and congregate together as they try to understand and explore who they are. Their explorations also involve examinations of teacher practices and expectations. When the teachers are White, they often have no experience with the kind of identity concerns that their students of color have. This sets the stage for misunderstandings, conflicts, and rejections. Thus we find White teachers responding to the identity explorations of their Black and Brown students with admonitions to "not wear those clothes," "not listen to that music," "not walk that way," and "not sit together in the cafeteria." The lack of understanding from White teachers and school administrators about the need for non-White students to congregate can result (as it did in the former excerpt) in the unfounded idea that this coming together is a defiant, dangerous act.

In the following excerpt we learn about an African American female who transfers from a predominantly White school to a multiracial public school. She is complemented about her intelligence and her "niceness" but the complements have a hollow ring to them, as the teachers act surprised that a Black high school student could be "so nice" and "so bright":

I went to a predominantly White private school until the sixth grade. "Predominantly White" meaning that I was usually the only minority child in my grade, and I don't remember there being more than five Black students at the school during any time when I was there. So I faced social isolation as a Black child. I was always different, could not possibly fit in, and had grown up feeling so much like an outcast and against the norm. So when I suddenly moved to a public multiethnic middle school, I still didn't fit in. Not only was I different because I was a "goody goody" private school kid, but I was a Black girl socialized to be White. Since I had gone to school with nothing but White kids my whole life, I didn't know what it was to be acculturated as a "Black girl."

Upon arriving at the public school, my peers wondered at me, painting me with their expectations of what a Black girl should be. "Why do you talk so proper?" they asked repeatedly. "Why do you act White?" I did well in school easily, but my self-esteem dropped. "You're not like other black girls. You're the nicest Black kid I've ever met." "You are so gifted and bright," the teachers told me again and again, as if they couldn't believe it. (African American, female)

In a final excerpt, a young Mexican American male is presented with the expectations that his White teacher has for him:

I was in tenth grade and I asked my history teacher a question and for no reason at all he said to the classroom "why do Mexicans study? They are all going end up being janitors anyways." I was in complete shock and I just stood silently, unable to do anything. I just sat down and went back to my work. I asked myself if I had just experienced racism? Why can't this teacher just learn about the Mexican race before he says stuff like that? (Mexican-American, male)

Although the efforts to demolish segregation and to achieve integration in high schools have been extensive, what do the results show? What might we expect when we integrate children from the same socioeconomic status? According to a national study of public high schools, Crosnoe (2009) indicates that African American and Latino students show smaller academic gains in high-income schools than in low-income schools. He calls this the "frog-pond effect." The students of color are either stigmatized in the high-income schools or lose out in the face of stiffer competition. This suggests that a new form of segregation within schools is occurring. The benefits that should be derived from socio-economic integration are undermined as low-income students in high-income schools remain socially and academically isolated and are unable to compete for resources.

COLLEGE

Most college students believe that they are less racist than their counterparts who have not moved forward beyond high school. While college may have some positive impact upon reducing racism, the impact tends to be rather small. As we shall see, the elite public University of California, Los Angeles (UCLA); two Cal State Universities, Channel Island and Northridge; the University of Southern California, a private school; and community colleges still teach and perpetuate racism.

In this first excerpt, a college student endures the racist ranting of a counselor. She enters the office and is "greeted very warmly." When the counselor begins to lambaste Mexican Americans, she is stunned, and unable to respond immediately. Once she leaves the scene and calms down, she begins the process of seeking justice:

> On my first day of summer school at SMC (Santa Monica College), I needed a permission code to enroll in a statistics course. I waited patiently for my turn to meet with the first available counselor. When I entered the counselor's office I was greeted very warmly. For some reason she, the counselor, began to converse with me about many different topics. One of the "topics" turned into one of the worst experiences I have ever gone through in my life. She began to talk about the local high schools and how the Mexicans drop out before even graduating. At this point I sank down in my chair and couldn't fathom what I was listening to. I wanted to scream; a million thoughts ran through my head about what I should say. She continued to talk to me, her fellow "White comrade" and explained how "Mexicans are lazy people who drain the economy." It didn't stop there. She said "their main focus was to have a big family; none of them go on to college." I wanted to scream at the top of my lungs. I wanted to tell her that Mexicans are the hardest working people; that many Mexicans achieve higher education. What this woman didn't realize was that she was talking about half of my family. I am Mexican-American and I am proud to be Mexican-American. This woman in her ignorance caused me to feel so much anger and hurt. I thought long and hard about a very eye-opening retort, but since I needed a permission code from her to register for my class, I remained silent. Once she finished, I asked for her card. I am now in the process of writing her and the president of SMC a very heartfelt letter about my experience with a counselor who instead of helping to guide a student to achieve everything she dreamed of in life, felt the need to degrade and humiliate an entire race. (Mexican American, female)

In the next excerpt, a biracial female/honor student is exposed to the lower expectations that her professor has of Latinas in contrast to the White students he is mentoring. She feels that he is doing "charity" and is supporting her research interests because of possible funding, not because she is deeply concerned about the impact of media stereotypes upon Latinos:

So just last week I had an experience with a professor that made me feel like shit. I actually almost felt like crying after the office hour appointment. So every Tuesday, I meet with my professor who is my adviser for my independent research project for Departmental Honors. I meet with him along with three other students who he is also advising for research projects. So I had already gotten the vibe from him that he really didn't understand where I was coming from and could already tell he was categorizing me when I first proposed my research topic to him which was about the stereotypical portrayals of Latinos on television and its effects on Latino adolescents. This was a "minority" issue that was rarely addressed and he noted as "important" to the field of Communication Studies. I kind of felt like he looked at me as a charity case and the only reason he accepted me as an advisee was because he would be "helping" me. He mentioned to me that he didn't have much experience with the topic of "Latinos" but that this kind of research would look amazing if I was planning on going to graduate school because not many people research topics revolving minority communities and media studies, and so there was a lot of potential funding in the research. I was a little thrown off by this statement because I was doing this research because this was a community that I loved and cared for and wanted to make change for, not because I knew there would be "funding" in the topic area.

Well, during this particular meeting we were wrapping things up with our papers and asking last minute questions. And then the Professor started asking each of us what our plans were after graduation. So he went down the line, and each person talked about the various job opportunities they were applying for, etc. And then he completely skipped over me. I felt completely invalidated. The professor may have not meant to do this but I felt like he didn't expect much out of me and so assumed there was nothing to hear about "my future plans." I do not know why I let this get to me but it did. And after walking out of the meeting I almost felt like crying. I had one of those moments where I questioned my abilities to be a successful UCLA student.

Reflecting back on this experience I am really upset at myself for allowing this professor to affect me and to devalue my experiences and potential.

This experience also made me think about exactly how I would want to talk to my future students if I become a teacher or professor. I would NEVER want to make them feel the way this professor made me feel and I also want to make sure I am careful with every word I use because words do make an impact. I also want to make sure I am a strong support system for ANY student who comes looking to me for that kind of support. I will make sure to value their experience and voice to them how much they have accomplished and how much they will accomplish in the future. I think that is what hurt the most; feeling like a superior didn't believe in the possibility of your future. In that moment he kind of crushed my dreams. I vowed to myself to never invalidate a student's dreams but rather to empower them to dream bigger and let them know that I believe in their capabilities immensely.

In this next account, a UCLA freshman's experiences with fellow students from all over the world are changed from feelings of deep satisfaction to fear and helplessness. The experience happened immediately after 9/11, near the co-ops at UCLA. She feels powerless in light of the anger and rage that is being directed toward her. Although she understands that she is a good and kind person, she knows that the fury of a fellow student is blind. He is unable to see her for what she is:

> I was living in the student co-op housing across the street from UCLA during my first year of college. Most of my friends and neighbors in the three buildings that make up the co-op were students from Santa Monica College, UCLA, and UCLA Extension and a large majority of them were foreign students from a vast array of countries—Italy, Nigeria, Cuba, Poland, Singapore, and many others. It is for this reason that I wanted to live in the co-ops—where else in Los Angeles could I befriend and learn from such a diverse group of fellow students outside of the classroom? Although the experience of living there for a few months was truly rewarding, it is sadly overshadowed by my most vivid memory of the co-ops, which occurred on September 11th, 2001.

> That day dozens of us in the co-ops were sitting in front of the big-screen television in the cafeteria, stunned by the images of the planes crashing into the Twin Towers. After a few hours of watching and discussing the attack with my roommates and others in the co-op, I remembered that I forgot my purse in my car, which was parked down the street. I walked alone to my car a few blocks away and as I passed one of the fraternity houses on the way, a tall White male walked about towards me. He was staring me down and had a weird look on his face. I tried not to make eye

contact with him, but as he came closer he said directly to my face, "you better watch where you're going." Automatically I said, "Excuse me?" to him, hoping that I misunderstood or that he would just walk away and leave me alone. But he didn't go away. He replied very angrily "Don't you see what your people are doing to our country?" After a long pause and stare of disgust on his part, he shrugged and finally walked away, but under his breath he said "You're just lucky you're a girl." Even though my family is of Latino and Italian heritages, my physical features made this disgruntled man mistake me for someone of Middle-Eastern decent, which in his mind made it okay to vent his anger and hate towards me at that moment. Although I can look back and understand that there was some underlying fear in this man's eyes towards "my people," I realized that even in the most diverse of places, stereotypes and xenophobic attitudes can still arise. I know I am a very harmless person, but the rest of the world thought otherwise on September 11th. What if I was male and I was attacked by this man? Would I have fought back? What if he had a weapon? I was scared for weeks. (Bi-Ethnic, female)

In the following excerpt, a UCLA woman talks about her difficulty in feeling guilty about her privileges but also feeling upset that others don't seem to recognize that her life involved struggles. She does what many Whites do when confronted with their own privileges and the lack of privileges for students of color. She talks about how hard she has worked and that her story of her difficulties does not benefit her in the way that it has benefitted students of color. As one African American woman at a Cal State University wrote in her journal after listening to White students talk in class about how hard they worked and how tired they were of hearing Black students "play the race card":

> If the race card works, how come so many of us still do not get equal pay, equal promotions, and the same treatment as they get when they go into department stores?

In the following excerpt, the student does not mean to demean or disparage people of color. Unfortunately, she has not reached the point where she is able to see that she has some benefits from her White skin[2]:

> I could completely understand the perspective in class from one of the students who claimed to feel guilty about being white. It seems in our society that because white has always been 'good,' we now have a responsibility to make other races understand that they too are 'good.' There is nothing

2 For an excellent set of readings that talks about the invisibility and power of Whiteness, as well as the ways in which White people can confront their own racism and become allies to people of color in the struggle to end racism, see Rothenberg, Paula S. (2011). *White privilege* (4th ed.). New York: Worth Publishers.

wrong with this because of course this is true; however, it then makes me feel guilty, and at times frustrated, for being white and having a different life. Growing up, I was a privileged white girl. I didn't ask for any of the things I was given, I was born into it. As I got older, and specifically when I applied to college, I felt more and more guilty in a sense for just being who I am. I also felt angry because it seemed like one of the ways you get into college these days is to share a story in which you struggled. Is it really a bad thing to have had a blessed life where I really haven't had to overcome any hardships? It made me angry to feel like I would be judged differently from someone who had a different life because although I was privileged, I had a lot of responsibilities and pressures that people who endured other hardships did not experience. It was kind of the burden of being an overachiever I guess I could say. Financially my life was easy, but I was still a teenage girl and was growing up in an environment where people were so obsessed with image and success (academically, athletically, musically, financially), and that life definitely had its own stresses. I guess the guilt and anger combine sometimes when I think about this because I feel guilty when I think "Why doesn't anyone ever feel sorry for me and the 'hardships' I went through? Or how can people judge me and belittle all of my hard work in school and extracurricular activities and disregard it as actual stress?" I obviously know that my issues growing up were not the same as someone coming from an underprivileged background, but I just don't think that it should be looked at so differently. We are all people with struggles, but who is to judge which 'hardships' are harder? To me, they're just different. (White female)

Students of color are often told that they are lucky to have struggles to talk about, especially for college applications. One Salvadoran student describes an incident in her high school A.P. English class. The students were writing their college personal statements and shared them with other students who would do a peer review. The following is the reaction from a White peer:

When H read my personal statement for my college application and found out that my family came to the United States because they were fleeing the Civil War in El Salvador, she said "You're so lucky that you have something to write about. This will help you get into any college." I couldn't believe that she said this. I was lucky? I remember H got a brand new car when she turned sixteen. When I was sixteen I had to wake up at five in the morning and take three public buses to arrive at school on time. I think that luck was definitely on her side. (Salvadoran female, UCLA)

This White student stresses the benefits of obstacles as a way to get into college. She minimizes the pain and difficulty of the Salvadoran woman and interprets these obstacles as a benefit. It's hard for her to believe that the woman's abilities, without such obstacles, would have also brought her to UCLA.

In the next example, a UCLA female student is bothered by seeing and hearing her two Asian classmates speaking a language other than English. She expresses her private beliefs in a journal about this experience. While saying that she doesn't want to take anything away from anyone's culture, her private feelings indicate just the opposite. She has no idea why the two women are communicating in a language that they feel comfortable with and can communicate more easily perhaps than in English. She has difficulty sympathizing with the possible reasons that bilingual people might enjoy speaking a language other than English. Wanting these two Asian classmates to speak the language she speaks is her way of saying "Why can't you be like me?":

> This past week, I was in one of my classes when I saw something I haven't seen before. I bring my laptop to most of my classes to take notes—a common occurrence at UCLA. In front of me were two Asian students and I noticed that they were speaking what I think was Chinese to each other before class started. Partially through the lecture, I saw over one of the girls' shoulders and noticed that she was taking notes on her laptop in Chinese characters. I was pretty surprised and started to have thoughts about why she would need to do this. I know that we live in America and there are people here from a lot of different places. It's possible that she could have been an exchange student or recently moved here. But let's say that this is not the case and that she has been raised in the U.S. and speaks English. I don't mind people being able to speak another language. But sometimes I do get a little offended, or annoyed might be a better word, when two people are speaking and I can't understand what they are saying. And as far as the notes go, that's just another extension of the same type of feeling…I definitely wouldn't want to take away from anyone's culture, but don't you think we should all be speaking and writing English when we go to UCLA and live in the United States? (White, female)

What happens to this ongoing assault on students of color? How are Whites who send these microaggressions perceived and evaluated? A recent study shows that White men are perceived as racist or ethnocentric. This was the most commonly held stereotype among Latinas/os and African Americans and the second most common stereotype among Asian Americans (Conley, Rabinowitz, & Rabow, 2010). If the outcome of this study, which was done in three different universities, can be generalized, it would help us understand why it's so difficult to engage in an honest dialogue about racism without confronting stereotypes, hurts, guilt, and anger.

THE MEDIA

The entertainment industry surrounds us with images of fair-skinned, blond-haired, and blue-eyed picture-perfect actors, models, and singers. Even if the media chooses to present differences, it does so cleverly by still maintaining its one-dimensional image of beauty. When non-White celebrities are shown, they are displayed with light skin and light hair. This treatment of people of color by the media has a twofold function. Its depiction of one-dimensional beauty stresses the beauty of Whiteness, while simultaneously teaching men and women of color that their beauty is less beautiful. When minorities are used as models, they will minimize darkness and emphasize Whiteness. This is true for real celebrities who are men and women of color. For example, when African American or Latino celebrities are selected, they will only be chosen if their skin color is atypically light. In the May 2001 edition of *People's 50 Most Beautiful People*, the chosen few were almost exclusively White. While one may dismiss the importance of this particular magazine, its message is extremely potent; the most beautiful people in the world are White. We could even go a step further and argue that the true symbolic message here is that only White people are beautiful. *People Magazine* is not alone in its depiction of White beauty. On the contrary, this overrepresentation of Whites can be found in all of our magazines of choice, from *Vogue* to *Vanity Fair* to *The New Yorker*.

Additionally, the entertainment industry, with its narrow image of beauty, enjoys a pervasive nature that reaches us all, particularly those of us who do not fit its image of perfection. While White children flip through the pages of *People Magazine*, their own positive self-image is affirmed and this simultaneously confirms their place of privilege. They are in the pictures and scenes of wealth, happiness, and comfort. People of color are rarely included. When they are depicted they tend to have White features. This experience is completely destructive for the non-White child, who yearns to identify with the images presented in the media.

White students rarely have to think about what skin color is beautiful. For them White is beautiful. In the following excerpt a White UCLA female describes her awakening to the awareness of the significance of skin color in American culture. She has been stimulated by class discussions about skin color and decides to do a little piece of research:

> I have never been subjected to the idea that one skin color is more "beautiful" than another. Or so I thought. I decided to open my GQ magazine and look at all the ads to see how many of them had only White models and how many had models with a skin color other than white. I was very surprised. Of the 85 ads in the magazine, only 2 ads had models who were a skin color other than white (1 ad with an Asian female and African

American male and another ad with white male and African American male). Although many of the models might be of various ethnicities, they clearly were not representative of what a person who normally comes from that ethnicity would look like. The theme across the entire magazine was to have models who looked white (many were very pale) or to have minority models look as white as possible. I have been reading magazines for a long time and I never thought twice about the ads. What I took from this is how prevalent the 'White is beautiful" idea actually is without many of us even noticing it. Although I never felt like I was being led to believe this way of thinking, I was fed this idea for years without even knowing it. (White female)

In the following excerpt, a Filipina discusses how Asian faces were simply not present on television when she was growing up. Therefore, she was forced to shape her own identity based on the White characteristics that she was bombarded with by the media:

> All the faces I saw on television were White and Black. Asian faces were invisible. I modeled my identity from the characteristics that I was constantly being exposed to. (Filipina, female)

The media's emphasis on Whiteness is damaging as it brainwashes minority children into viewing themselves as inferior or less desirable. In the following excerpt, an African American woman describes how the media has impacted her. The student is so unaccustomed to seeing Black actors engaged in love scenes that when presented with this rarity she actually finds it "gross":

> I remember thinking that love scenes between two Black actors were gross. I didn't want to watch it but I could watch two White actors without a problem. (African American, female)

In the next excerpt, a Chicano male describes how he internalized the media images of Whiteness as the superior ideal:

> I mean how can you not want to be like the guys on TV commercials, or on billboards, these are guys I would refer to as 'firme' in Spanish? What else could a young man want to be like if that is all he sees being advertised as attractive? Even today, as I walk along campus and see White guys and how some resemble the images on TV, I continue to believe that they look better. (Chicano, male)

An Arab male recalls how the media's depiction of sameness affected his self-image and created a desire to deny his cultural roots and identity:

> My attitude was that if only I looked more like them, then I could rule the world . . . I unfortunately have to admit that I desperately wanted to deny my own cultural roots and identity and immerse myself in and become the White culture I saw on TV and at school. (Arab, male)

In the following excerpt, an African American female recalls how the media only depicted light-skinned Blacks as worthy of attaining fame and fortune:

> Growing up I was secretly told that the darker the skin tones, the deeper the problems. Not by my parents, but by my peer group and my surroundings, the billboards, the commercials, ads, beauty queens. If he/she was Black, famous, and had money, they were "light skinned." (African American, female)

As we have indicated earlier, institutions reinforce each other in their message of racism. In the following example, a young woman describes how school, peers, and the media taught her about herself:

> I knew since elementary school that it was not desirable to be Chinese. Chinese people were unpopular and looked down upon. I knew that by the way people would talk about us or imitate us. Aside from the typical slant-eyed faces that I watched non-Asian kids make, I always heard kids making fun of the Chinese language by caricaturizing it in their imitation. This continued into intermediate school (grades 5–8) and did not stop when I left school. At home I would see the same caricatures on TV. (Chinese, female)

The classic movie *Little Mermaid* is also a cause of self-loathing:

> When I first saw the animated movie *Little Mermaid*, I instantly fell in love with the movie and the songs. I fell in love with Ariel, the mermaid and her Prince Charming. I would watch the movie over and over again. As I watched these animated movies when I was 13-years-old, I had a hard time accepting who I was and what I looked like. I thought to myself, "Why do I look like this? Why can't I look like Ariel?" Even my friends were always ranting and raving about her pretty hair, voice, and figure. We knew it was just a cartoon. However, the thought did not occur to me that Ariel was a drawing, and most White girls do not even

look nearly as pretty. However, to me, having a nice figure, long wavy hair that blew in the wind, big eyes, and the voice of an angel would make me the most beautiful person in the world.

I decided that I was going to look like Ariel even if it killed me. I wanted a beautiful figure and a beautiful face. I was determined that during the summer vacation, I would look like Ariel and then when I made the transition to high school, my friends would be shocked and I would just impress the world. It was then that I decided that I would stop eating to make my figure look like the animated drawings that depicted the ideal beauty in my eyes. I lost over twenty pounds in the two months of vacation. I put nothing in my stomach, except water. I was ready to die because I wanted to look beautiful, and in order for me to look beautiful I thought I had to look like those White models on television, the movies, magazines, or even animated movies. I had to have a figure like them. I had to be tall and skinny. Because of my irrational thought and my irrational decision, I lost a huge part of my life. (Asian, female)

In the next excerpt a Chinese male describes what he believes to be the media messages for Asian men and women. He understands the historical treatment of Black women by the media and suggests that Asian women are the new forbidden beauties:

My Asian brothers and I are taught by the media to hate ourselves. We are taught to look in the mirror and despise our slanted eyes, our yellow skin, and our pudgy nose. We are told that we have small penises. We are told that we perform so badly in bed that the Asian women need to turn to the White man for sexual satisfaction. We are taught to think that we are ugly. And guess what? It worked. Most Asian men internalized it. It saddens me when the males of a race think that they are so ugly, and believe me, this sentiment comes out whether it is subtle or someone is simply joking—it comes out, and it saddens me. We are also taught that we will never be quite as good as White men. We are taught that White women are the epitome of beauty, and that we will never be able to have them. My Asian sisters, you are taught to be sexy for the White man. You are exotic; you are submissive; you are great in bed. You are taught to fawn over White men, because they are perfect in ways that Asian men are not. You are taught to despise your culture; dye your hair blond; wear blue contacts; and stand next to the White man, so that you might be a little lighter, a little more accepted, A LITTLE MORE WHITE. Your delicate, exotic beauty is your special sexual pass into mainstream acceptance, but only when you accept the stream of the White man's semen. This society has raped your body and mind, and left it covered in the sticky ejaculation of submission, of fawning, of bleach. I can go into a million theories about why this phenomenon occurs in American society, but in the end, most agree that it is just another expression of White male privilege. In this, and many other historical cases, it translates into sexual politics. These stereotypes have been branded on us. And while Asian women get the better deal, it is still a stereotype that has been given, and not created, and can be taken back whenever society pleases. Any stereotype is a bad stereotype. Once, Black women were forbidden and White men pursued them. In our generation, it is the Asian woman's turn to be raped. (Chinese, male)

A student begins to recognize how being White has afforded him with privileges not similarly shared by other races, particularly regarding representation in the media. This male begins to question the overrepresentation of Whites on television and in movies, newspapers, and magazines. More importantly, he questions what the lack of minority representation in the media must feel like for other races:

I was completely unaware of my privilege as a dominant group member of an oppressive society. I thought that my life experiences were the same as all the others, never thinking about race. When I walked into a store and received plenty of help and paid with a credit card and wasn't even asked for identification, I thought that is how it was for everyone. I never realized that if my Black friend walked into the store, she may have been watched suspiciously, and asked for several forms of identification before her check was accepted. It never even entered my mind that band-aids are supposed to be skin colored, but they really only matched my white flesh. I never realized that what I saw in the media were people of my race, and what it would feel like to be a minority who only sees Whites on TV, in the movies, in the newspaper, and in magazines. When I was searching for an apartment last year, I never had to think about the fact that someone would not want to rent to me because of my race. (White, male)

In the next example, a White female describes her previous assessment of Black magazines as an example of self-segregation:

I never understood why magazines like *Ebony* were popular. I thought that Black people were further alienating themselves by creating a separate magazine, instead of subscribing to the "general" magazine. I did not realize that these "general" magazines are simply White magazines. Now I see a woman's magazine and not only see the size of the models, but the color. In flipping through, I see mostly Caucasian models, with an occasional "token" light-skinned minority. The makeup advice is obviously geared towards White women, and most of the hairstyle suggestions would never work on someone who does not have Caucasian hair. Occasionally a magazine will show one hairstyle for African-American women, but this is a side-note, instead of the rule. (White, female)

LAW ENFORCEMENT

Law enforcement officials are typically extremely humane and courageous people. They risk their lives every day to ensure safety for all. Unfortunately, as is true of every profession, there are some officials who maintain racist ideals and prejudices against certain minority groups. The only difference between a racist policeman and any other racist professional is that the former typically has greater power to abuse under the guise of the law. Sometimes this power turns deadly.

Most Whites learn of police racism and brutality through the public exposure generated by the Rodney Kings of the world. Whites have little firsthand experience with being harassed, beaten, and even murdered at the hands of the police. This is part of that privilege enjoyed by Whites. This is not the experience of other races, particularly African Americans and Latinos who often report feeling targeted by law enforcement because of their skin color. In the following excerpt, an African American student describes the fear that the police instilled in him when he was handcuffed on the ground and told that he might be a possible shooting suspect simply because of his race:

> I still have fear going through the wrong neighborhoods at times, not so much because of the people, but because of the police. In a sense, I never feel safe when I drive. I have always had a fear of the police because of the power they possess. I have had only one run-in with the police and it was major. I was riding with a friend who lived near me and all of a sudden the police were right behind us. We had three people in the back seat, and one of them lived in the predominantly White neighborhood near our school. As we turned off of the main street onto the residential neighborhood, they turned on their sirens and pulled us over. While I was wondering what we could have possibly done wrong, two officers behind their car with their guns drawn asked us to put our hands up. I was handcuffed on the ground and explained that we were possible suspects of a shooting, which occurred earlier that day. It was one of the most humiliating and scary experiences that I've ever had in my life. They checked our car for weapons and only found schoolbooks. They had to let us go. It looked like a White woman in

the first police car was trying to identify us. This did not make me feel very good because I heard one of the cops say that they were looking for a black, gray, or blue car with 2–5 Black male passengers. And they really thought that they would find the people who did this. How many people fit that description? I felt like I was a threat to society. (African American, male)

Another student recalls his frightening run-in with the police. This African American male and his friend were stopped, told to get out of their car, and then instructed to get on the ground with their legs spread. The reason for the interrogation was the same as in the previous example: skin color:

Out of nowhere a cop car came behind us and began flashing its lights. We were pretty shocked because it was so sudden. We were told to get out of the car with our hands up. We were then told to get on the ground with our legs spread. At this point I had no idea what was going on and my feelings of being intimidated slowly turned to feelings of anger and resentment. They had absolutely no right to conduct this procedure on us. They checked to see if we had illegal substances on us. They looked at my ID and checked my background and they found that I was clean. Knowing this, they let me go on the curb. My best friend however, did not receive the same fate. He did not have his ID on him so they began questioning him about a million things such as where he was from, what was his address, where he went to school, if he was in a gang, and whether he had any tattoos, just to name a few. After about a half hour of trying to figure out who he was, the police officers decided to let us go. Before leaving the scene I demanded a reason as to why we were put under such circumstances. He said that the car we were sitting in (which belonged to me) "fit the description of a vehicle stolen earlier in the day" and that my friend "fit the description" of a youth they had been after for burglary and drug dealing for quite some time. (African American, male)

The sentiments expressed by students are artistically captured by Jay-Z's depiction of a run-in with a police officer: http://www.azlyrics.com/lyrics/jayz/99problems.html.

The experiences that White students have with the police are often very different. It would not be surprising if White students believe that the code of "to protect and serve" is applicable to all. In this next excerpt, a CSUN student describes the benefit he gains from having White skin:

I came into this class not believing that I had any privileges because of my Whiteness. I've worked very hard all my life—my family was very poor—

but when people were sharing their encounters with the police, one particular incident comes to mind. I remember when I was 16 and had just gotten my license I went out one night on my way to pick something up from a store in a neighboring town. There's this one stop sign in the town I grew up in that comes into a blind turn. I was driving my new Prius, blasting classical music, and coming out of that stop sign when I almost crashed into a police car. Then, while looking exceptionally white and nerdy I said through rolled down windows, 'Sorry, officer.' All he said was 'Be more careful next time.' Then he drove away. This was an instance where I clearly would not have gotten away without so much as a ticket if I'd been in a different neighborhood with different colored skin. (White, male)

In this next excerpt, a White student recalls how he and his Black friends were painted. A policeman tries to teach the White student that he should not be socializing with African Americans. Shockingly, the officer is African American:

I remember a time I went with some of my Black friends to a high school football game. At the game there were some police officers that made sure nothing happened after the game. My friends and I were standing around after the game just talking. I remember seeing a Black officer staring at us. I thought he was going to question us because one of my friends was drunk, talking loudly, and being obnoxious. The Black cop motioned for me to go over to him. I went to him, and he looked at my friends and then me and asked me what I was doing with them. I was so shocked by this question that I asked him to repeat it. I was not sure what he meant by it. "They're Black and you're White. What are you doing with them?" I searched his face for some sort of hint that he was joking or being sarcastic, but he was serious. Shocked, I simply said, "They're my friends!" and proceeded to go back to them. I felt so many emotions. A Black officer asked me why I was hanging out with Black guys. To me, it made no difference what color they were, but for some reason, the fact that they were Black and I was White was important to him. I could not understand why he would question my association with them. For the first time in my life, I knew what it felt like to have my actions questioned simply because of my skin color and who I was with. (White/Armenian American, male)

In the following excerpt, a Chicano student describes his experience with the police. A medical emergency is neglected and the stereotype of Latinos and Indians as drug users is implemented:

After chatting for a while, my friends and I decided to go out to a bar near the beach. We were all happy, none of us had been drinking, and all we wanted was to enjoy the time we had available because it is rare when we have the opportunity to spend time together. So we drove off expecting to have a good time. Suddenly, the driver began to have convulsions and the car went out of control. After we got control of the car we immediately dialed 911 and we all exited the car. I followed directions from the dispatcher. He was unconscious, shaking, and foam was coming out of his mouth. The paramedics came to the rescue and took control of the situation. They asked questions and we cooperated with them. Minutes later, the police arrived. They saw a new car with three Latinos and a Hindu lying on the ground out of control. They assumed it was a drug overdose and began searching the car and interrogating us. One police officer pulled me aside and began asking questions.

"Have you been doing drugs?" he asked. I answered, "I just got back from UCLA, I'm a student there, I don't do drugs and we haven't been drinking." While this was taking place, the second officer kept searching the car, in hope of finding some illegal substance. At the end of the night, we all came to the conclusion that the police officers were not concerned with the well-being of our friend. When they first arrived they saw three Mexicans panicking and in shock. They assumed this was a drug-related incident and wanted to find evidence. Despite my effort to cooperate with him I was confronted with prejudice. I found that these officers who are supposed to serve and protect did no such thing. Instead, what I encountered was racial profiling and intimidation. (Chicano, male)

This last example reads like a horror movie. It starts out with friends hoping to celebrate Christmas Eve until the police arrive and threaten the lives of the Black young men who are waiting outside. Fortunately, this story does not end with gun shots, but rather with a sarcastic farewell:

When I was 19-years-old, some friends and I went to a mutual friend's house to celebrate the Christmas Eve holiday. When we got there, he wasn't home yet so we stood near my friend's car while waiting for him to arrive. While we were waiting, a police car drove by and shined their lights on us. I immediately had that "here we go again" feeling come over me. It was commonplace in 1995 for police to interrogate people on sight in Baldwin Hills. So when the police shined their lights on us, no one was surprised. During that period in my life, I was probably pulled over and searched about once every two weeks. As a result, I resented the police with a passion. They made me feel like I was some kind of threat to society.

Two Black police officers exited the car with their guns drawn and ordered us to put our hands in the air. We did. The officers then approached us and frisked us individually. Once they found out that we had no weapons, they asked us to put our hands on the hood of the car. They then emptied our pockets and went through our wallets to take our driver's licenses to run our names through the computer to see if we had any warrants. The younger officer kept referring to the older officer as "pop," and the older officer called the younger one "son." When I noticed that they had different last names, I realized that they were going through some kind of sick bad-cop/good-cop routine. While we were waiting for our names to clear, they started to tell us how much they hated car thieves.

"Pop, there's nothing like whooping a car thief's ass," said the younger one.

When we tried to explain that we were in front of a friend's house, we were told to "shut the fuck up." It turned out that a warrant for me and a friend came back on the computer. We had both forgotten to pay a traffic ticket.

"Ah, they steal cars and don't pay tickets," said the older one.

They began to tell us how much they hate gangsters, and claimed that they beat up two of them about an hour ago. They said all the local "bloods" know not to "fuck" with them. I had heard many threats made by police before, but something about the tone of their voices scared me. It was like you could tell that they were telling the truth. Perhaps it's just a stereotype of mine, but it seems like some Black cops feel like they can get away with more brutality against other Blacks simply because they are the same color. The younger officer then looked at me while putting a hand on his gun and said, "Go ahead, run away." I didn't know if he was testing me or letting me go. The blank stares on their faces told me that they were just as unsure as I was. Knowing that my friends were scared too only made me more frightened.

"It's a good thing you didn't run, cuz I would've blown the back of your head off," said the younger officer, with a grin on his face. (African American, male)

THE WORKPLACE

In addition to the influence of the media, school environment, and law enforcement officials, students also recalled learning to be painters when they entered the workforce. In the following example, a White female remembers her duties working at a club in West Hollywood. A major part of her job was to promote racism per strict orders from her boss:

I worked at a very high-end club in West Hollywood, called the G. I was the VIP host for an exclusive room, so it was my job to decide who could and could not come in. My manager would often, very often, come and yell at me because I had let too many Persians in the room and/or that the room looked like shit because I had let unattractive women and men up there. I used to really cringe when he said these things, but I heard it all the time and I was expected to enforce his racist and "look" standards. And he had the same rationale that the rich White people would not want to come up there and spend a lot of money if there were not good looking women and people of the "right" race up there. I only stayed because I made a tremendous amount of money, bigwigs tipping me for reservations and/or tables in this very sought-after club. But I didn't have my soul while I was there. Every night I would come home upset about things that occurred. I just can't believe that Persians and Arabs are so discriminated against in Los Angeles, and even worse that I was a part of it. I perpetuated being the oppressor in this way and perpetuated racism by thinking twice before I let "too" many Arabs into the VIP room. Oh, I just remembered, he was even worse about Blacks. They usually never even made it in the club at all, and into where I was. There were a limited number of Black regulars, but of course they were either well connected or had money. I was yelled at for letting too many Blacks into the room as well. Basically, I was in the position that would discriminate against all unattractive people unless they were "somebody" or had lots of money, and all races, except Whites. I eventually quit and I've never walked into a club since. (White, female)

Similarly, another student describes how African American customers were treated in the store in which he worked. This student, also an African American, recalls how people of color were suspected of stealing and thus watched and scrutinized at every turn. What is most concerning about this example is that this racist ideology regarding the trustworthiness of African Americans briefly caused this student to view members of his own race as thieves solely based on their skin color:

I was seeing discrimination take place at my work almost twice a week. People of color are seen as not being able to pay for many of the articles that they try on. Since the area that I work in is very wealthy there are not that many people of color that come into the store. It seems that when they do my manager tells everyone to keep an eye on them. I've often heard the other employees say that the reason why they watch them is because they look suspicious. After a period of time I too began to feel and think that the people of color that came into my store were stealing.

But I never thought that I'd see what I saw during the holidays. I was working in the afternoon with the manager and one of the employees when a group of three black males entered the store, two of which were carrying big bags. The manager quickly came over to us and told us to keep an eye out. After they perused the store for about 20 minutes and were about to leave, the manager went over to them and asked to look into their bags. They did not seem as though this was the first time it had happened to them because they simply opened it up and let her examine the contents. She did not find anything from our store so she politely said sorry and they left. (African American, male)

In the next example, an Asian female discusses how she learned the culture of racism when she worked as a waitress. Her co-workers taught her to predict her tip based on the customer's race:

All of us who wait on tables think that we can look at the customers and predict the kind of tip we will receive and this makes it hard to approach each table with the same enthusiasm. The general consensus at my work is that African Americans are the worst tippers. There are always exceptions and then I feel bad for having thought differently. But the majority of African American customers are very hard to wait on. They seem very demanding, they complain about their food and, their (watered down) alcoholic beverages, and regardless of the amount of their bill, 10 dollars or 40 dollars, the tip is always the same—1 dollar. A guy at my work who is Black himself started the phrase "groove dollar." He even says that most Black people do not tip well. (Asian, female)

In this last excerpt, a Latina student pays the price for being assertive. As an unsatisfied customer in a florist shop, this student asks to speak with the manager and is faced with raw racism:

"May I help you?" "As a matter of fact, yes you can. You see my cousin here had ordered a simple bouquet. I just want a bouquet that's ready but just add a rose. Just one simple rose." She smiled and sighed, "You see hon, I don't think that's possible." I smiled and replied, "Isn't that what florists do though? Can I ask your manager to see what he or she thinks a florist does?" At that point I felt a tug at my dress and my cousin whispered that it was all right, and to drop the request. As I turned once again towards the florist, she was beginning to dismantle a bouquet and she inserted a rose in the middle. As she did she murmured something I would never forget. "You can't just come in and ask for something, damn

Mexicans!" That really insulted me, and I didn't want to argue with her anymore. I told her to excuse me as I proceeded to look for the manager. As I found him I told him that I wanted service and how I felt personally insulted as a person of color by the florist. As we both walked towards the florist the bouquet was done. She told me the amount and asked "Cash?" "Credit please." I smiled. But I knew that it was too good to be true, to just pay and leave. And as we left, I heard some remarks that just showed me that racism is alive everywhere. "Go back to where you came from. Lazy mother-fuckers, just come here to cause trouble." I turned around as and saw a little boy look me in the eyes saying "SPIC"! (Mexican American, female)

In this woman's excerpt there are three painters. There is the employee who has painted the student as a "lazy mother-fucker" simply because of her race. There is a manager whose silence allows the painting to occur. More frightening, however, is the child bystander who has already learned to paint blatant strokes of racism.

PUBLIC SETTINGS

The learning, teaching, and *practice* of racism also occur in public settings.

Research has carefully documented how people of color receive racist comments in restaurants, retail outlets, and on public transportation (Feagin, 1991). The experiences of our students corroborate Feagin's research.

In this first excerpt example, a donut shop is the scene of a public lesson in racism. A customer levies his racism at a Cambodian student working in her parents' store:

> When I tell people that I am Cambodian, they automatically assume that we are dirty people, killers, and deviants because of our past history with the Pol Pot and Khmer Rouge. People judge me on the basis of my ethnicity even before they get to know who I am, which makes me annoyed at them for prejudging me. Two to three weeks ago, when I was working at my parents' Donut Shop, a customer of ours, an elderly Persian man in his sixties, asked me about the kind of food I eat. I told him the usual kinds of food: beef, pork, chicken, vegetables, and fruits. The same type of food everyone eats, it is just cooked and prepared differently from American food. Then, out of nowhere he asked me, "Do you eat dog?" I was shocked and mortified at even the thought of eating a dog. I could

not believe that he just asked me that ridiculous question. The question was a surprise attack on me. How can someone accuse another person of such a horrible act of animal cruelty? To say the least, I was dumbfounded. "Was he joking or was he serious about it?" I mumbled to myself. I asked him if he was joking and he said, "No." I told him, "I have never eaten a dog in my whole life and I would never eat one in the future either." I asked him why he asked me that and he said, "I thought all Asians ate dogs." I told him, "People would only eat cats and dogs if they were desperate for food and they had nothing else to eat." This was what I had to say in defense of all Asians. That was enough for me; my opinion about him dropped tenfold. He incorrectly judged and insulted me, and on top of that, all other Cambodian and Asian people on the planet too. I was at a loss for words. Afterwards, I realized that he did not know any better; that is why he said those words, out of ignorance and myths. Probably, nobody has ever taken the time to tell him that dogs are not a popular entree in Asia. I hope he has corrected his misguided idea after our conversation. I am still shaken by his words. Now, I walk around thinking if other people think I eat dogs. (Cambodian, female)

A frequent and contradictory set of experiences often occurs for men and women of color. They can be either ignored or carefully scrutinized while shopping. In the following, a woman visits a very popular shopping area in Los Angeles. Her entrance into the store is greeted with neither warmth nor interest. She is not taken seriously and is ignored for 10 minutes. When the salesperson finally approaches, she is treated as if illiterate and deaf and is called a "Spic." How ironic that this student is fluent in three languages:

I recently visited Victoria's Secret at the Beverly Center in Beverly Hills, CA to make a purchase but soon saw that I was not welcomed. I waited for about ten minutes to get some assistance and the only thing I got for those ten minutes were dirty looks, which I did not pay any mind to. I guess I have become accustomed to stares and snickering behind my back as well as dirty looks from White women. After waiting for so long finally a White lady approaches me and tells me, as if I am deaf and illiterate to her words, "I WILL GET YOU A SPANISH PERSON OK?" I was horrified beyond belief and wanted to jump out of my skin. My Spanish blood kicked in instead and the only thing I could say to her was, "Just because I look Spanish doesn't mean I can't understand you, so no, NO SPANISH PERSON IS NECESSARY." I could not stand there any longer and deal with her ignorance so the next best thing I could do was turn around and walk out of the store. Her reply back to me was, "That's the problem with the Spics . . ." I wish I could have stayed longer to finish hearing the rest of her genius words but if I stayed I know I would have done something I could not have been proud of later. (Japanese/Colombian, female)

In the following excerpt, an Iranian student reports how frightened she was to return to her regular place of employment. This student is confronted with the dilemma that many of our Middle Eastern and South Asian students who wear clothing and religious symbols deal with. These symbols, which are representations of these students' core identities, become the stimulus for attacks. She returns to work with a strategy for minimizing potential attacks. Unfortunately, this strategy fails. A customer complains to a manager about their employment of "such people." The woman is unable to respond to her attacker and unfortunately her frustration is redirected at herself and her people:

> After I returned to work, I maintained minimum amount of contact with my co-workers for fear that one of them would ask me: "So does Islam teach Muslims to be terrorists?" However, that question came from a customer that I was serving a week after the attacks. A middle-aged, Caucasian woman whom I was helping noticed my pendant and proceeded to question me as to its meaning. It so happened that I was wearing a pendant that said Allah (God) in Arabic. She became quite irate and began to spew a plethora of hateful comments. I was flabbergasted at first for although I had expected them, I was never prepared to respond to her comments. I had not prepared a response because a part of me believed what she was saying. A part of me was ashamed of my religion and my people. The woman refused to be served by me and informed my manager that she ought to be ashamed of herself for employing "such people"! (Iranian, female)

In the next example, a biracial young woman who grew up in Hawaii is introduced to racism when she visits her cousins in Seattle. Her Japanese Korean heritage was firmly accepted in Hawaii, but her cousins tell her about the "real world":

> I grew up in Hawaii with my parents, and in an extended family of aunts, uncles, and cousins. In middle school when I was 12, my parents decided to send me to Seattle, Washington, to visit more relatives. My parents felt that it would be a good experience because I had never left the islands. Born and raised in Hawaii as a fourth generation Japanese/Korean, I've never considered myself a foreigner because in Hawaii, Japanese people were the majority. During my visit to Seattle, there was one incident that sticks out in my mind. My cousin, who is a year older than me, and I were walking to McDonalds for dinner. A car pulled up next to us with four White college-aged students. One stuck his head out the window and yelled sounds of the Chinese language at us "Ching Chung . . ." He was trying to make fun of

us and to insult us. (Might I add that neither of us was Chinese.) Meanwhile the other people in the car, a male and two females, were laughing. As they drove off I told my cousin how shocked I was about what had just happened. I also told her that it was absolutely racist. She told me to let it go because we were not in Hawaii but in the real world. She told me to accept what had just happened and not to fight it. It amazed me that she was accepting of this and that she also wanted me to feel inferior. I thought that we are not better off in the 'real world' because we were not like those people who insulted us. (Japanese Korean, female)

In Chapters Two and Three, we read how family members, peer groups, the media, teachers, law enforcement officials, and persons in the workforce teach us lessons about racism. These painters teach us the basic lesson that "difference" means "lesser." Once we become aware of the efforts to paint difference as less, we can use this self-realization and can begin to examine our own internalized prejudices and hate. These teachings do not have to remain permanent. Instead, understanding the lessons that are learned as being incorrect, unjust, and cruel can begin a process of self-awareness, in which we acknowledge the painter within all of us, and then commit to learning how to put the paintbrush down. Two artists urge us to stop painting and to speak up. Bob Marley urges us to stand up for our rights in his song, "Get Up, Stand Up." (http://www.lyrics007. com/Bob%20Marley%20Lyrics/Get%20Up%20Stand%20Up%20Lyrics.html)

Bruce Springsteen also provides us with a song about standing up to the government. This song was originally recorded by Pete Seeger who spoke about bringing home the men and women fighting in Vietnam. Springsteen doesn't mention Vietnam but the reader can supply the other countries where we are currently involved. http://www. springsteenlyrics.com/lyrics/b/bringthemhome.php

In Chapter Four, we describe how painters are trained to not just paint indiscriminately, but to paint particular differences.

*"In the end, we will remember not the words of our enemies, but
the silence of our friends."*
—Martin Luther King Jr., "The Trumpet of Conscience," 1967

"Brown-Eyed, Blue-Eyed" Exercise

Instructors:

The Brown-Eyed/Blue-Eyed Exercise was developed by Jane Elliot in an all-White rural classroom for public school children. Her work has received national and international attention and has achieved enough prominence to have worked its way into Wikipedia. Her work has resulted in a documentary, "The Eye of the Storm" and two books written by William Peters: *A Class Divided* and *A Class Divided: Then and Now*. The experiment originated in the Warsaw ghetto when eye color was used to send or not send people to the gas chamber. Elliot was inspired to teach her fifth-grade class about racism the day that Martin Luther King, Jr. was assassinated. Elliot divided her class randomly into a privileged group and a nonprivileged group. She conducted this experiment over 2 days with the privileges and lack of privileges alternating between the groups. The nonprivileged group was treated poorly with rules limiting its access to the ordinary activities that the privileged group engaged in and took for granted. The video depicting the young children indicates their sad and depressed looks and their feelings of isolation and abandonment. Elliot learned something important about her students' test performance. She discovered statistically different performances between the groups. Those lacking privilege performed more poorly.

How can a college instructor replicate this study? I imitate her work with the following exercise: To start the experiment, I put an equal number of students in each group. This is easy to do if you just draw an imaginary line in the classroom that divides the students approximately in half. I try to get as many students of color into the brown-eyed "privileged" group and as many White students in the blue-eyed "nonprivileged" group. I don't want to make this obvious so I leave a few Whites and a few students of color in each of the groups. You should feel free to move a few select students around.

We ask our students to identify where their parents were born. Then we ask them about grandparents, about great-grandparents, and about great-great-grandparents. By now, we have lost most of them. We then ask them to go back much further where everyone in the class comes from. When they are able to identify Africa as the place where we all came from, we can begin to conduct the following scenario.

"At this point we are all dark-skinned and brown-eyed. With the beginning of migration into Northern African and Europe and into Asia, our skins and eyes became lighter. After many hundreds of generations many of the people were now blue-eyed. The problem for the blue-eyed people is that the sun penetrated the iris into the brain and destroyed brain cells." (We usually pause at this point to make sure that they've absorbed this point. Of course, there are no scientific bases for this point.) We continue: "Because of the destruction of brain cells, we know that blue-eyed people are more stupid than brown-eyed people. Because they are more stupid, they are lazier, less ambitious, and less well-mannered." (At this point I look at the blue-eyed people to find out and point out that they're wearing hats in a classroom or sitting slouched or chewing gum or texting. I do this to embarrass them and make them feel frightened.)

I then ask all students to take out a piece of paper and to write on the paper in cursive "The Listening Exercises." After doing this, I go and examine blue-eyed writings to discover: who has printed the text instead of writing it in cursive, whose spelling is poor, and whose handwriting is atrocious. I make comments to these students about each of these defects and of course, when we walk into the brown-eyed section, we try to find students whose handwriting and spelling is excellent. We compliment them and give credit to their parents for providing them with a good education. We continue with the next direction, which is "Write the Roman numeral I and next to it write 'The first listening exercise involves paying attention.'" We repeat the harassment of the blue-eyed and the positive regard for the brown-eyed. Because we have paid so much attention to the "lazy, poorly educated blue-eyed students" we ask the class, "What could we do with this group that's holding us brown-eyed back?" If you're lucky, a brown-eyed will suggest that removing or separating them from the class and providing them with special education would be a good idea. If you don't get this from a student, you might turn to a facilitator for this suggestion or you may have to say it yourself. To suggest that we are fair and that we believe in meritocracy, we search for a blue-eyed paper that is well written and neat and ask that student if he or she wants to move over to the brown-eyed group. If the student resists moving we often try to be more active in urging the student to see the benefits of belonging to a smart, ambitious, hard-working group of peers. Occasionally one of the brown-eyed people will speak up to defend "his or her fellow classmates." We usually put that student into the blue-eyed group, since he or she has such a strong feeling of concern and empathy.

The second listening skill is, "In paying attention it is important that you hear the words and the music." If at this point in the exercise someone has challenged you, the instructor, by indicating that he or she plans to go to the dean, ACLU, or chair of your department, it is time to end the experiment. In our experience, however, this has only happened three times in over 30 years. If no one has challenged you, you have to judge whether to end the experiment or not. It is most important, however, that you leave time to process the feelings. When we end the experiment we apologize to the students whom we have hurt, insulted, or offended. We talk about how difficult it is to do this and how it must be done early in the semester before a deeper sense of trust between students and faculty has been established. We can then move to processing the feelings that students have. We usually ask the nonprivileged group to talk about how it felt. Feelings of helplessness, being trapped, and anger are usually expressed. There is also recognition that no matter what they did, they were going to get the short end of the stick. We also ask them to express their feelings of how it felt when one of their own went over to the other group, or vice versa. Feelings of resentment, envy, or anger usually accompany that probe. Before turning to the brown-eyed group we make the point that this unfair, cruel, mean, belittling effort can only occur with the silence of brown-eyed. We emphasize how silence can often function to allow injustice. When their feelings are explored, they talk about how lucky and safe they felt, and most importantly that they wanted to protect their privilege. For many students of color having privilege and enjoying it and realizing how others who have it may feel was a powerful experience. For many White students realizing how trapped they felt was equally powerful. If you're lucky enough to have a student challenge you to the point where you must stop the experiment, you will discover that so many students wished they could have done the same thing. Also, in the discussion, students will often say that it was only an experiment and therefore they didn't take it seriously. We usually respond by pointing out that the name calling we did, the belittling, the insults that were made were experience as real. They were seeing and witnessing prejudice and discrimination and had done nothing.

This experiment integrates very nicely with Milgram's work on obedience and Hannah Arendt's writing on the Eichmann trial where she argues that ordinary people can commit extraordinary evil. It also can be used to analyze Lieutenant Wiliam Calley's defense, "I was only following orders."

CHAPTER 4

The Strokes of Difference

"Do not fear your enemies. The worst they can do is kill you. Do not fear friends. At worst, they may betray you. Fear those who do not care; they neither kill nor betray, But betrayal and murder exist because of their silent consent."

—Bruno Jasienski
(1901–1938, Polish poet and leader of the Polish futurist movement)

In a song written and performed by Randy Newman called "Short People," the artist ridicules short people. He can write this song without being harassed or boycotted because in fact there is no formal history of oppression toward short people. Though they may have suffered by feeling that they are not as attractive as taller people, they have not been pulled over by the police for "driving while short." Indeed, there is no long history of names that are derogatory for short people. Newman is using "short prejudice" as a way to point out the ridiculousness of all prejudices. A few decades ago, however, serious song lyrics demeaning different groups of people were not a rare occurrence. It is not hard to imagine that the adjective "short" could be replaced by Black, Latino, Asian, Jews, or Middle Eastern in the Newman refrain "don't want no 'short' people, don't want no 'short' round here." A link for the lyrics of the Randy Newman song is provided below.

http://www.lyricsdepot.com/randy-newman/short-people.html

Once children learn to paint and become adept with the paintbrush, what strokes do they make? Our students indicate that as painters, they take aim at all who are different. Families, peers, and others instruct painters to respond to the differences that distinguish themselves from subordinates. In this chapter, we examine the ways in which subordinate differences are selected, evaluated, and painted by dominants. Difference is equated as "less than" in the painter's eyes, heart, and mind. This difference often allows the painter to justify a canvas of racist ideologies and practices.[1]

Table 3 summarizes the excerpts in this chapter to those who teach difference, those who learn these lessons, and those who are targeted. Teachers include family members, peers, school teachers, as well as the self. The students who are learning are from four major ethnic and racial groups and the lessons are about four ethnic groups. The painful lessons or brushstrokes are of varied ethnic features and names.

TABLE 3

The Teachers, Learners, and Targets of Racism

Teachers		Learners		Targets	
Superior/Teacher	4	African Americans	3	Ethnice Features/Names	18
Peers	4	Asians	3	Asians	1
Family members	5	Latinos (as)	13	Latinos(as)	3
Other Society	9	Middle Easterners	3		
Total	22	Total	22	Total	22

---

1 Edward E. Sampson. (1999). *Dealing with differences* (Fort Worth, TX: Harcourt Brace College Publishers), gives an excellent description of categorization and the way in which items may be assimilated or differentiated. When items fall within a category, they will be perceived and evaluated as more alike than they may actually be. This is the process of assimilation. When items fall into different categories, their differences are exaggerated and so they may be perceived as more different then they may actually be.

YOU'RE DIFFERENT!

The possession of power by the painter results in the painted being treated as abnormal, inadequate, and unwanted. Our metaphoric White paintbrush works on people in much the same way as it does on walls. It carries standards of Whiteness: skin color, facial features, language, accents, and body types. When it passes over White people, it glides on easily. However, when it passes over people of color, their differences still show through. These differences become obvious and problematic as the paintbrush easily determines who fits in and who doesn't. Because Whiteness is the standard to which we are all held, people who are different are marked as inferior. Dominants frequently treat the skin of people of color as something that is undesirable, unattractive, and ugly. Over and over, students write about remembering how their skin color was treated as less beautiful.

You're Different—Your Skin Color Isn't White So You're Inferior

Because race is so salient in our country, the paintbrush actively searches for the racial identity of subordinates. This is done most easily and frequently when children are young and skin color becomes noticeable. A Chicano male relates how he was forced to focus on his skin color. He also describes the pain and hatred he developed toward himself and others:

> I have been scarred by all these differences or should I say my culture! Many of the students [in class] spoke of the way they looked at themselves in the mirror and how they probed their features, hoping to sculpture them into the ideal. This brought back a vivid image of myself when I was in front of the mirror hoping to shed my skin because it was too dark. Why did I not accept my darkness? I guess I have always known. Not until this class have I really looked at the reasons behind it. My darkness made me feel different. In the middle of playing or talking to a classmate I would get asked, "Why are you so dark?" or "You're dark!" As if I had an explanation for this. Now I have scientific and geographical explanations, but that's not what they were looking for. They were looking to make me feel different, not to be seen as one of them. With that came the pain and hatred towards them and myself. (Latino, male)

White children are rarely asked about their skin color; it is usually assumed to be "normal." Being a different color is constant in the lives of children of color to the point of internalization and self-hatred.

In the following example, a Latina describes her family's positive response to her fair complexion. It appears that even her own family has succumbed to the dominant ideology: Whiteness is superior and preferred:

> One of the biggest prejudices that I learned from my family as a child was the notion that people of color were somehow inferior to people of white or fair complexion. I never questioned this concept for I was very fair in complexion. Everyone in my family was very fair and some of us had green eyes, which made the remarks more believable at age seven. I remember my parents telling me, "you're so pretty because you're White." I never quite understood what they meant by the statement, until years later. The notion that Whites were more beautiful and smarter was ingrained into my mind and myself. All this learning was taking place in the comfort of my own home. In the eyes of my parents, you had to be fair in complexion to be accepted or beautiful. My aunts and uncles have similar views except that their offspring were darker in complexion. Their children would always get compared to me, "Why can't you be more like B. She is so nice and smart." The constant remarks and comments I heard in my living room became my truth. I trusted my parents, my aunts, and my uncles. I figured that maybe there was some truth to what they were saying. They had power and authority over me and so I mimicked their actions and attitudes. Similarly, I began to relate beauty and smartness to skin color. However, I never saw or considered myself as racist. I imagined everyone thought the same way my parents and I did. (Latina, female)

White is not just a skin color, but translates into a measure of beauty and intelligence. While the brush seeks to paint non-White skin because it is different, the paint penetrates deep beneath the skin. The effects of being painted are illustrated in the following excerpt. A woman's hatred for her skin color reveals a degree of self-loathing that is palpable. In the following example, a Black woman cannot see anything beautiful or attractive about her dark skin. For her, any other color would be preferable:

> As I grew up, I began to hate being dark. I thought, this is not who I am. I hated it. I'm brown not black. In school I would always emphasize that my color was not like the crayon black, but like the crayon brown or sienna, anything but black. Once, I colored a self-portrait of myself orange because the brown crayon was gone, anything but black, even purple would have sufficed. (African American, female)

Students of color are constantly being bombarded with the message of the superiority of White skin. This image is so pervasive that many of the students of color report an internalized sense of inferiority, shame, and self-loathing. In a brilliant experiment conducted in 1947, Clark and Clark focused on young Black and White children, 3 to 7 years of age, who were living in interracial neighborhoods in both the North and the South. The children were shown two dolls, one Black (the word "Colored" was used in 1947) and one White. They were asked four questions: Which doll do you want to play with? Which doll is a nice doll? Which doll looks bad? Which doll has a nice color? The results were striking, in that 60% of the Black children thought that the nice doll, the doll with the nice color, and the doll they wanted to play with was White; 59% of the Black children said the doll that "looked" bad was the Black doll. The need to challenge this internalized view of White superiority prompted Black educators to develop a program for Black children that emphasized a slogan, "Black is Beautiful." This program was introduced in some schools in the 1960s. The program challenged dominants' views of IQ tests, equal opportunity, and equality in education. It challenged the brush's standards for evaluating clothing, dress, and speech. It was a political statement and helped organize collective sentiments of pride and action. Can such a program change the way in which children of color view themselves? Yes it can! In a replication done in 1970 of the 1947 experiment, Hraba and Grant found that 60% of the Black children preferred the Black doll and approximately 70% thought the Black doll had a nice color.

While programs to help children of color with their self-esteem can be helpful, slogans may not be strong enough to erase damaged aspirations and self-esteem, and the constant daily attacks on skin color.

In the following excerpt, a UCLA student describes her reaction to a political slogan and then goes on to discuss her deep feelings about her childhood, experiences in a predominantly White private school, dreams about finding love with a White boy, and the dramatic impact of television and other media on her identity as an African American woman. She ends her personal exploration with her feelings about White society and European culture. This shame of Blackness penetrated so deeply that it caused her to wish for a total change in her racial identity. It would be hard to imagine that a political slogan like "Black is Beautiful" could have helped her overcome her belief that Black people were anything but beautiful:

> I didn't think that Black was beautiful. I thought it was ugly, full lips, Gheri Curls, kinky hair that won't fall straight, everything. I thought all that was White was pretty and because I looked different, I was ugly. So when I would look at my face in the mirror and see what I thought were "Black features" becoming more prominent, I would get upset and think, "Please don't let me look ugly like those girls." It took me a long time to get comfortable with my Blackness.

I remember that when I was younger, I wanted to be White. Not necessarily a White person, but I wanted to have white skin and straight hair. That was a very painful time for me. It was so hard to look in the mirror and wish to see something other than my own reflection. I never really questioned this desire that I had, but I knew to keep it a secret. I knew that I shouldn't let anyone know about how I felt about myself, especially my family.

When I think about why I wanted so badly to have white skin and straight hair, I remember instantly my experience at a predominantly White private school. I was never teased for being an African American and no one ever called my attention to that fact, but it manifested in the form of exclusion. For the first year or so, I didn't have any friends or anyone really to play with on an everyday basis. I never went to school expecting to play with any one child in particular. My memories are of being alone, reading, and sewing and observing the things around me. Whenever we would play tag games, no one wanted to catch me. It was kind of like, "oh she's it." I didn't let that get me down though . . . not as much as my desire to be White got me down. It was bad. I had this white shawl and I would put it on my head and pretend like it was long hair—shaking it and flinging that stupid thing everywhere. I hate to even remember that.

In my dreams I was a pretty White girl discovering love with a White boy. I still remember his name. I would look at television and commercials and imagine that I was the cute little White girl on the screen. I would look through *Seventeen* magazines and identify characteristics that I wanted to possess. I would circle the picture and pray to God and wish on the stars that someday I would wake up. I hate to even think about that now. This feeling of guilt was from wanting to be White, and why did I want to be White? I felt excluded, unloved, and unhappy in my world. Inclusion, love, and happiness were portrayed only in the lives of White people. "Leave it to Beaver," "The Brady Bunch," the commercials, the movies, the magazines were the White world. I was in the Black world. My people were on the evening news, in still pictures showing their faces and their profiles. My people were the robbers and rapists in the movies. My people were in the ghettos and the slums. Whenever I saw my people outside of my limited environment, they looked like I felt—unloved, unhappy, excluded. So who am I mad at? White society! European culture! They have portrayed my people like this. (African American, female)

We would like students who are reading this book to recognize that their own skin color is very likely to be different than the color that their ancestors had. Anthropology Professor Nina Jablonski from Penn State explains that "skin has changed color in human lineages much faster than scientists had previously supposed, even without intermarriage. By creating genetic 'clocks,' paleontologists and anthropologists can see that for many families on the planet" it took only 2,500 years to develop a different color. A shorter explanation can be read in the following link:

http://www.npr.org/templates/story/story.php?storyId=100057939

We expect all of our readers to understand that all of our ancestors can be traced to Africa. If we go back about 100,000 years, we would see ourselves as dark-skinned people.

The standard of Whiteness is more than just about skin color. In fact, skin color is only one way that White painters attack difference. The following sections detail other characteristics that are found by painters and used to paint individuals who don't conform to a White standard. The first section details student experiences of other physical characteristics that do not conform to the painters' arbitrary standards. The next section further explains the effects of non-White names on students.

Your Other Physical Characteristics Also Indicate Your Inferiority

If only skin color was painted, lighter skinned people of color could "pass." This would be dangerous to the dominants' set of beliefs and practices. Passing would mean that some non-Whites could participate more fully in American life. This would in turn affect our definition of what it means to be American. The opportunity for all people of color to be validated is threatening to dominants. If skin color was not treated as "less," then the norm of Whiteness as being more beautiful, more intelligent, or more motivated would be challenged and indeed eradicated. A non-White appearance is attacked on a number of dimensions. In the following example, a Filipino male is belittled and denigrated for both language and eye shape by his neighborhood peers:

> When I was about eight-years-old, I was walking up my street to play with some kids around the block. There were two kids who were walking towards me. As I was walked past them, they both squinted their eyes with their fingers and in a voice, loud enough for me to hear, mimicked an Asian language in a degrading way. While they were doing this, I thought to myself they couldn't be doing this to me. I never felt that I looked Chinese or Japanese, so I turned around and looked to see if they could've been teasing someone else, but there wasn't anyone else around. I remember that my first thoughts were not anger towards the boys, but angry at getting teased and confused for another Asian. This is the be-

ginning of many experiences that have made me internalize oppression about my race, as well as the Asian race. (Filipino, male)

Like skin color, this young man's eyes were not only depicted as different but as strange and ugly. By looking around him and seeing the dominance of "Whiteness" and White features, this young man accepted this evaluation. Rather than taking pride in his appearance and his ethnicity, he turned his anger on himself. Instead of standing up to the people who belittled him, he learned to hate members of his own group.

In the next excerpt, a Filipino female indicates how "Westernized" features were emphasized in her culture. As this Filipina found, sometimes one's own parents wield the brush:

> Growing up, I was taught that the more "White" you looked, the prettier you were. If your nose was sharp, if your skin was light, if your eyes were more rounded, you were praised for having such characteristics. I grew up with the mentality that dark was ugly, or just not as socially accepted by my family and relatives. Even though most Filipinos have darker skin, the ones who were lighter were deemed beautiful. I remember telling my girlfriends that I wanted to marry a guy who was White because my kids would be beautiful. This is an example of the self-hate that is found in various cultures. I find myself not appreciating the beauty of my own culture, the beauty of my own unique features. It's terrible how my culture has succumbed to deeming "White" as beautiful, even after the cruelty Filipinos have endured, especially when Filipinos first migrated here. In my Filipino American experience class I learned of the hatred and discrimination Filipinos had suffered. And it made me angry when my mom praised my cousin for having more Westernized features. It's like we try to downplay our own beautiful, natural features. (Filipino, female)

In the next excerpt, a Latina discusses how her parents did not accept her hair and eye color and how they, unknowingly, reinforced White painters' standards of beauty:

> When I was in second grade, I joined our local swim team. I went swimming every day and because of the chlorine, my hair would turn light. On top of the chlorine, my mother put Sun-In in my hair to lighten it as well. What kinds of messages were being sent to me through this? By the time I got to high school, I was putting Sun-In in my own hair and eventually dyed it. My hair was basically blond, and my mother kept telling me how much she loved my hair color and how she wanted me to keep it light. Later, as I got older and I needed glasses, I got contact lenses. I remember coming home from my optometrist saying, "Dad, I'm getting contacts." The first thing out of his

mouth was, "You should get colored lenses," and he wanted me to get blue contacts. So, not only did he love my hair light, he wanted me to look even whiter. Even today, I sometimes feel as though I favor blond hair and light eyes as my idea of beauty. (Mexican American, female)

Another Latina learns from her mother and aunt that White features are superior. She also describes how she internalized these standards of beauty to the point where she hated herself, her culture, and eventually her own family:

I learned to hate darker skin and I think that that is perhaps part of the reason behind me having an adolescence filled with timidity and shame in my culture, my appearance, and my family. I hated being Mexican, dark, short, and having brown eyes. This self-hatred was heightened during this point of life. I learned to feed into what my family believed. I remember how I hated those "beaners" and "indios," as my mother called them. The saddest part in all of this was that my mother had dark skin, brown eyes, and was short. I grew ashamed of her too. The seeds had been planted so deeply by then, that they allowed me to hate my family. (Latina, female)

Young people are naturally concerned about the shape and size of their body. Body image is a very key aspect of developing identity. In the following excerpt, a Latina describes her experiences with her ethnic body type:

Although skin color never really was an issue for me because my peers admired my ability to tan so easily, my body type was an issue. My basic body shape, which would later find some affirmation by women and men of my own ethnic background, was not the norm amongst the White women who were my peers. Tall and slender was the ideal. Knowing this and seeing the preference for this type definitely gave me a sense of being unattractive. As a young woman I was very uncomfortable in my own skin. Struggling with my body image has been a long, difficult personal struggle. It took a long time to change this. It wasn't until I moved to California that I was able to overcome my deep sense of being undesirable. Once I moved to California and saw other young women, I wondered what my self-concept would have been like if I had grown up with other young women who would have been more like me or if the media had affirmed my looks. (Latina, female)

A focus on one's "defects" can sometimes lead the painted person to obsess about being different. In the following excerpt, a Black woman yearns for a different eye color. Her hope was, and still is, that this would make a difference in her life and would bring her greater adoration:

> I have always wanted a different eye color. Now I can see where that is coming from because when society looks at a person, eye color and skin are examined first. No one ever comes up to me and says "gosh, your eyes are so beautiful" because they are just brown. But I often compliment people with beautiful green or hazel eyes and I begin to picture myself with those same eyes. I know guys who love black women with green, blue, or even hazel eyes, just as long as they are not brown. Because of this I still want an eye color other than brown. This is what I have come to realize as my internalized oppression to be something that I am not. I think that as a light-skinned Black woman, most Black men already accept me, but if I had green eyes I would be even more adored. (African American, female)

The above student is similar to the major character in the 1970 work by Toni Morrison, *The Bluest Eye*. Pecola Breedlove, the protagonist in the novel, believes that a new pair of eyes will change everything, including how she sees things and how she will be seen. Her deepest desire is to have the bluest eyes in the world. The young girl's innocent wish is marked by her perception of a world where the cruelty and hardships she suffers are a result of her appearance as an ugly black girl with dark eyes. She imagines that having blue eyes will earn her respect and possible admiration. Black women of this novel are presented as the victims of the White beauty standards of society and some of the characters develop Stockholm syndrome[2] and, consequently, start loving and adopting the ways of White people. In the book many of the Black characters love White people more than themselves.

Like the characters in *The Bluest Eye*, a UCLA student described how she obtained green contacts for her dark brown eyes during her freshman year. She began noticing immediately that her female friends were describing her as having "beautiful green eyes" and as she feels more confident about herself she is able to get rid of her "green eyes":

> When people told me I had beautiful eyes I felt weird. I knew that what they were responding to weren't my eyes. I acted polite of course and accepted the compliment graciously but underneath I wondered what they would say if they saw me without contacts. I decided to get rid of

---

2 The Stockholm syndrome refers to the ways in which people held hostage develop an affinity for their captors. A lack of abuse is seen as kindness and increases acceptance of the captors' views. The authors of this book feel that many Black, Brown, and Asian women come close to having symptoms akin to the Stockholm syndrome.

them when I began to feel more accepting of myself as attractive and that I shouldn't have to rely on green colored contacts to make myself feel beautiful. I was getting tired of shopping for green contacts and feeling embarrassed when I went into the store. I also felt I wanted to stand up for myself and against the wide held belief that having light eyes is beautiful and better than having dark eyes. (Salvadoran, female)

In the next excerpt, an Arab male wonders how a White appearance might affect areas of his life:

I remember staring at the male models in the pages of magazines like *GQ*, and wondering how different my life would be if I had their features. Maybe then I could command the respect from White America I felt I deserved. I felt that the good looking White boys in junior high not only got the best looking girlfriends, but they were given way more respect, positive feedback, and encouragement from students and faculty than I was. I always thought that I was smarter and funnier than all of them and therefore I should have been the recipient of such praise, but that didn't happen. (Arab, male)

Trying to measure up to dominants' vision of Whiteness, subordinates often fantasize how other aspects of their lives might be different if they looked more White. Wishing to be lighter skinned and possess "Whiter" features caused many students to wonder about how their non-White appearance affected their personal relationships, education, and job opportunities. Feelings of envy and of longing to be White can consume time and energy, which is not productive or healthy. In the following excerpt, a young woman expresses her wish to be White and fantasizes about lost opportunities:

Sometimes I wish I was a little lighter, or that my hair was not so dark. I wish I had finer features. It would be pretty nice to experience some of that White privilege. Sometimes I envy my roommate because she looks white. I honestly believe that she is able to get away with a lot because of the way she looks. I often wonder how my life would differ if I looked White. Would I have more opportunities? Would I have been put in seventh grade algebra class if I looked White? Would I have gotten a different job? I do not know. But I think my life would be a little different. I know that I would be treated differently by some people. (Mexican American, female)

An entire industry built upon allowing people of color to look more like White people exists in this country. This business will flourish as long as women and men of color feel that their hair, their eyes, and their skin are less than adequate. In the following two excerpts a Chicano and a Latina express their desire to be more attractive. Both are concerned about their hair; the male wants his hair curlier and the female wants her hair straighter:

> Now that I look back, high school and junior high school was a time when I wanted to be White. I see how many of the things I did were ways of trying to live up to a societal expectation of beauty. For example, I always wanted my hair to be lighter and curly. So, in junior high, I got a perm. It was one of the most horrendous hair blunders in the history of mankind. Yet, I did not learn my lesson. I continued to believe a perm looked good on me until I came to UCLA. For a couple of years in my life, I wish I had been born less brown. (Chicano, male)

> When I was in high school, I was on the dance team and almost every one of the girls either had straight hair or straightened their hair every day. I hopped on this bandwagon and purchased a $200 straightener so that I could have silky, smooth, and straight hair, which was much more appreciated than curly and wavy hair. Thankfully, since I am too lazy to straighten my hair every day, my hair is still curly. However, one of my friends who straightened her hair every day no longer has curly hair. I can't believe that I felt like I needed to change my natural hairstyle just to fit in and be considered beautiful. (Latina female)

Men and women of color spend money because they want to fit the dominants' standards of beauty and because they feel less handsome or beautiful.

When people are in pain, they can often fantasize and imagine how it might be if the pain or the painting ended. Pervasive self-hatred is often accompanied by a wish to be free of pain and self-hate. For students of color, there is often a belief that Whiteness is the solution to ending the pain. In the following excerpt, a Mexican man describes how he felt when he was called White. This "good" feeling never existed when he thought of himself as Mexican:

> I eventually got a job with the company and was getting along with all the workers. On our daily trips to the sites I would always have conversations with my boss and other colleagues. One day my boss said that I was not Mexican, that I was White. I felt good that day. I felt that I was some- one in this country of ours. After years of being called a "wetback" or a "Mexican," it felt good to be called White. (Mexican, male)

For this young man, having a dominant strip him of his heritage and background felt like a compliment.

Your Names Don't Sound Right: Another Indication of Inferiority

The paintbrush not only identifies physical features that set subordinates apart from dominants; it also recognizes and looks down upon accents, different types of foods, and ethnic names. In the same pattern of physical characteristics, other racial and ethnic markers come under attack, and subordinates often find themselves wanting to change these as well. This can happen even if the change means denying their heritage and giving up part of their identity.

It is very common for children with ethnic names to pick up "American" nicknames. It is also common for dominants to suggest or even insist that a subordinate be referred to by a nickname. Dominants do not always want to go through the trouble of learning to pronounce or remembering a foreign sounding name that may require some effort on their part. They wish for subordinates to accommodate to them.

In the following excerpt an Armenian woman describes how teachers "butchered" her name for many years. Although she acted politely, her anger was always under the surface. On the day of her graduation, the teacher once again ignored her name. Below is her journal account of a fantasy in which she recounts what she wishes she said:

> My last name is very long and difficult to pronounce. All throughout my education in the United States, I have received comments on how hard my name looks. I had gotten accustomed to it in high school, but the whole ordeal always made me feel like a foreigner. I would tell my new teachers not to worry, that I understood if they butchered my name, but I was only being nice about it. I did not want to rock the boat. Although I had suppressed the anger I felt at my name always being ridiculed, I never said anything at all. The ultimate example is my graduation from a Law and Government Magnet School. My counselor of four years was calling out the names of graduates, and when she reached my name, she said, "I'm not even going to try." She only said my first name. I approached the podium, received my certificate and felt completely insulted and angry. Four years of hard work, four years of showing constant respect to this woman, and she could not even attempt to say my full name at my own graduation. After that day, I always had fantasies of having caused a scene. If I could live it all over again, I would grab the microphone and say that I think she should try. I would say, "She should at least try folks. Wouldn't you all like to hear Mrs. F. try to say my name?" (Armenian, female)

Dominants often select and assign a new name for the subordinate without thinking about what they are doing. They believe they are simply changing someone's name. But a name is given by your family, it is yours alone, and it is who you are. When you change someone's name from Katya to Katy, Jose to Joe, from Eliazare to Elly, Yuseph to Joe, Zalika to "Z", LaShell to Shelley, Trang to Tina, Ijeoma to Ida, or Paulino to Paul,[3] you take away a piece of their identity.

In the following example, a Latino has a name that he values because it belonged to his deceased grandfather. His peers and his boss continually mispronounce his name. He feels they're taking away his uniqueness. Eventually he grows angry and tired of having to teach dominants:

> Growing up, I was ashamed of my name because it is not very common in the United States or in Latin America. My name is Blas, its Basque—a region in northern Spain. Not only is my name special to me because it's unique, but it also has sentimental value. This name belonged to my paternal grandfather who passed away before I was born. However, because my peers teased me, I chose to go by my middle name, Humberto. Even then, my peers were not satisfied and continued to mispronounce my name. Despite my effort to acculturate, I was unable to satisfy anyone. I recall that when I got my first job, my boss changed my name from Humberto to Bert without my permission. He claimed it sounded better and was easier to pronounce. It really pissed me off but I stayed quiet. As time progressed, I got tired of not being acknowledged and tired of justifying who I was. (Latino, male)[4]

A Mexican American male discusses his efforts to make it easier on Whites who struggle with his name. He also reveals his respect for people who struggle to pronounce his name correctly:

> I went through a time when I wanted to be White due to the fact that I wanted to be accepted with the other White kids. Nevertheless, as I look at it now I realize how close I came to becoming one of those "White washed" individuals who never discloses his or her own raza (people). I also fell into the role White people put me in. For example, my name is Roberto, not Rob, Bob, or Bobby. I never corrected anyone about calling me something different than Roberto because of respect and because I just felt that many teachers had a hard time rolling the "R" in Roberto.

---

3   These unsolicited examples were all mentioned in my classes. They come from students at UCLA and CSUN.
4   This student felt that the reader could benefit only if his real name was included in the excerpt.

Even today, many people who do not roll the "R's" will still call me Robert, but those who try to say Roberto and do not roll their "R's" will get more respect from me than those who either do not try or whom I have already corrected. (Mexican American, male)

Those who wield the paintbrush can also make children suffer by merely mispronouncing their names. In the following excerpt, an Arab student's patience with helping and correcting others pronounce his name has worn thin, and prompts him to adopt an "American" name, thus yielding a part of his identity:

> One painful memory that will stick with me forever is that I did not correct people (students, teachers, etc.) for incorrectly pronouncing my name, and even allowing them to give me a nickname to make it easier for them. The most painful memory I have is one time I was making a collect call home for a ride, and remembering all the horrible experiences I had with the phone operators. They would ask for my name to accept the call and then would say stupid things like, "What did you say your name was?" or just repeat something that sounded nothing like my name. I decided just to say my name was Mark and speak up when a family member answered the phone. However, my father answered the phone and would not accept a call from a Mark, even when I was talking over the operator saying it was me. I called back and got the ride. On the way home, I felt like my father was disgusted with me. He said that I needed to be proud, to force people to deal with my culture and me. (Arab, male)

Dominants, of course, have a language that is seen as superior. Names for their own children are "normal," easy to learn, and pronounce. Mispronouncing the names of subordinates or changing them to a more convenient nickname is often demeaning to students of color. The following student learned to hate her last name because of her teachers' insensitivity and ignorance:

> In grade school, I always hated when a new teacher or substitute would wrongly pronounce my last name whenever it was time to call attendance. I distinctly remember a third grade substitute asking me with a look of impatience and disgust after wrongly pronouncing my name, "so are you Chinese, Korean, Oriental, Japanese?" When I told him I was Filipino, he just looked at me and said, "what is that??!!" I just felt so embarrassed in front of the whole class. From this point on, I remember wishing I had an American last name, just so that I could fit in, just so that people wouldn't look at me as though I was an alien. I hated being different! (Filipina, female)

IMITATING THE DOMINANTS

We recognize that subordinates also use and practice prejudice, racism, and stereotypes. Why would this happen? What causes subordinates to paint other subordinates? We believe that one of the reasons that subordinates paint other subordinates is because they have often been caught up in the dominants' message of White superiority. This is the internalized racism previously mentioned in Chapter 1. Racism occurs in all institutions (political, economic, educational, and religious) and at all levels of society (cultural, social, and psychological). This constant participation and exposure to prejudice teaches and prompts us all to be racist. In other words, if Latinos are continuously exposed to dominant stereotypes about African Americans as lazy and if Asians are exposed to stereotypes about Arabs as terrorists, they will often adopt the views of the dominant painters without recognizing the source or cause of their beliefs or actions. Although some members of subordinate groups can resist dominant messages, the participation in all of the major institutions of society, family, peers, education, and religion tend to reinforce the superiority of dominance and the inferiority of subordinates. Thus, subordinates often enact prejudice on other subordinates because of what they have learned.

The internalized oppression that can fuel externalized prejudice was described by writer and activist W.E.B. Dubois in 1903. In *The Souls of Black Folks*, Dubois discusses the "double consciousness" that Blacks, and today many other non-White individuals, learn to possess when they live in a country that measures people against a White standard. Non-whites not only experience themselves and the world through their own ethnic eyes, but also develop the ability to see themselves as Whites see them. Sadly, this added awareness doesn't serve to enhance the subordinate's experience. It merely emphasizes that who they are and how they look is deemed as substandard. It is a peculiar sensation, this double-consciousness, this sense of always looking at one's self through the eyes of others, of measuring one's soul by the tape of a world that looks on in amused contempt and pity.

We do not believe that prejudice from a subordinate, such as a female, is in any way equivalent to the prejudice of a dominant male. While the pain may be equivalent in kind, the impact and lethality of racism from a dominant is much more potent than its subordinate counterpart. Imagine that you are a White privileged male student and you were called a "honky" or "peckerhead." Most White students would laugh and think of the other person as either stupid or telling a joke. They are less likely to feel deep pain as students of color do when they are called names. Another example that illustrates the difference in oppression that comes from dominants to subordinates, versus subordinates to subordinates, can be illustrated with gender oppression. If you as a male have been called a pig or a dog it may sting and even hurt, but there are no institutional supports from the courts or from peers that will threaten you. When women get called "bitch," or even worse, they not only feel the sting but because they know that a history of violence has often accompanied that word, they may feel powerless and afraid to respond. So, the oppression of those with greater power (dominants) is far more consequential than the painting of subordinates to other subordinates. Subordinate-on-subordinate oppression is painful to the recipient but is also powerful as it supports privilege and dominance. This is illustrated in the research study of grown children of Korean and Vietnamese immigrants. The terms "FOB" ("Fresh Off the Boat") and "whitewashed" were commonly used to denigrate their fellow subordinates as "too ethnic" or "too assimilated." These children had adopted a view of what they called "normal" and which the authors call "the bicultural middle." This "intraethnic othering" is buttressed by the concept of internalized racial oppression (Pyke & Dang, 2003). An excerpt from their work shows how a Vietnamese woman differentiates FOB women from those who are whitewashed:

> When I see a girl FOB, my friends and me call them the "Bolsa" girls, they always wear their dressy black shoes and black slacks and they won't dress down with tennis shoes or sweats. They always have to be trendy and proper. Even though they are skinny, they are not fit. They don't want to tan because if you are tan back in Vietnam it means you have been working in the field. Whitewashed girls here like to get tan.

This prior example points to the universal tendency to want to increase one's value at the expense of others. If one subordinate group practices racism against another group, the former increases its own sense of empowerment and entitlement to maintain its hierarchical place. In doing so, the oppressive subordinate group imitates dominants in their practices of racism. Not surprisingly, dominants often encourage this imitation. This lack of unity between subordinates serves to empower dominants. Furthermore, dominants can use subordinates' actions against each other to justify their own racist beliefs and actions with statements like, "What's the big deal? We are only doing what they already do to each other?"

In the next example, a Mexican American woman remembers making fun of immigrant men who were field workers:

> I can remember when I was about eight-years-old, my family would drive past places where men were out in the fields working. I had forgotten about this, but I recall my cousin jokingly yelling out the window "La Migra, La Migra." At the time, I thought it was the funniest thing. We would laugh hysterically thinking that all the men would stop what they were doing and run and hide. Gosh, I can't believe we used to do that. Granted we were just kids with no clue, but did we ever think about what we were doing? Or if they could hear us, how it made them feel? And

what about our parents, why didn't they say anything? (Mexican American, female)

As she recalls this experience, this student realizes that what she and her cousin were doing was hurtful, and that the fun they had was at others' expense. This excerpt also demonstrates how children of color teach each other how to paint like dominants. Just as Whites make ethnic jokes to show their superiority, subordinates often find ways to laugh at those who they feel are inferior to them. The paintbrush is handed down and thrives from one racial group to another.

The reader who is not a person of color can probably imagine a time in their lives when peers and parents and teachers ridiculed them. They were called names, or told they were too fat, too short, too skinny, four-eyed, or nerdy. The pain that accompanies those slurs is similar to the pain felt by the students you have been reading about. However, the qualities that you were ridiculed for are ones that you could either outgrow or modify while the qualities and characteristics that children of color are ridiculed for are permanent. Name calling of White children is not institutionalized as a regular, ongoing form of discrimination. (The terms "White trash" and "redneck" come close to being institutionalized.) Also, the prejudicial slurs insult the individual and not their whole culture, family, or history. For the students of color, the names, slurs, and innuendoes are repetitive; often occur daily; and attack the basic identity of the person. The oppression is more significant, not necessarily in its pain, but in its consequences and frequency.

In sum, the White paintbrush—the paintbrush of racism—often instills in children of color the belief that their skin, facial features, hair, and body type are ugly and unattractive and that their names are peculiar or un-American. For subordinates, their social identity is often evaluated as undesirable. Subordinates are made to feel that their differences make them inferior to dominants. In our next chapter, we will discover how subordinates are lumped together and treated as the same by dominants and how differences are ignored between and among subordinates. This is the double bind that students and people of color often have to deal with. Sometimes their differences are emphasized and other times their differences are completely ignored.

In our experience on teaching classes on racism we have discovered that our concerns with oppression and discrimination cannot be limited to race and ethnicity. After all, if White women have the privilege that goes along with being White they are also subordinates to males. And of course, women of color are often treated as subordinates by men of color. My first efforts to teach in a transformative matter and focus exclusively on race were challenged by my female students. They were right and we offer these gender exercises to the instructor who wishes to look at oppression as a fact that occurs across genders regardless of color.

GENDER EXERCISES

Gender Fantasy

Instructors:

In this exercise students are asked to close their eyes, become quiet, and get centered. It is advisable to turn the lights off, but not make it so dark that you cannot see students' faces. Your job as the instructor is to take them through the life cycle of members of the opposite sex. You start out by asking them to go back in time to when they were in their mother's womb. You mention the first trimester, second trimester, and third trimester. Do this slowly. It should take up to 1 minute for this part of the exercise. You then tell them that they are about to enter the world. The water breaks and they do enter the world, but this time they come into the world as a member of the opposite sex. I often use "with a penis or a vagina" to make sure they get it. Their birth order in their family is the same. These are the prompts I use, providing at least 30 seconds after each prompt.

Reactions of family members to your gender:
Who's happy? Who's disappointed?

Reactions to your first steps walking.
Any discipline? Who does it?

First day of school: What does it feel like? Who takes you?

Second or third grade: Who are you friendly with? Which sports or subjects do you like? Which subjects do you do well in?

Getting along with siblings: Fights?

You're 10 years old. Chores in the house? Helping with dishes? Mowing the lawn? Laundry? Cooking? Who do you confide in?

You're 11 or 12 and your body is beginning to change as you enter puberty. Describe changes for students in terms of body hair, menstrual period, erections, wet dreams. Who do you discuss these issues with, if anyone?

You're 14 and beginning high school. What are your favorite subjects? What's your GPA? Do you have any part-time jobs? Do you help around the house? Who are you close to? Do you play with the opposite sex at school? Do you play sports? Any clubs in school?

You're 16 and have had your first date. Take them through a dating experience including who is coming to pick up whom. Parental reactions, decision making regarding where to go and what to do, and a kiss good-night. Have them imagine their feelings.

Junior year: How are you doing in school? What is your best subject? What are you being disciplined for at home? What are your guidance counselor's suggestions for after high school? What colleges, if any, are being recommended?

The summer before you start college do you work? If so, where? Is it your money or do you contribute at home?

First year of college: What's your GPA? How much drinking do you do? How much sex do you have? Do you live at school or commute?

Third year in college: What's your major? How's your GPA?

You develop a very serious and committed relationship: How does that feel? What do your parents or friends say?
This relationship continues until you graduate, at which point the male partner decides to break the relationship. How does that feel?

What do you do after graduation? Do you go on to graduate school or are you employed? And if so, what kind of work are you doing?

Jump ahead to the age of 32. You are now in a committed relationship and there is a pregnancy. Open your eyes in order to see whether is it is a boy or a girl.

This exercise can reveal how gender expectations for boys and girls in the same family are communicated. In general, the women in the fantasy love having more freedom than the boys while growing up, but also feel more responsibility in selecting a major that will earn more money to provide for their family. The boys in the family have menstrual cycles and are afraid of giving birth and discover that they have to be very protective with females. They can also pick majors less oriented toward economic stability. The fantasy can provide numerous moments of reflection, especially if the boys are asked about getting pregnant. The major insight has to do with the way expectations have been communicated regarding education, occupation, as well as different norms of freedom and safety.

Gender Realties

After students have begun to think about becoming anti-racist, they still are being challenged by the women in the class who now can use "male privilege" as a concept instead of White privilege. The following exercise engages these and other gender issues. All the men come to the front of the class and sit on the floor. The women sit above the men in their seats. The men are told they cannot speak, ask questions, or make comments. Ask the men to comment on how it feels to be on the floor and pose the same question to the women about their being seated. We introduce this exercise in the following way: You have learned after reading Jean Baker Miller's article (1998) on the relationships between dominants and subordinates that dominants know very little about subordinates, their world, difficulties, fears, and concerns. You have also learned that subordinates always have to be concerned with what dominants are planning, so here is the opportunity for you dominants to learn from subordinates. You will listen and you will not be allowed to interrupt.

We suggest to the women that they are going to inform the men about their experiences as women. We have found that having women begin by talking about their purses is a good way to commence the presentation of information—that is, how it feels to carry a purse around and the comments they receive about their purse. Please allow time for this topic to be exhausted. There is much they have to say! After this, we bring up the issue of safety without calling it by that name. You, the instructor, may ask the women to volunteer what it has felt like to walk in an elevator with only men, a parking lot late at night, or an underground garage. After this issue is explored and expressed we suggest that the instructor ask the women to describe the comments they have received from men about their menses. They will probably report being ridiculed and made fun of. The women should also be able to explain how they are often treated in public—being stared at, whistled at, and cat-called. Experiences in clubs are also a possible reporting. The more serious issues are yet to come; I will leave it up to the instructor to handle the delicate issues that are underlying women's realities regarding date rape and other sexual violations. In our experience, we have always found that at least 25% of the women in the class have been raped or sexually molested. Please allow the tears to flow and do not interrupt. Sometimes the women talk to each other about how they need to not bad-mouth other women and instead support each other. Make sure that there is enough time for the women to express themselves about this issue. The instructor can take some time to remind men of how little they know about women. Isn't this an excellent example of the relationships between dominants and subordinates?

We often end this part of the exercise at this point and plan to continue in our next meeting. We start again with the men on the floor. We ask if there are any further comments that the women wish to make before we turn to the men. Some of the women will point out that men may have laughed while the horror stories were being told. After the women have fully exhausted what they want to say, the men are allowed to speak and are encouraged to describe their feelings and responses. They are asked whether they realized that the realities that their female classmates are describing were the same realities of their sisters, mothers, aunts, and grandmothers. The instructor should aim to have the men talk about their feelings upon learning about their female classmates. The men will often express the idea that they would never rape or whistle or make jokes. As an instructor you can ask them if they have seen or heard their friends whistling or cat-calling, joking about women's menstrual cycles, or making fun of their irrational fears without doing anything. It should be noted that their silence supports the sexism and exploitation they have just learned about. The instructor should not ignore the possibility that the men have been sexually molested or raped also. This is very important for the men to express and the women to see. Finally, each group is asked to huddle and come up with six things that they want the opposite gender to know about them.

In doing this exercise, every instructor should realize that some deep wounds are being opened. We offer free counseling to anyone in the class. We suggest that if the instructor cannot make this offer, that the student go to student services for counseling, stressing the idea that all wounds can be healed. This exercise can be used successfully in any Social Psychology, Gender Studies, or Oppression

Theory class that emphasizes different realities and the information and perceptions that individuals have by being limited to their own view of truth.

The song performed by Gwen Stefani and written by her and Tom Dumont, called "Just a Girl," illustrates many of the concepts that students will have expressed in these two exercises. The instructor, or the student, can go to the following links to listen and read the lyrics:

http://www.youtube.com/watch?v=PHzOOQfhPFg.
(http://www.azlyrics.com/lyrics/nodoubt/justagirl.html)

CHAPTER 5

The Strokes of Sameness

"Stereotypes are devices for saving a biased person the trouble of learning."

—Unknown

The previous chapter revealed how the paintbrush highlights differences and then uses those differences to demean and humiliate subordinates. The paintbrush not only paints subordinates as different from dominants, but also works to make sure that they are defined as inferior. In this chapter we show how generalizations and prejudgments of subordinates as being "the same" are equally damaging and degrading. Evaluating subordinates as similar includes grouping them together by character, intelligence, morality, and ambition. This lumping ignores their uniqueness, talents, and potential, and makes success more difficult for subordinates.

Richard Pryor describes this phenomenon in his 1977 album, "Who Me? I'm Not Him." Pryor loved being a kid and then it all changed:

> I like being a kid very much. I do . . . I really love it—'cause if you was a kid, you didn't have to be anything else. I was a kid until I was about eight . . . then I became a Negro.

In this quip, Pryor describes the "grouping and lumping" phenomenon. He implies that White children are just children and that children of color are "marked." The racial category of "Whiteness" leaves White children unmarked by Whites but noticed by people of color as being White. They are not described by White people or the media as being White. They are not set apart. These unmarked White children are differentiated from each other based on their uniqueness. We notice and comment upon what those children do and accomplish. In contrast, subordinate children are grouped together. They are not just children, but Black children, Latino/a children, Asian children, or Middle Eastern children.

Generalizations made about others are most commonly known as "stereotypes." These are fixed and oversimplified images or ideas of a person. In this chapter we will discuss stereotypes that are ascribed to students based solely on their ethnic, racial, or religious identity. These stereotypes can often cause harm. Professor Claude Steele demonstrates how stereotypes cause harm in the classroom. Steele (1997) developed the concept of "stereotype threat." This theory states that a person's "social identity"—defined as group membership in categories such as age, gender, religion, and ethnicity—has significance when "rooted in concrete situations." Thus, stereotype threat can result in tangible consequences for students of color. For instance, African Americans face the stereotype of being racially inferior, a stereotype that has long been entrenched in American society. African American students quickly learn that being seen as good students by teachers and peers is difficult to achieve. One student recalls how she experienced this battle in the seventh grade:

> I remember that I was always finding mistakes made on the grading of my chemistry tests and I had to correct the teacher. On every single test that I took, she marked correct answers wrong and I would bring it to her attention and every single time her response would be "I guess I over-looked that." I started getting the feeling that I was different and that it was not necessarily a good thing. It went against everything my mother taught me about how my being different was a great thing. I hated the feeling I had when my teacher was around. She made me feel like I was not important and that was very strange to me. I was always a good student who was praised for my work but no matter what I did, she refused

to give me recognition for it. I dreaded going to that class but I still went because my grades were very important to me. I will never forget that seventh grade teacher. (African American, female, California State University, Northridge)

This student carries an extra burden—a burden that can lower her academic performance. Many will argue that in situations such as taking a chemistry exam everyone is treated equally. This assumption seems especially reasonable in the case of "standardized" cognitive tests. After all, getting a good grade on an exam has nothing to do with opinions or feelings. Yet even something as "objective" as a chemistry test can have a different meaning for Black students. They must battle the negative stereotype of being racially inferior. These thoughts interfere with their cognitive energy while taking the test, which results in lower scores. Many of our students of color have spoken about taking lower-level classes instead of being one of the only few students of color in honors classes solely for the fear of being singled out in order to justify their place in the class. Even in a regular class, students of color can feel intimidated about speaking out because they are afraid their abilities are being judged.

To establish the validity of the stereotype threat, Steele and Aronson (1995) asked Black and White sophomore Stanford students to take a 30-minute verbal test from the Graduate Record Examination in literature. Although both group of students were statistically equated on ability level, the Black students performed dramatically worse than White students. They hypothesized that if stereotype threat was the cause of these students' poorer test performance, then reducing that threat should naturally lead to higher test results. A second group of Black and White sophomores, again statistically equated on ability level, were given the same test. Steel and Aronson told the students that this exam was not a test of ability, but a "problem-solving" task that had nothing to do with ability. This made the stereotype about Blacks' ability irrelevant to their performance on the task. The results of the test did not measure ability. This simple change of instruction profoundly changed the meaning of the situation. It indicated to Black participants that the racial stereotype about their lower ability was irrelevant to their performance on this particular task. The outcome was that Black and White Stanford students performed equally.[1]

The threat of being stereotyped, as described by Steele (1997), characterizes the daily experiences of Black students on predominantly White campuses and in a predominantly White society. In the following excerpt, an African American student at UCLA describes his reactions toward indicating his race in standardized tests that he's taken:

---

[1] Recent research suggests that one of the better ways that educators can reduce stereotypic threat is by focusing on dominant groups' disadvantages. This focus allows subordinate groups to remain engaged in the academic task. Lowery, Brian S. & Wout, Daryl A. (2010). "When inequality matters: The effect of inequality frames on academic engagement." *Journal of Personality and Social Psychology*, *98*(6), 956–966.

There have been countless times where I haven't filled in that portion of the test because of my own imprudent thoughts of the graders separating certain selected ethnicities and sending them to a 'special' factory to be 'specially' graded. Crazy, yes maybe, but not impossible. Think about it. The times when I filled in the 'African American/Black' or 'other' bubble, I can confidently say that it was in the back of my mind that I had to do especially well in order to 'positively represent my race/ethnicity.' This personal act correlates to the reading in the sense of an effort to overcome stereotype threat by disproving the stereotype, which was exactly what I was attempting to do. (African-American, male)

Steele's research shows that stereotype threat can undermine the test performance of any group that is negatively stereotyped.

Another experiment is less about stereotype threat and more about expectations. In *Pygmalion in the Classroom* (Rosenthal & Jacobson, 1992), the teacher's expectations were altered just by being told that their Black and Brown students had high IQs. In this creative experiment, teachers in the Oakland, California, school district were told by a Harvard Ph.D. that there was a new culture-free IQ test. After administrating the test, the teachers were informed about which of their students of color had high IQs. Miraculously, students began behaving more positively in the classroom and increased their academic performance on standardized California exams. The truth is that there was no culture-free test. The information presented to the teachers was false. Yet, it had the power to change the teacher–student dynamic in an extremely positive way. The teachers believed that these students were bright and gifted in ways they may not have believed before. Having a Harvard Ph.D. validate these students' academic abilities was enough to get the teachers to think differently about them. Thinking about the students in this new way, as having high IQs, led teachers to behave differently towards their "newly gifted" Black and Brown students. Their prior expectations were drastically modified as they now had higher expectations for their students and gave positive reinforcements for any signs of learning or intelligence. Students responded to these new higher expectations with improved grades and improved behavior in their classrooms. It is unfortunate that there isn't always a Harvard Ph.D. around to defend the intelligence of so many students of color.

Many Americans believe that African Americans are less intelligent. This belief is examined by Jared Diamond (1999), in his Pulitzer Prize–winning work, *Guns, Germs, and Steel.* Diamond examines the causes of domination and racism, and addresses the biological explanation. He concludes that there is no sound evidence for the existence of human racial differences in intelligence, even though many continue to believe in a racist biological explanation privately or subconsciously.

What are the other ways in which subordinates are treated and labeled as all the "same"? Following are questions and answers expressed by dominants who already think they have the answers:

"Why don't you just speak English?"
There is something wrong with you for not rushing to adopt White language and standards.

"Why do you need your own day or month for history—why can't you just be content with regular American history?"
You should just accept American history and not try to rewrite a history that distorts our reality.

"Why can't you work hard like I did?"
The fact that you are not in honors classes, have a good paying job, and live in a good neighborhood proves to me that you are lazy, want something for nothing, and are not willing to work hard.

"How come you are always bringing up slavery and why are you living in the past?"
You would rather play the race card and talk about the past as a way of providing an excuse for your shortcomings.

When Tim Wise (2004, 2009), a White activist who has been publishing about White privilege and racism in America and teaching diversity education to Whites, hears statements like these, he wonders aloud and challenges the members of his White audience. He retorts, "Why are you people bringing up the American Revolution, Independence Day, and the Boston Tea Party and living in the past?" Dominants are often frustrated when subordinates do not want to be just like them; they want subordinates to think like they do, believe as they do, dress and speak and dance like they do. They get upset when subordinates want to maintain their individuality and want to create new, alternative ways of life, or challenge the dominants' views of history and social justice. Most of all, dominants want to make sure that their views and ways remain the norm. This latter sentiment is achieved by purposefully ignoring all that is unique, original, or different about subordinates.

Table 4 summarizes what we discovered in our student journals. Students were painted as similar most frequently by peers, educators, and police officers. The learners come from every major racial group, including biracial students. Efforts to lump students as similar were mostly aimed toward African Americans and Asians.

TABLE 4

The Teachers, Learners, and Targets of Racism

Teachers		Learners		Targets	
Teachers	7	African Americans	9	African Americans	12
Peers	12	Asians	9	Asians	10
Police/Government	6	Latinos (as)	2	Latinos(as)	5
Media	2	Middle Easterners	7	Middle Easterners	8
Neighborhood/Landlord	4	Whites	4		
Parent	1	Bi Racial	4		
Business/Store	3				
Total	35	Total	35	Total	35

YOU'RE THE SAME—I DON'T NEED TO KNOW YOU AS AN INDIVIDUAL

Painting by dominants of subordinates highlights, pathologizes, and ignores people's differences. In the United States, we celebrate individuality and we strive to be unique. But in many cases, it is the privilege of being dominant that allows people to be noticed and to feel unique. In the following excerpt, a Filipino reacts to the dominants' lumping of all Asians:

> One of the biggest problems is how whites lump us into the Asian category. They say, that we all look alike, sound alike, and eat the same food. But they are wrong. It hurts to think that they cannot and do want to differentiate identities. (Filipino, male)

In the next example an Asian male describes the ways in which he is continually being painted as nonathletic, musically gifted, a nerd, and a thug. He is none of these:

> I have been treated differently because I am Asian and different than the White majority. Asians are stereotyped as being nonathletic, musical, and either nerdish or thuggish. Sadly, I have little to no musical ability. I slack off way too much. I tend to be fairly athletic and aggressive when playing sports. I do not fit into the nerd or thug roles. For some reason, understanding math or English never came easy to me as young kid. When I was 7, a guy in my class asked if he could study with me and I was happy

to say yes. He didn't know me very well but I suppose he knew I was Asian and thus assumed that I was intelligent and knew the answers. He expected me to finish the work for both of us. He was disappointed as I was hoping that he could help me with the problems. Even at that age I felt bad that I couldn't live up to people's expectations of me. At the same time, I felt pressured to fulfill the stereotype though I didn't know how I could. (Chinese, male)

The privilege of Whiteness allows dominants to be recognized for their individual qualities. The media is frequently guilty of slighting and ignoring individuals who are not White and classifying them into a single category. In the following example, an Asian man describes his anger at the media's one-dimensional depiction of his murdered friend. The television reports simply referred to the deceased as "Asian," in striking contrast to how White victims were portrayed:

> The American media is biased. Two weeks ago, my friend T was brutally murdered. When reporters reported the story, none of them mentioned that he graduated from UCLA with honors and was waiting for an acceptance letter from medical schools. I was so upset when I didn't hear any description of my friend's achievements. I am upset because if this had happened to a White person, something positive would have been mentioned. For instance, two days ago a (White) couple jumped off a cliff. The news reporters spent time telling us how great these kids were (e.g. they got straight A's and were outgoing). I was infuriated when I realized that the same newscaster only spent a few seconds reporting my friend's murder. This reaffirmed my thought that the dominant society has not yet fully recognized Asian people. My friend needed to be recognized as an individual, as someone who had worked hard in school so that he could attend medical school, as an ex-president of the Vietnamese Student Association, as an inspiration for his friends. Instead, people who saw the news coverage of T will probably remember him as a product of the growing violence among the Asian community. Whatever it is that the public remembers him as, they won't remember him like they do the self-destructive White couple. (Vietnamese, male)

For dominants, Whiteness or race is neutral. The identities of Whites become tied to the subjects they major in, the sports they play, or the careers they choose. On the other hand, the identities of subordinates are submerged in the lumping process. When they are noticed, assumptions are made about their personalities, their morality, and their behavior. When parents ask their daughter about her new boyfriend, they want to know what he looks like, how he treats her, what he's interested in, and perhaps they are also curious about the socioeconomic background of the suitor. If parents find out that the boyfriend is Black, that's often enough information. They dislike him immediately because of all the images that are conjured up by his skin color. Drawing on a non-race example, when people find out that the daycare worker is homosexual, they often yank their children out of preschool because they assume that all gay people are sexual deviants. In everyday life, the things that mark subordinates as "different" allow dominants to group them as all the same. It then becomes the subordinates' responsibility to prove that they are "exceptions."

YOU'RE ALL THE SAME—DEROGATORY NAMES APPLY TO YOU

Calling someone a name is a very powerful experience. The category "mom" evokes many more images than simply that of a woman who has given birth to a child. Presidents remain "Mr. President" even after having served their term as a form of respect. Just as these titles evoke images, the names that we give to racial categories similarly embody deep symbolism. While the word "mom" can have a positive connotation and "Mr. President" implies respect, racial names of subordinates carry negative ideas of low intelligence, poor morality, lack of ambition, and immigrant status.

All people belong to one or more official racial categories. When White people do things, their race goes unmentioned. For instance, "a teacher was arrested for sexually harassing students" as opposed to "a young Black male stole a car." On the other hand, a range of names marks non-White races. By marking non-Whites with derogatory names, the paintbrush highlights all subordinates as the same—and such sameness often translates into an image of deviance. Because of a history of exploitation, many terms for racial categories become so loaded that with just one word, the impact can be seared into the psyche of a child forever.

In the following example, an 8-year-old female describes the great time she was having in a snowball fight with her friend until she is called a name. The situation became worse when her friend's siblings joined in the name calling. She knows this word is horrible and degrading despite never having heard it before. The name she is called places her in a category that refers to "all Black people":

> As a child, I can remember having a good friend named J, with whom I did everything. We were the best of friends. J was White and I was Black but that was never an issue. One day we were in her backyard playing in the snow. We were having a great time. I remember starting a snowball fight. Well, we were getting wet and cold from the snow and were ready

to stop. I threw my last snowball and it hit J in the face. J became mad. All of a sudden she shouted, "Nigger" into my face. She kept repeating it. Soon her little brother and sister joined in. I started to cry. "Why were they saying this to me?" I felt so scared and helpless. I ran all the way home. That day I knew that I was different. (African American, female)

Names are not limited to Black children. Most subordinates involuntarily join the ranks of "the labeled."In the following excerpt, the terms used for a young Korean are incorrect, but they nevertheless hurt her:

> As horribly blunt as children can be, I heard insults such as "You little chink! Why don't you go back to your own country?!" and "You think you're so smart you little nip!" hurled at me. Even the other Korean children would tease me because I seemed to look more Chinese than Korean. I can clearly remember numerous instances when I would come home crying and hating that I was Korean. (Korean, female)

This quote shows the power of labeling. By naming people and allowing their racial background to be the primary form of identification, these children were labeling all people who look Asian as the same.

In the next excerpt, a spray-painted word on a new house frightens this Korean student. He learned that who he was must be undesirable. The fact that his family was highly educated, affluent, accomplished, or highly moral was irrelevant. Only race mattered to the painters:

> I remember in 1982, when I was eight, my grandmother's sister and her family moved to Arcadia, a predominantly White, middle-to-upper-class neighborhood. When we went over to see her house, someone had spray painted, "Fuck You Nip" on the front door. I was so puzzled as to why anyone would write such a thing. I was even more confused because the neighborhood looked so quiet and nice. I asked my mom if auntie and grandma's sister would be safe living here and I remember my mom saying, "I sure hope they will be." Her answer frightened me, but when she said this, I also knew that I would have some tough battles ahead of me. (Korean, male)

In the following, a biracial female recalls her age, year, place, and the individuals who were involved when she was first subjected to a racial slur. This specificity suggests the traumatic impact of the event:

I was six years old at the time, living with my mom and sister in Garden Grove, a city in Orange County. My elementary school had a diversity of students: Whites, Hispanics, and Asians. The majority of the Asians were Vietnamese. My White friends would call them "nips" or "gooks." I was even guilty of this myself. Even though I am half-Japanese, I did not look very Asian; not one of my White friends noticed that I was part Asian. One day after school my friend Jane came over and saw that my mom was Asian. She did not say anything at that time but I can still visualize the shock and surprise on her face when I introduced this little Japanese woman as my mother. The following day at school, she came up to me with a few of our other friends and said, "My daddy said that you are a 'nip' too because your mother is Asian." Shocked by what she had just said to me, I tried to defend myself by stupidly saying, "But my mom is Japanese, not Vietnamese." J followed with, "That doesn't matter because my daddy said that all them Asians are the same. They are all 'gooks'." I did not continue to argue with her because there was no point. I was so embarrassed because our other friends were just staring in disbelief. I was very angry and hurt—this big secret that I was withholding from all my friends had just been revealed and I was not prepared to really defend myself. I could not believe J would call me those same awful names that we called out to the Vietnamese students. (Biracial, Japanese White, female)

Often, subordinates think and feel as though they are dominants until forcefully reminded otherwise. Before a slur was applied to her, this student found it fun to call other children racial names. Clearly, to dominants, name calling seems benign. It seems like a game, especially to young children. To subordinates, the name calling and group labeling (which they face everywhere they go) deeply affect their self-image.

Ongoing name calling created difficulty for this young Middle Eastern male who was unable to focus on his education:

Sometimes I got called "mean Arab" and other such things, especially during times when the Middle East was heavily covered in the news. These children didn't know any better. It came naturally to them. I remember being occupied with worries about being different and inferior. There were many times I can remember not being able to think straight days after a confrontation. I was too worried about what the other children were thinking. For many years this worrying affected my performance in school no matter how hard I tried. (Arab, male)

Naming and grouping someone is an exercise of power. The power by dominants to re-name and regroup subordinates is rarely done in a complimentary fashion. Racial names are derogatory and designed to make the other feel less worthy, less valued, less attractive, and less desirable. A name that others hold as something you are has an impact on the self. The name becomes part of the subordinates' identity, reminding them of their sameness and their place in the world.

YOU'RE ALL THE SAME—MY JOKES ARE "ALL IN GOOD FUN"

In addition to slurs, the paintbrush uses jokes to respond to, accentuate, and belittle subordinates. These jokes treat all members of ethnic, racial, and religious groups as similar. In fact, many of these jokes rely on shared stereotypes in order to be funny in the first place. These jokes are very difficult for young people to challenge. It's hard to stand up for yourself, especially when everyone else is laughing. The painter often believes these words to be funny, and as a dominant, may not realize that they reemphasize similarity and pain. In the following example, an Asian student recalled jokes aimed at her race. Her objection to the jokes demonstrated how deeply they impacted her. She recalls one from high school and another from college. Both jokes are equally painful for this student:

Setting: junior or senior year in high school
J: "How did Chinese people come up with their last names?"
L: (going along with it) "How?"
J: "When someone dropped the silverware down the stairs, it went ching chang-ching-chang-etc."
L: "F-you!" (not too serious, but not too facetiously either)
J: (laughing)

Setting: I was either 18 or 19 years old having lunch on campus with my White roommate.
J: "Why do Chinese men walk with their hands behind their backs?"
L: (with a reluctant look on her face like she's thinking to herself) "Why are you saying this to me?"
J: "To protect their wallets, get it?"
L: (just looks at Jennifer, upset and unamused)
J: "Oh relax! Don't get all sensitive!"

It was from this last joke that I first learned of the stereotype that all Chinese people were considered cheap and "protective" of their money. The jokes were painful, but I usually left such remarks alone. Besides a look of disapproval, I never pursued the issue with J. It would have been difficult to talk to her about it, and I always felt that she would be too stubborn to own up to it. (Chinese American, female)

Dominants can laugh at jokes about subordinates. The jokes often reinforce stereotypes but can also remind subordinates of a very painful history. In the movie *Guess Who*, Ashton Kutcher, a White male, has been brought to his girlfriend's family home for a family celebration. After being encouraged to repeat jokes that he has heard in his own family, he decides to proceed with the idea that open discussion is necessary to break down barriers. His joke is in the form of a question: "What are three things that a Black man can never get?" His answer is: "a black eye, fat lip, and a job." Did you laugh at this joke? Do you think your laughter has anything to do with your race? Do you think White students were more likely to find humor in this joke than students of color? If you are a person of color, you probably were offended, as were the father and grandfather in the movie.

Subordinates are frequently called "too sensitive." This ignores the pain, frustration, and anger that accompany knowing that you must work that much harder for people to see you "differently" than they do your entire race. Perhaps their sensitivity derives from their awareness of the history of persecution, murder, lynching, and physical exploitation that they know has occurred. If all citizens, dominants and subordinates, were aware of the human costs of slavery, of the horrible exploitative conditions under which Chinese laborers built our railroads, of how the four states of California, Texas, Arizona, and New Mexico belonged to Mexico before the United States forcibly took them, how we lynched African Americans and Mexican Americans, and how 400 treaties were broken by the U.S. government with Native Americans, than perhaps "insensitive" would not be used to belittle the feelings of minorities. In the song "Strange Fruit," Billie Holiday sings that many Americans find it difficult to listen to and want to dismiss such horrors. While it may be from the past, it haunts those whose ancestors received a common fate. This song could be used as a discussion about the history of lynching in America. What is your reaction to this song and that idea?

Please review the lyrics at: http://www.bluesforpeace.com/lyrics/strange-fruit.htm (http://www.elyrics.net/read/b/billie-holiday-lyrics/strange-fruit-lyrics.html)

Billie Holiday's lyrics refer to the lynching that was so prevalent in the South. It was not just Black men who were hanged. One author notes that Mexican Americans faced a rate of lynching equal to African Americans in the Deep South. The figure of 27.4 Mexican lynching victims per 100,000 of population for that period exceeds the statistics for Black victims during the same time period in some southern states and nearly equals that in others. Between 1880 and 1930, the lynching rate for African Americans in South Carolina and North Carolina was 18.8 and 11.0 per 100,000 of population, respectively. In

Alabama, the figure was 32.4. These figures show that Mexican Americans faced a similar risk of lynching as African Americans.[2]

For students who are unaware of the history of the colonization of Native Americans, Howard Zinn (1999) provides us with a description of how we brutalized 9 million "Americans." According to Zinn, the methods used to kill Native Americans during this genocidal period included lynching, the introduction of diseases by the colonists, and forced migration. As a protest of dominant cruelty, in November 1969, a landmark event occurred: A group of Native Americans landed on Alcatraz Island in the San Francisco Bay with the intention of occupying it. They "offered to buy Alcatraz in glass beads and red cloth, the price paid [to] Indians for Manhattan Island over 300 years earlier" (Zinn, 1999). The federal government responded with federal forces that invaded and physically removed the Native Americans. This event, which occurred over 40 years ago, confirms that historical oppression and violence against Native Americans is still prevalent and that feelings of White supremacy that fueled the colonists are still prevalent in the U.S. government. All these historical experiences for men and women of color can make them quite sensitive about racial jokes.

Another horrific historical American experience is the internment of Japanese Americans in the 1940s. After the December 7, 1941, Japanese attack on Pearl Harbor, President Franklin D. Roosevelt issued Executive Order 9066. This act permitted the military to bypass the constitutional safeguards of American citizens in the name of national defense. The order excluded persons of Japanese ancestry living on the West Coast from residing and working in certain locations. This traumatic event culminated in the mass evacuation and incarceration of most Japanese Americans, most of whom were U.S. citizens or legal permanent resident aliens. They were detained for up to 4 years without due process of law or any factual basis. They were forced to live in bleak, remote camps behind barbed wire and under the surveillance of armed guards. Japanese American internment raised questions about the rights of American citizens as embodied in the first 10 amendments to the Constitution. When they were released from the camps they discovered that their houses had been sold and property had been confiscated. Money had been made after their deportation.

There are many ethnic groups that we have left out from this brief history of the oppression that Americans have inflicted upon other Americans. Arab Americans, Vietnamese Americans, Central and South Americans, Pacific Islander Americans, Middle Eastern Americans, and other groups have all been the brunt of oppression and jokes. As this is not a textbook about history, we recommend that students who are interested in the hidden history of oppression read *Lies My Teacher Told Me* (Loewen, 2007) and *A People's History of the United States* (Zinn, 1999).

---

2 Carrigan, W. D., & Webb, C. (2003). "The lynching of persons of Mexican origin or descent in the United States, 1848 to 1928." *Journal of Social History*, 37(2), 411-438

Along with additional readings please see the links below for music and lyrics of a song that summarizes colonialism and describes the impact on the Americas. We suggest listening and reading lyrics of Randy Newman's "Great Nations of Europe."

To Read: http://www.lyricsdepot.com/randy-newman/great-nations-of-europe.html

To Listen: http://www.youtube.com/watch?v=d_IA3stJRoE

People may find it difficult to challenge racist jokes, especially when directed at their own group. In this next example, a Vietnamese woman described a dinner with her boyfriend's family who proceeded to make a set of derogatory comments about Cambodians:

> At my boyfriend's family dinner, the sons were talking about the Hmong people of Cambodia and making derogatory comments that they were stupid because they ate dog. Suddenly they looked at me and said, "Oh my gosh, T, I'm sorry. You're not Cambodian, are you?" I was shocked. When they were making these comments, I felt very uncomfortable, but I did not say anything. Instead, I just sat there like a passive victim. However, when they realized their blunder, I walked out. It never occurred to me that they were ignoring me because of their White privilege. My boyfriend walked out with me and asked me why I didn't say anything. I just told him to forget it, that it didn't matter, and that it wasn't going to make much of a difference. Now I wish that I had spoken up. I wish I had told them how hurt and angry I was that they stereotyped Asians that way and that they had the gall to say things like that around me. (Vietnamese American, female)

As this example brings to light, no matter how hurt and angry you are, it's very hard to confront dominants when they are busy labeling and grouping your ethnicity into one category. In the following, a UCLA student is subjected to her university professor's comments. While the professor believes that his jokes are in good fun, the student is aggravated and furious at this racist humor. She deeply regrets that she was unable to speak her mind:

> Last year in my introductory American Government Political Science class, I had a professor who was very racist (although he probably would not consider himself racist). He made several comments in front of the class of 350 students, of which maybe 5 were African American. One example sticks out in my mind. He was lecturing on the Constitution, talking about the amendments, and said to the class in a joking tone of voice, "So, for any of you out there that want to own slaves still, I'm sorry

but you can't." The professor obviously thought that he was being very witty, but I was furious. I honestly, very naively, could not believe that a professor said something so racist in front of the class. I didn't know what to do. I did not have the courage to raise my hand and say something in front of such a large group. I thought about saying something to the professor after class, but didn't. The fact that he was a professor and I was his student intimidated me. In short, I did nothing except get angry and talk to my friends about it. I don't think I will ever forgive myself for not saying something. It really bothers me that I was unable to speak my mind, so much so that I burst into tears when relating this story to a different professor of mine a few weeks ago. (White, female)

YOU'RE ALL THE SAME—I CAN ASK YOU ANYTHING I WANT

We would like you, the reader, to take a moment and think about a question you would ask someone you have just recently met. Picture the person as being White. Now picture the person as a person of color. Do you think you would ask the same questions to each person? It is our experience that questions posed to Whites are different than those posed to students of color. If the student sitting next to you is White and seems friendly you might ask them what their major is or if they live on campus. If the person sitting next to you is a person of color, you might be hesitant to ask a question or you might pose a question that is indicative of the stereotype that you have. One stereotype held by dominants is that they believe that one member of the subordinate group can speak for every member of the group. Again, they are using the paintbrush to lump subordinates together. Not surprisingly, then, subordinates often experience being singled out and asked to speak for their entire race. The assumption that there is no variability within a racial community is, of course, ignorant. There are a whole host of questions asked of people of color that would never be asked of Whites. These questions might be considered valid and legitimate, if there were an established relationship between the discussants. Dominants feel that their curiosity gives them the right to inquire of subordinates about anything, even when there is no established relationship or trust. We have collected a set of intrusive questions from student journals that reflect the insensitivity of the speaker.

Are you here because of affirmative action?
Don't you love sushi? Or collard greens?
Don't you love tacos with those beans?
Doesn't Colin Powell prove that you've arrived?
Why are you people all so smart?
How do you wash your hair?

Please tell us about the African American experience.

Are all Arabs Muslims?

How do you feel about your people killing Christ?

Why must you bring the ghetto with you?

Who wears the pants in your relationship?

You don't act like you're Mexican. Are you?

Aren't Jews a race?

Wasn't it horrible to grow up without Christmas?

You can probably tell me everything about China, can't you?

Do you people really eat dog?

Oh, you're getting married! Are you pregnant?

Why doesn't your dad wear a turban?

When you nurse your baby, does your milk come out chocolate?

Everyday actions, such as filling out a bubble-form that asks one's race or ethnicity, points out to many subordinates that dominants assume they are all the same. These forms force subordinates into categories that often don't match their racial identity. In the following a White woman relates a quandary that an Iranian classmate shared with her:

> The girl I was sitting next to in class today explained that she was Iranian. She said that it was very difficult for her because she did not know where she fit in. Was she White? Was she Black? Her entire culture/ethnicity has been overlooked by American society, so she has to check "other." How would I feel if I had to check "other"? I don't think I would take it as well as she did. (White, female)

As this example shows, dominants (who of course make the forms) expect people to conform to their definitions of racial and ethnic groups. By forcing subordinates to fit into the categories that dominants provide, subordinates are forced to ignore their entire culture and identity.

As stated at the outset of this section, people of color often find themselves being called upon to act as the "spokesperson" for their race. They are asked to speak for all African Americans, or all Asians, or all Latinos, a task, which of course, is impossible. This task is particularly daunting for people who are not comfortable speaking out. In the following excerpt, a biracial female relates a story of a shy young man who was constantly called upon to give the "Black perspective" in his sociology class at UCLA:

> There were about 30 students in the class but T was the only African American. In this class, our professor tended to always call on T, singling him out, but I don't think that he was even aware that he was doing it. T is a quiet guy and was never really one to participate in class discussions

but it seemed like, in this class, he had no choice. For example, we would watch some sociological movie on a troubled kid (who happened to be African American). After the movie, during discussion, the professor would specifically ask T what he thought about the movie or other questions about what he thought the kid was feeling or thinking at specific parts of the movie. When this happened, I could easily see the discomfort in T's face. After class, he would tell me how much it bothered him because he felt like he was being singled out because he was the only Black guy in the class. Just because he was Black and so was the main character of the movie, did not mean that they have some kind of connection or that T would experience the same feelings as this kid in similar situations. T did not want to be a spokesperson for his entire race . . . he was not an expert. He also felt that when we talked about racism in our class or anything else that had to do with African Americans, that people in class tended to look at him. (Biracial, Japanese White Female)

This biracial Japanese woman expresses the feelings encountered by the students in Chapter Three who were always called upon when the topic of slavery came up and expressed so eloquently in *Freedom Writers* (also in Chapter Three).

Subordinates are not only asked for the perspective of their entire group, but also often challenged with everything that dominants find puzzling or irksome about their race. They are, for instance, asked to justify Black politics, or explain how people can possibly eat a popular food in their culture. In the next example, an African American woman reviews her own experience with being bombarded with intrusive and racist questions from her White peers in high school. She has also grown tired of being asked to represent the opinions of all Black people and finds a way to accommodate her White peers and make them comfortable. She decides to not threaten them with the knowledge she has about the sufferings of migrant workers, slaves, and even poor Whites:

> Because I was one of the three Black people in my high school (the other two being my sisters) I was, for many people, their only encounter with a Black person. I was the standard of Black that all of my friends and acquaintances thought Black people should try to achieve. Every time there was a racial issue that was burning the covers of newspapers and magazines, I would have to be the voice of all Black people, everywhere. They would ask me, "Why are Black people still so stuck on slavery? That was 400 years ago." So as not to rock the boat, my reply would always be, "Some people just can't stop living in the past." I would always try to give an acceptable answer. Not the answer that would make me look like an activist or something. They always thought they were paying me a com-

pliment by saying that I wasn't like the other Blacks and that I was different. The White people loved me. I was always "that cool Black girl." I was extraordinary, because my parents had money and I didn't speak "that ghetto shit." It was okay for the most racist people to be friends with me because I wasn't like the other "jungle bunnies." I was different because I wasn't a threat. I didn't remind them of the millions of people that are still stuck in hell because of racism and slavery. I don't remind them that they are where they are today because they stand on the bones of migrant workers, slaves, and even poor White people. I was never really comfortable in my own skin because I believed that someone else's skin was more special than mine. I no longer believe that. I love the person that I am, skin color, hair, lips, and all. (African American, female)

Many of the questions posed from peers to college students of color are derived from stereotypes. In the following example, a White male talks about how he and his wife, a woman of color, are hounded by questions. The questions his wife has been asked are astounding for their ignorance, their intrusiveness, and the way the speaker turns the subordinate into an object. She no longer is identified as a student, a daughter, or a wife. Rather, she is continually pigeonholed by the stereotype of a Japanese woman:

My wife of seven years is Japanese. Some of the things said to and about her have ranged from ignorant to downright stupid. On campus, a person asked her if she was a mail order bride. Another asked her if she eats dog. If these people were being mean, at least I could understand it, but in most cases these people are being honest. The most common response I get from men when I tell them that my wife is Japanese is a knowing nod, followed by "she does everything for you doesn't she?" (White, male)

Sometimes, a casual encounter in a public setting begins with an innocent-sounding question that can quickly evolve into an attack that reveals the bigotry of the individual. In the following excerpt, a Cal State University–Northridge Iranian student is confronted by a truly shocking belief expressed by a man at a coffee shop:

As I stood in line at a coffee shop in Northridge, a white male of about 50 who stood before me struck up a conversation, which leads from a mundane discussion regarding the warm weather to his involvement with the Bush administration. I was curious and so I questioned him regarding his dealings with George W. Bush. He began to tell me about what an amazing individual President George W. Bush is and emphasized his perception by stating that he was the only President to learn Spanish. Failing to understand the significance of such a gesture, I questioned him further regarding the matter and he explained that it was a means of establishing rapport with the Spanish-speaking communities in the United States of America. Still quite baffled, I informed him as to the absence of significant changes made by the administration to alleviate the unique struggles faced by the Latino community. Besides, given that he is the President of United States, he ought to be well versed not only in English but also in various languages so as to facilitate diplomatic relations. Irked, he stated, "Imagine what it would be like if he learned Ebonics, or worse yet Arabic. That would be equivalent to having a banner stating, 'All terrorists are welcome here.'" Astounded by the man's utter bigotry, I walked away. I felt angry and hurt that people held such notions about Middle Eastern people. The incident crystallized the notion that the perceptions that arose regarding people of Middle Eastern descent in the aftermath of the attacks on 9/11 would not dissipate. Time and again, I was faced with individuals who were suspicious of Middle Eastern people and were eager to report "any suspicious activity." (Iranian, female)

YOU'RE ALL THE SAME—YOU HAVE NO FUTURE

The most common, demeaning, and perhaps the most consequential stroke that painters deliver to subordinates is that they are not destined for success. They are painted as less intelligent, less motivated, and less capable. Even when subordinates prove these stereotypes false, dominants minimize the success of subordinates by labeling them as an exception. Because dominants are typically in positions of power, their paint job often works. Moreover, in their efforts to preserve self-interest, dominants promote their own beliefs about who should be successful. The brush is used to paint "F" for failure on subordinates' talents, abilities, and hopes. There is no need to paint a white "S" for success; success is synonymous with Whiteness. The brush must work to ensure and justify how failure and denied opportunities are designated for some, whereas security and prosperity are designated for others. The painters teach subordinates their proper place in the collective; a collective in which subordinates of varying racial backgrounds are categorized as being the same.

In the following excerpt, an 11-year-old learns about his occupational future from his sixth-grade teacher. Success is not in his future:

> I know now the teacher was probably racist and had no care in the world about my feelings when she told me it would be hard for me to become successful because I looked Black. (African American, male)

In a similar example of blatant racism, another African American student's teacher equates his Blackness with failure, stupidity, and an inability to achieve his dreams:

> At school, I learned all about racism and becoming prejudiced. The town nicknamed "Klancaster" (Lancaster, CA) possessed some very racist teachers. In the sixth grade, a teacher said to me that I would never become a lawyer because I was Black. (African American, male)

For many dominants, it is a given that teachers will be kind and supportive and will push them to achieve their full potential. Sadly, for this young man, and others like him, teachers and other adults placed obstacles in their path of progress and success. Teachers and counselors can even do damage when they feel they are being kind and understanding. In the next example, a Latina student describes her experience with being racially stereotyped by her college counselor. The college counselor's expectations of Latinas are that they should not be pre-med majors:

> I needed to drop a class because I was having family problems and could not handle 12 units. I made an appointment with a counselor, who was a big White lady in her 60s. When she asked me why I wanted to drop the class, I confided in her and told her about my problems at home and how it was too stressful. I could not believe what she said. She said that it was typical of students like me to go through such problems at home and that I shouldn't worry. "Students like me!" What did she mean by that? This made me so angry but what made me even angrier was when she saw the notation on my folder that I was pre-med. She tried to convince me that with the problems I had, I probably would not be able to handle pre-med, and that I should consider going into another career. I was pissed but I calmly told her that I was sure that these kind of problems would not be there forever. "Trust me," she said . . . I know that she was referring to Latinos in general. She was stereotyping me as coming from a broken family full of problems that just never go away. She also inferred that because I was Latina, I was a high risk of dropping out. I was so mad. I thought that this type of discrimination from a UCLA staff person could not happen to me. (Latina, female)

Students of color recall, with great vividness, incidents where others degraded their intelligence and limited their opportunities. The internalized pain and rage is enduring. In the following, an African American male talks about his fifth-grade experience with racism. He learns that success and good grades were only designed for White students:

> When I received my report card it was usually safe to assume that I received straight A's. There was no reason for me not to get straight A's. I

excelled to the top of my class in every subject. To my surprise I glanced at my report card and Miss W had given me a B. She did not give me a B+; she gave me a B in spelling. I was very disappointed. She suggested that I talk to my mother about my grade and possibly have a conference with her.

When we arrived at the school my mother asked Miss W why I had received a B instead of an A. When Miss W showed her my test they had mostly received grades in the high 90s. When my mother questioned why I received a B with such high test scores, Miss W said it was because I missed some homework assignments.

When my mother asked which homework assignments I missed Miss W said she had those records at home and that my mother would have to take off work again to schedule another meeting to see them. My mother knew that I had turned in all my work. She had already talked to my math teacher who told my mother that I should have received an A and that Miss W was grading me very unfairly. As my mother and I walked back to the car she talked about how Whites treat Blacks unfairly because they are prejudiced and don't like to see Black children excelling past White children in the classroom. (African American, male)

We often like to believe that grades are objective measures of our achievement in the classroom. As this example demonstrates, teachers have a great deal of arbitrary power. Though there is often solid evidence, such as tests and homework that can be used to either "prove" or "disprove" a teacher's assessment, they can choose to make it hard for students and their families to have access to these materials. For instance, this student's mother was forced to take 2 days off work to try to investigate her child's grade. The myth of "objective grades" is one of the factors that lead some people to vehemently oppose programs such as affirmative action, which try to compensate for disadvantages and discrimination that students of color experience throughout their education. However, as these excerpts show, for many students, the struggle to get good grades means more than doing assignments and studying for exams. It also means uncovering and battling prejudice.

For many students of color, arrival at the university suggests that they have overcome a great deal. Unfortunately, they are rarely given a warm welcome. It is as if the paint is continually reapplied to newly emerging identities. When students describe their experiences in college, they report how the paintbrush operates in their classes and in their everyday life with peers and professors. In the following excerpt, a Korean woman articulates what many dominants express when they encounter students of color on campus:

I grew up thinking that all Mexicans were meant to work for us (Koreans). I have to admit that when I first came to college, I wondered how most Latino/as got to UCLA. I worked my ass off to get into this school, they probably got in by affirmative action. Then I actually had an intelligent conversation with a Latina. I was ashamed to think what I had thought. All my life my family and my community, had labeled them as inferior, as illegal immigrants. How could I change my beliefs now? I realized I had to. I would be destroyed by my own prejudice if I couldn't change it. (Korean, female)

This woman's experience is fairly common. White fears and cries of reversed discrimination have made all minority admissions seem suspect. Concerns about preferential treatment start in high school:

One incident I clearly remember regarding my ethnicity occurred my senior year of high school. W, a girl who hung out with my group of friends, made a comment to me about not having to worry about getting into UCLA because of my last name. When she made this comment to me I remember being very offended. Immediately I defended myself. I felt that she was wrong for making such a comment and wondered why my friend would say such a thing to me out of spite. She was also applying to UCLA and was afraid of not being admitted. That day, I recall comparing our grades, scores, and activities and once we had finished, W had nothing to say. She knew that after we had compared our applications that I had a better chance of being admitted. This incident that I have just briefly explained was the first time I had ever been bothered by my last name. I did not want the last name Chavez because I felt like it automatically screamed out "minority, please let her in." These feelings made me want to change my last name on my college applications just to prove to everyone that I could get into the school of my choice based on my academic merit and well-rounded involvement. (bicultural, Mexican Portuguese, female)

Affirmative action is designed to help disadvantaged students through the consideration of factors that show that a student is ambitious, hard working, and intelligent despite their having "inferior" education. This challenges dominants' sense of their own privilege. The anti–affirmative action sentiments made by dominants attach a stigma to it. This often causes subordinates to feel insecure and pressured that they have more to prove. These fears are often confirmed as students interact with professors, who also assume that they are not as competent or need more help than their White counterparts. In the following example, a university professor's assumptions about students of color are immediately apparent in his greeting to a Mexican Portuguese woman:

I was discriminated against by a professor my freshman year at UCLA. When I went to my professor's office hours to discuss a paper assignment, he assumed I was there to talk about a midterm I had taken the week before. When I told him my name he replied with "oh, did you do poorly on your midterm and want to see your exam?" Although he was nice, he assumed I had done badly on my midterm and suggested going over the areas I didn't do well on. I was offended. He heard my name and then assumed I did not do well. He made an assumption based on the stereotypes society has placed on Latinos, which are that Latinos are not intelligent, they may struggle in learning, and very rarely excel rank in the top 20% of their classes.[3] (Mexican Portuguese, female)

While this professor was not as openly racist as the elementary school teachers discussed earlier in this section, the assumption that the student must have done poorly on the exam due to her race is a stereotype that was damaging to the students' self-esteem.

Subordinates do not always accept the messages they receive about their inferiority. Poets, writers, and citizens often speak back and protest the assigned roles and the lack of a future. One artist that addresses this issue is Nas. In the song "I Can," Nas sings about a future that is possible. Again, we do not believe that the singing of songs or repeating of slogans can change self-conceptions. When songs and slogans are part of a larger culture that emphasizes the accomplishments of subordinates and the history of subordinates, and when these accomplishments and histories are not relegated to a single day, month, or year, then changes in the self are more likely to occur and more likely to be positive. This is not an impossible task for teachers, educators, professors, and school districts.

Here is a link for the lyrics.
http://www.azlyrics.com/lyrics/nas/ican.html

In the last verse of "I Can," Nas reminds his listeners of their history. This is a history that is often denied to children who grow up in America. In his artistic and creative way he is summarizing the work of Howard Zinn and James Loewen.

---

3 This professor assumes that Latinos fall within the category of less capable. When individuals do this categorizing, known as cognitive assimilation, individuals are seen as more alike than they may actually be (see Sampson, 1999).

YOU'RE ALL THE SAME—YOU'LL RUIN OUR "GOOD" NEIGHBORHOOD

In 2009, the U.S. Census Bureau reported that "the moving rate for renters was 27.7 percent, compared to 5.4 percent for people living in owner-occupied homes." When dominants move, they expect to be greeted with a "welcome wagon" committee knocking on their new house and helping out with small gifts and information about schools, shopping, and places to worship. They also want information about the percentage of subordinates in the area. Moving and buying is perceived by dominants as a basic right belonging to everyone. It is a right that is denied to many families of color. When people of color move into a predominantly White neighborhood, they are often treated like a plague or disease that will surely destroy property values:

> I moved in with my grandmother's sister and my aunt when I was ten. I grew up in Arcadia all the way up until high school and I would overhear people say throughout the entire time, even some of my own friends and their family would say things like: "I can't believe all these Asians are storming in. These people are taking over our neighborhood." I found this so hurtful that it made me cry. Why was it their neighborhood? My family worked so hard with their blood and sweat to buy the house. Was this not America, the land of equality? This invisible racism is worse than the blatant form, for things are sugarcoated to seem like everything is equal, when in actuality it is not. I did not know it at the time, but this type of prejudice created much internalized oppression inside myself and therefore I felt this great pressure to fit in. I think this is why most of all my friends were White in elementary, junior high, and high school. (Korean, female)

Even when subordinates go out of their way to prove that they are friendly neighbors, they may still find themselves confronted with prejudice. In the following, a female student extends herself to her new neighbors. She goes out of her way to be helpful and informative, but when she asks to borrow a vacuum cleaner, she is unashamedly rebuffed:

> Last year, a White couple moved into our building. Now, you can just imagine that when they saw me they were a little surprised. So, I was cool. I let them know that it was not safe to park in the lot, etc. etc. But, one day I wanted to borrow their vacuum, so I asked. The husband goes and gets it for me and he begins to hand it to me. Right then, the wife walks out and says, "Oh honey, don't you remember the vacuum doesn't work?" He looks at her like "what the hell are you talking about?" And then she leans forward looks him straight in the eye and raises her eyebrows and

says, "Remember, it's broken." Then he says, "Oh." Right then I knew, I shouldn't even try to deal with them. My encounters with them thus far have included a nasty encounter regarding my poor parking, refusing to answer the door when I needed help, and quick stares when I am nearby. They (or she) have a problem with my race, and they did not even need to tell me. I know, just by their actions. (African American, female)

Like the couple just described, many dominants stop short of being openly racist, but their acts make it clear that they don't like or don't want to have anything to do with minorities. An African American woman describes the pain associated with looking for apartments near UCLA:

I remember one incident when we were in Palms looking for an apartment. We were trying to get the feel of the area in terms of price range, so we went to a couple of dumps, i.e., places we knew we weren't interested in, and asked about the cost of rent. We got to this one place, and went to knock on the manager's door. No one answered. We could hear noises inside. In fact, to this day I'm sure the manager looked through his peephole. Well, we heard the TV, so we kept knocking, persistently. Finally, this big, stinky, old White man with no shirt on comes to the door and very rudely says "Yeah? What's the problem?" I said, "We're inquiring about the two bedroom apartment for rent." He said, "You got a job?" I said, "Excuse me?" He said, "What do you do?" I was shocked!! So my friend asked "And how much is the rent for?" He said 1,100 dollars a month. After that we just left. I knew that place was not worth that much. In fact, it could not have been more than $650. I was so hurt! I kept voicing my astonishment to my friend. She was not even moved by the situation. It was like it didn't even bother her. I couldn't imagine how anyone could be so cruel. Even though I didn't want to stay in that dump, I felt limited. I hated that feeling. (African American, female)

For this young woman, being a student and part of the UCLA community was not enough to guarantee her equal opportunity to rent. Because of her skin color, she would not be given a choice of the full range of available apartments. Her choices were circumscribed.

The geographical area surrounding UCLA is similar to the area surrounding CSUN in that students of color have to develop strategies for obtaining apartments. An African American woman from CSUN describes such a strategy:

I have learned that I can rent an apartment when I send my White boyfriend ahead to sign the lease. They're much easier about credit and when he says that his apartment is both for he and his girlfriend, they never think of asking about race, which they can't because it's illegal. When I show up with our furniture the look of shock is palpable. (African American, women)

YOU'RE ALL THE SAME—YOU LOOK SUSPICIOUS, AND I CAN'T TRUST YOU

Subordinates are continually subjected to inspection and suspicion. The mere sight of a subordinate can lead dominants toward erroneous conclusions. They are lumped together as criminals and thieves.

In the following excerpt, an Iranian student not only feels the persecution at a personal level but also understands what is going on at an institutional level. The passage of the Patriot Act and required registration by the INS has resulted in detainment, persecution, and loss of jobs for many innocents:

> At this moment, I cannot find words that articulate the frustration that I feel every time I am stopped at an airport terminal for a "random security check" of my luggage/car or asked as to what "jihad" means. And I feel especially disconcerted when I find that the prejudice against Middle Easterners has not ceased, rather it has merely become subtle and more importantly institutionalized with the Patriot Act and special registration that the INS required of the immigrants from Islamic countries. The implementation of various laws hid under the guise of the protection of freedom for its veritable purpose was to seek out all people of Middle Eastern or South Asian descent who were Muslim and therein permitted discrimination based on religion or race. (Iranian, female, University of California, Los Angeles)

In the next example, a student accompanying her father observes how he is closely scrutinized. Her father playfully but painfully acknowledges this inspection when he failed to pass the border patrol's scrutiny. One can only imagine the self-degradation:

> Two months ago, the border patrol stopped my dad and me in San Clemente. The officer asked if the car, which I had bought recently, was his. As my father reached for his license, the cop reached for his gun. My dad said, "I'm just getting my license." The cop responded, "Oh! You have a license?" At first I was shocked. Then, it was followed by outrage. I told the cop I had a license, too. The cop checked both of them and they just

waved us through. We drove about a mile in silence and then my dad said, "I guess we're too brown today." (Latina, female)

In the next account, a Pakistani female seeks to protect herself by limiting her public encounters. Her concerns go beyond name calling and the questions that our previous student recorded. She is concerned for her physical safety:

Following the attacks on the World Trade Center, I confined myself to my apartment. I refused to go to classes or to a store for bare essentials for I was extremely concerned for my safety. I was certain that hate crimes and bias against hijabi Muslims would rise exponentially due to the terrorist attacks. Amazingly though, a few of my friends chastised me for being a recluse, stating that by refraining from part taking in my daily activities I would be allowing the ignorant people to win. Easier said than done. I am the one asked if there is a bomb in my backpack. I am the one greeted by comments such as "I hope she doesn't blow the place up" when I enter an ice cream shop. I was the one flipped off by strangers. I am the one who was called Saddam. I am the one who was refused service when I attempted to purchase a watch from a major department store in Northridge. I am the one who causes a 21-year-old Caucasian female to request a change of seat on an airplane. I am the one who was kept waiting when I went to dine at a restaurant. I am the one that is the target of all "patriots." I AM the one who is treated as evil and inferior EVERYDAY. (Pakistani, female, University of Southern California)

Although not all inspections are life threatening, fear and suspicion of people of color often lead to outright mistreatment. In this next excerpt, an African American student describes her humiliation at the hands of a dominant, who never apologizes for the false accusation:

I know how it feels to be on the other side of the White privilege. When I was younger, I went into a store and the White owner served other White people that came in the store even after I was there for ten minutes. He never asked if I needed help. He did not really acknowledge my existence. After I looked around for a while, I walked out and he followed me into the next department store. In front of everyone, he asked me to empty out my purse on the counter because he thought I stole something from the store. I was embarrassed and ashamed. I was standing there with everything I had in my purse, by myself, with everyone watching me and not one person defended me or tried to help. They just stood there as if I had done something wrong. He never apologized for embarrassing me. He just walked away without a word. (African American, female)

Sometimes mistrust and suspicion translates into institutional behavior that is overwhelming and threatening for subordinates. In the following excerpt, an Afghani female explains the effect of painting on her family and friends. The hatred extends beyond racial slurs to physical violence directed toward members of ethnic communities who are threatened at gunpoint and stabbed. The student also understands that the backlash is permitted at an institutional level through the various policies that threaten the mobility and freedom of these individuals:

> My interactions with my family and friends have allowed me a glimpse of the extent of the damage that has been done to the South Asian community as of 9/11. The devastating effects of profiling and hate crimes have risen to cause severe physical, psychological, and financial injury. A close friend of the family, who operates a business in the downtown Los Angeles area, was beaten and stabbed following the attacks on the World Trade Center. A friend who operated a few stores in the Southern California area was forced to shut down his business for an extensive period due to community members who threatened him at gunpoint. The community "patriots" felt it was "unjust that a terrorist should profit from their neighborhood." The lack of income led to the demise of the business, causing him to shut down the stores all together. Also, the special registration mandated by the INS was quite injurious to the South Asian community for it led to the deportation and imprisonment of various individuals, while others were restricted from leaving the country. In one particular instance, a friend of the family was disallowed from leaving the USA even when his family members, who lived in Afghanistan, passed away. The feelings of helplessness are often overwhelming. Although the attacks caused an increase in the number of hate crimes and state violence, it certainly would be naïve to imply that these acts were merely due to the attacks. Rather, it allowed for the dramatic expression of vile thoughts. Even the pleas made by the Bush administration to stop hate crimes and the harsh prosecutions of criminals who commit such crimes are NOT ENOUGH, especially when racial profiling by security officials in airport terminals follows them! Members of my family have not only been selected for "random" baggage searches but airport officials have also detained them for two to three hours of questioning. (Afghani, female, California State University, Northridge)

Stories about hatred, insults, economic discrimination, and state violence are not the ultimate form of racism. The ultimate form is murder. The loss of a loved one has devastating impacts on family and friends. A student had to deal with the loss of her uncle due to the hatred and anti-Muslim fervor that continues to rip through America and Americans.

If ever there was a voice of pain, the subsequent writing expresses her profound and intense anger at what our country has allowed:

> The country I live in taught me how to discriminate, hate, and judge those who are different. It is a country that requires its citizens to fit into a mold. If they deviate, they are deemed fanatical, non-conforming, and erroneous. However, the problem is that the country in which I live is the United States of America and the people that are victimized, criticized, and seen as different are my people and me. After the attacks on September 11th, 2001, we as a country stood together with patriotism in our hearts and revenge on our minds. We united against the evil that caused our demise. However, I was unaware that we classified evil solely on the basis of physical appearance. If I had known I would have been a good American and tried to prevent the terror by turning in my family. I would have arrested all baptized Sikhs, who wear the ceremonial sword symbolic of fighting injustice and protecting the weak. I would have thrown rocks at my father, my uncles, and my brothers because the turban that they wear, which symbolizes a rise against oppression, reminds this country of Osama Bin Laden. Finally, I would have shot the convenient storeowner, who is my uncle. The impact of this murder still affects me. Whenever a male friend or family member who wears a turban and has unshorn hair accompanies me, I receive either a cold stare or a hateful comment. (Sikh, female, California State University, Northridge)

In this next selection, skin color and suspiciousness are once again reasons for a California Highway Patrol officer to harass a young man driving the speed limit in his brand new car on a highway that most Californians are very familiar with. An African American male is pulled over and is questioned, harassed, and degraded. When he told this story to his classmates at Northridge, every other African American male confirmed that a similar experience had happened to them and to their Black friends:

> I was so happy because I had just purchased my new car. My friends (all Black males) and I decided to take a road trip from Southern California up to the Bay Area to the college where I would be starting my PhD program. As I was driving up the 5 freeway, just past the grapevine, I saw cop lights in my rear view mirror. I knew it could not be for me because I was driving the speed limit in my new Escalade - just relaxing.
>
> I was wrong, the lights were for me. The policeman (who was white) pulled me over and when he got up to my vehicle I said "Excuse me officer, why am I being pulled over?" He said "Don't ask me any questions,

I'll ask the questions." I said "Okay sir." He then began to ask each of us if we had any drugs in the car and if we had been drinking. I answered "No sir" (mind you it was 2:00 in the afternoon). At this point I was beginning to get frustrated because he had not told me what I was getting pulled over for. I asked him again "Sir, why did you pull me over." His response to my question was to tell all of us to get out of the car and he still had not told me what he had pulled me over for.

I was very upset and continued to ask him why he was pulling me over. My friends started to tell me to shut up because they didn't want any trouble, but I couldn't because I knew that I did not do anything wrong. I was abiding by the laws and following the speed limit. The officer then made my friends lay down on their stomachs on the side of the road in the dirt. Many cars were passing by and here were my friends in their new clothes (some of them expensive pieces of clothing) being made to lie face down on the dirt.

I said "Sir, this is my car, I just bought it and all the paperwork has my name on it. What am I being pulled over for?" The officer answered "Boy, if you don't want any problems just stand there and shut up." He proceeded to search each of us and then told them to get off the ground. They had to get up and get into my new car with dirt and gravel all over them. I was still standing outside my vehicle. I was so angry but I was feeling utterly helpless because there is nothing I could do but take it. Then the officer told me to leave and yet he still had not told me why he had pulled me over.

As the officer walked back to his car, I began to call my lawyer but my friends asked me to stop because they did not want any more problems. I did not do anything wrong and I did not deserve this shit. I drove on in complete silence feeling humiliated, abused, and completely powerless. I did not even want to finish our trip and I do know that I will never drive alone through Kern County again. (African American, male)

No matter how polite and respectful this young man acted, he was going to be treated suspiciously. It did not matter that he was on his way to UC Berkeley—that was irrelevant to the police officer. His Black skin guaranteed that he would be subjected to humiliation.

The recognition that you are going to be perceived as a threat may push you to think of ways to avoid a stereotypic reaction. These efforts rarely change the hearts and minds of those acting in anger, ignorance, hatred, or violence. The desire to avoid violence and to survive leads some to accommodate to the dominant culture. Brent Staples (1995), in his autobiography *Parallel Time*, describes his experiences as an African American graduate student at the University of Chicago. He talks about walking down the street dressed as a student and realizing that his mere presence made Whites uncomfortable. Whites would avoid him or walk across the street, so as not to pass him. He learned that whistling a theme from Vivaldi, a composer of classical music, would make the White person more comfortable and made his experience less tense and awkward. He was using Vivaldi to deflect that stereotype. When White people heard him whistling Vivaldi, they believed he was a man of culture and refinement.

Our own students also describe a way they respond to knowing that they are often perceived as a threat. Many of our African American male students report that their fathers trained them to immediately put their hands on the steering wheel when they are pulled over by a police officer. This can reassure the officer that their hands would not be used to grab a weapon.

YOU'RE ALL THE SAME—YOU'RE UNIMPORTANT SO I NEVER HAVE TO NOTICE YOU

Sometimes, the paintbrush doesn't work to make difference obvious, but rather to make people who are different feel invisible—along with their pain, needs, and accomplishments. We eat fruit picked by migrant laborers, whom we don't think about. We enjoy dinners without noticing the bus boy. We enter our office everyday without thinking of the janitors who made it possible for us to continue to fill our wastebaskets. Subordinates often do the menial work of society: removing garbage, cleaning streets, mowing lawns, cleaning homes, and changing diapers. You do not have to be a menial worker in America to be considered invisible. Invisibility often occurs to students of color.

A Muslim woman describes her experience with being ignored at a makeup counter in a major department store:

> I was at the make-up counter at Macy's and there were two women behind the counter talking. I knew what I wanted to buy and I was just waiting there for someone to help me. But they never even bothered to ask me if I needed any help. Just then another woman (older, White) walks up to the counter and automatically one of the girls walk up to her and asks if she needs any help. Well, I'm not the type to cause a scene. I was so upset that I just left. I realize that maybe it wasn't my race, but maybe they thought that I didn't have the money to afford their prod-

ucts, whereas this older lady looked wealthy enough and old enough to afford it. (Middle Eastern, female)

Like many people of color, this woman was left to wonder—was it because of race that I wasn't helped? Or, was it because of something else? These questions, along with the accusation of "you people make everything a race issue," haunt people of color. But, the journals are clear on at least one point: Invisibility is a common experience, one that is even noticed by some dominants.

A White woman describes her experience in a yogurt shop. She sees and defends the invisibility of a Black man:

> I told the class about how this weekend I went to a yogurt shop. Four of my female friends and I had already been helped and the employees were asking the crowd of customers who was next (they help based on numbers so they were asking who had the next number). A Black man had the next number and he was telling the guy calling out the number. The guy behind the counter blatantly ignored him and continued to ask my friends and me what we wanted. I repeatedly told him that we had already been helped and that the gentleman waiting at the counter was next. The guy kept ignoring the Black man and I cringed. I finally screamed at him, "He is next! He has the next number. We were last, and he has the number after us. Can you not see him?" I walked out, telling them that I would never eat there again. (White, female)

People who work in retail or other service-oriented jobs have the power to determine who is worth serving. The consequence of this power is to be able to make people of color constantly question themselves. "Was it race or was that person just rude?" "Did I do something wrong?" These are issues that dominants don't have to deal with. For them, bad service is just bad service. They walk away and never have to think about it again. They can give a poor tip and be finished. They rarely have to be concerned about being judged by their race. They rarely have to adjust their view that life in America is fair, equal, and good.

We need to ask what happens when the person cannot be marked racially. In other words, what about those individuals whose physical appearance does not fall within the categories that have been established by dominants? Their differences and similarities cannot be readily identified and thus, they cannot be easily oppressed by those in power. Biracial and bicultural people challenge the dynamics of the dominant–subordinate relationship. The way dominants and subordinates respond and react to biracial and multicultural individuals are the subject of the next chapter.

ATTITUDE SURVEY

The instructor who is teaching about racism in a way that seeks to transform students will invariably confront sexism as well as homophobia. Just as we provided exercises for dealing with and talking about sexism, we seek to provide you with a way to introduce the topic of homophobia. Often it is not necessary to introduce this topic as it may have come up earlier. However, it would be important for the entire class to be involved in this discussion. Gay and lesbian students are not often eager to see if your classroom will be different than the other classes. To get the whole class involved, we have developed a questionnaire where students are asked about living, working, playing, and interacting with gays and lesbians as well as their views on gay rights and marriage. The class is divided according to their scores and students are asked to talk about their beliefs. One recognition that confronts non-supporters of gay marriage is the comment and challenge as to whether they realize that their vote or stance is hurtful to a fellow student. It is important that students fill out this questionnaire anonymously. If students wish to identify their scores they can. The higher the number, the greater the acceptance of gays and lesbians. This exercise is often one that can encounter deep resistance to thoughtful dialogue and understanding. The people who are anti-gay or anti-marriage have two major reasons that are evoked. They often repeat the arguments they have heard: "It's an attack on marriage" or "It's in the Bible." I have found that it's useful to ask why certain principles or laws from the Bible are believed in but not others.

Attitudes Survey

Please circle yes or no for each of the following questions:

1. I would be uncomfortable if my 8-year-old daughter was in Girl Scouts and her leader was a lesbian.   Yes   No

2. I would be uncomfortable if my 8-year-old son was in Boy Scouts and his leader was gay.   Yes   No

3. I would be uncomfortable living next door to a gay couple.   Yes   No

4. I would become very uncomfortable if the current teacher of my 8-year-old came out to the school.   Yes   No

5. I would have trouble working in close proximity to a gay male.   Yes   No

6. I would have trouble working in close proximity to a lesbian.   Yes   No

7. I would have trouble staying best friends with someone who just revealed he was homosexual.   Yes   No

8. I would vote against same-sex marriage.   Yes   No

9. If my 16-year-old child told me that he or she was homosexual, I would take him or her to a doctor to see if this were true.   Yes   No

10. If my 16-year-old child told me that he or she was homosexual, I would take him or her to a therapist with the purpose of trying to change his or her mind.   Yes   No

11. If I had a gay child, I would feel as if I were a failure.   Yes   No

12. If someone in your family tried to obtain the financial assets of another member of your family, so as to prevent their long-term gay partner from benefiting, would you oppose your family's actions?   Yes   No

13. If my long-term babysitter who has worked with me for 7 years revealed that she was gay, I would NOT let her continue to babysit my 9-year-old child.　　　Yes　No

14. If I had a close friend or family member who was gay or lesbian and this person asked me to march in a parade to support the cause, I would NOT do so.　　　Yes　No

15. I believe that allowing gays to marry destroys the importance and significance of heterosexual marriage.　　　Yes　No

16. I believe that gay couples should never be allowed to adopt children.　　　Yes　No

17. I believe that a child who grows up with either gay or lesbian parents will not be as healthy as a child raised in a heterosexual family.　　　Yes　No

18. I think gay people should "stay in the closet."　　　Yes　No

Count the number of 'NO' responses and write that number here: _____

CHAPTER 6

"I'm happy to challenge people's understanding of what it looks like to be biracial, because guess what? In the next 50 years, people will start looking more and more like me."

—Rashida Jones, Actor

We have documented how the power, privilege, and insulation of dominants allow them to either label subordinates as "different" or cluster subordinates as "the same." In both scenarios the "other" is less. The majority of subordinates receive these biased and racist messages on a daily basis. The lessons are quite explicit. The strokes of racism on individuals—Black, Brown, Yellow, Red—are repeated by dominants and often internalized by subordinates. But what happens when a dominant is not sure of a person's race? What happens when a dominant doesn't know whether to paint or what color to use? What happens to the biracial persons when a dominant cannot categorize the "other" into his or her schema of racial categories? This chapter will explore how dominants and subordinates treat people of mixed race and ethnicity and how multiracial individuals respond. Biracial and multiracial individuals pose a challenge to dominants and subordinates because their membership in any particular ethnic or racial group is not clearly discernible.

TABLE 5

The Teachers, Learners, and Targets of Racism

Teachers		Learners		Targets	
Teacher	1	African Americans	2	Bi Racial	34
Peers	16	Asians	1		
Government	6	Latina	4		
Family	2	African American/White	6		
Self (Internalized Racism)	8	Asian/White	6		
Business/Store	1	Latina(o)/White	4		
		Native American/White	1		
		Tri-racial/Multicultural	7		
		White	2		
		Other Bi Racial	1		
Total	34	Total	34	Total	34

Table 5 summarizes where the brushstrokes come from and to whom they are aimed. The table indicates that multiracial individuals are responded to mostly by peers (16) and that of the 34 multiracial individuals who were targeted, labeled, or called names, 6 of them were African American/White, another 6 were Asian/White, 4 of them were Latina(o)/White, and 7 of them were tri-racial or multicultural.

The first section of this chapter shows how dominants respond to multiracial persons with a set of questions. The next two sections show how dominants force categories upon multiracial people and describe the enduring and evolving naming process that dominants employ for multiracial individuals. The final two sections describe how subordinates also pressure multiracial people to choose a single identity and then demonstrate the responses of multiracial persons to their treatment by dominants and subordinates.

In the first excerpt, we learn what some dominants do when their schema for racial classification is challenged. A Japanese American White female describes the bombardment of questions she receives because of her name and her looks. For most of her life, she has coped with such inquiries that feel like an interrogation. Her name is a marker that has created a set of expectations for painters on how exactly to categorize her. The painters are often disappointed when they meet her in person. This woman struggles to find acceptance from dominants:

> I'm 3⁄4 Asian and 1⁄4 White and I consider myself biracial because my experiences have largely been shaped by my mixed backgrounds. I have a White last name, although I look mostly Asian. From elementary school and on, I have had to deal with people harassing me, asking for a detailed explanation as to why I have a White last name. It makes me feel almost as if something is wrong with me. Sometimes I feel like just saying that I'm adopted, just to make things easier for me. I'm 22 years old, and I would say that for a majority of my life I have had to explain myself, almost in need of justifying my existence. People are always asking me, "What's your last name?" or "Why is that your last name?" When I tell them, they proceed by asking more questions concerning my racial identity. It's as if every single person of any race needs to know how Asian I really am.
>
> It's amazing how my name has really affected me. My name is a racial marker, an identifier for other people. If I didn't have a White last name, no one would even assume I was anything other than Asian. I also feel that whenever I meet people face-to-face after having mentioned my last name prior to the meeting, I am disappointing them when they realize I'm not really White. For example, there was a time I was conducting interviews, I told the interviewees my name over the phone, and when I met them, their reactions made it seem like I wasn't good enough. I felt like they expected me to be White then realized upon meeting me that they DO NOT have me all figured out. Now, of course, this may be me projecting, but what is most relevant and valid about these personal experiences is that I do have to think about these things. Sometimes I think, "Should I tell people that I'm not really White, that I'm mostly Asian?" I cannot believe I'm in this position where I really think that sometimes, even though I know I shouldn't have to ever explain myself. The struggles I experience as a biracial woman are part of my everyday consciousness, because somewhere inside of me, I feel that I'm not good enough, that it's my duty to almost warn people that I'm Asian. As an employee, it's like telling prospective customers that what they think they are buying is not what they expect, that it is faulty in some way, that I am faulty in some way. (Biracial, Japanese American, female)

For biracial students being forced to select a racial category and explain their existence is an ongoing struggle. The backdrop to these ongoing interpersonal encounters is the issue of power.

Dominants are vigilant about preserving their power in society. They always ponder who shall be granted access and who will be denied entry. Denying entry to all people of color would turn America into a caste-like society. This goes against our ideals and values. However, treating all as equal is a threat to White supremacy and their power. A subtle way to preserve power is through granting access to a few subordinates. By providing limited access, dominants prove to themselves (and try to prove to subordinates) that they are open and willing to providing access to all. This is consistent with the ideals of the United States as an open, just, and meritocratic society. This helps dominants assert that they are "colorblind" and that race doesn't matter. This enables dominants to believe that America is a "melting pot," whereby recent immigrants and people of color are welcomed with open arms and assimilated into the dominant culture. When these beliefs about America as a meritocracy are challenged, the challengers are considered as either "too sensitive," "acting like a victims," or "playing the race card." Those who feel that America is a level playing field quickly point out Sonia Sotomayor, Colin Powell, Condoleezza Rice, Barack Obama to argue that racism is dead and that because they "made it" there is equal opportunity in America. The election of America's first biracial president is used as an example to argue that racism is dead. If Black or Brown individuals are at the bottom of the economic or educational ladders, they must be personally flawed. If all these "others" can be successful then dropping out of school or not having a job is proof that you have chosen to be a victim or be lazy. Multiracial and multicultural individuals pose a challenge to the traditional categories that dominants use to classify and oppress.

A multiracial student describes her frustrations when dominants expect her to explain and justify her physical features that are not typically associated with being African American:

> Although we are mixed with three or four different races, my parents and I consider ourselves Black. I have light skin and curly hair, which often encourages people to ask me, "What are you?" I mostly reply African American or Black. This never seems good enough for people. I guess because some of my features are more "White," I must justify why it is that I look different from other Black people. People always ask me what I am with an answer in mind and when they don't get what they expect, it's almost as if they feel cheated because my answer doesn't fit their expectations. I feel that this in a sense is the dominant's power over me to be dissatisfied by my answer. (African American, female)

Individuals from mixed heritage are continuously faced with questions about their identity and physical appearance. Their physical appearance is not easily classified and they are forced by dominants and subordinates to continually select one identity over another. When subordinates and dominants are confronted with a biracial person who cannot clearly be identified, they resort to questioning, naming, and categorizing as a means degrading the person who does not fit into preconceived and stereotypical racial categories.

An African American woman describes the hurt she feels when others question, tease, and challenge her racial identity:

> I completely understand about stereotypes within your own group. As a very light-skinned Black woman, people always assume that I am mixed with White, or that I am Black and Latina. I am used to questions about who I am coming from other racial groups. But comments from African Americans tend to be the most hurtful. Recently, a fellow Black student told me that I wasn't really Black; he said that I was "culturally" Black, but because I am so light, I am not ethnically or racially Black. He said that I must have more White in me than anything else. I have been called names like redbone, oreo, zebra, etc.—names that were meant as a joke, but were still hurtful, especially since I am not mixed. Would I be right for calling darker-skinned Black people names like darky? (African American, female)

Dominants seek racial identifications in order to assess an individual's physical ambiguity. Dominants want to hear answers that will explain a person's physical ambiguity, not which racial group an individual chooses to identify with. In other words, dominants do not view the multiracial individual's identity as a matter of their choice, but instead seek to impose an identity upon them linked to the racial category in which the dominants feel they belong.

Dominants prevent multiracial people from asserting their plural identities because, as dominants, they create the standards and assert what realities are true. They can insist upon their comfortable version of a racial reality. Though dominants in America have worked to establish clear boundaries about racial categories, race is less a matter of who is White and who is non-White, and more about who may be considered White (Hacker, 1998). There has been ongoing debates about racial categories and categorization. The 1900 census had five racial designations, the 1930 census had ten, and the 1990 census provided fifteen racial designations. The 2010 census used the following form for ascertaining "race":[1]

1 Images retrieved from: http://2010.census.gov/2010census/about/interactive-form.php

9. What is Person 1's race? *Mark* X *one or more boxes.*

- [ ] White
- [ ] Black, African Am., or Negro
- [ ] American Indian or Alaska Native — *Print name of enrolled or principal tribe.* ↗

[_____]

- [ ] Asian Indian
- [ ] Chinese
- [ ] Filipino
- [ ] Other Asian — *Print race, for example, Hmong, Laotian, Thai, Pakistani, Cambodian, and so on.* ↗

- [ ] Japanese
- [ ] Korean
- [ ] Vietnamese

- [ ] Native Hawaiian
- [ ] Guamanian or Chamorro
- [ ] Samoan
- [ ] Other Pacific Islander — *Print race, for example, Fijian, Tongan, and so on.* ↗

[_____]

- [ ] Some other race — *Print race.* ↗

[_____]

A careful reading of this question and the categories provided should shock you. Do you, the reader, believe that there are 14 or more races? Although the census bureau indicates that this information is important for purposes of allocating money to different communities across the country, these communities are treated as racial. What is also remarkable is that there's no place for Latinos in this race question. There is a separate question designed for individuals who identify themselves as Latina/o.

8. Is Person 1 of Hispanic, Latino, or Spanish origin?

- [ ] **No,** not of Hispanic, Latino, or Spanish origin
- [ ] **Yes,** Mexican, Mexican Am., Chicano
- [ ] **Yes,** Puerto Rican
- [ ] **Yes,** Cuban
- [ ] **Yes,** another Hispanic, Latino, or Spanish origin — *Print origin, for example, Argentinean, Colombian, Dominican, Nicaraguan, Salvadoran, Spaniard, and so on.* ↗

[_____]

This question on origins, while useful for administering bilingual programs for people of Hispanic origin, seems to contribute to the idea that there is a single race of Hispanics. This category might be convenient for the census bureau and comforting for dominants who prefer to think in simplistic "four racial" category terms, but is not something that illuminates our understanding of race and ethnicity. The categories are arbitrary and lack scientific evidence.

As the reader should realize by now, the concept of race is subjective, arbitrary, and created by human beings for purposes that have little to do with scientific merit. This is most clear in our own history of slavery. Slavery, as an economic system, contributed enormously to the wealth of the North and South. The justifications for it were based on maintaining the system that reaped enormous profits at the expense of human justice. A legal policy that provided justification and maintenance of slavery was the one-drop rule, known formally as "hypodescent." The one-drop rule states that a biracial or multiracial child is categorized under whichever parent is of lower racial status (Rockquemore & Brunsma, 2002). This rule prevented the offspring of slaves and their slave owners from inheriting property. This allowed slave owners to disown their own prodigy. The lack of scientific status of this rule is illustrated by the great American writer Langston Hughes. In his short essay, "That Powerful Drop," Hughes (1953) playfully illustrates the lack of scientific thinking about racial categories:

> Leaning on the lamp post in front of the barber shop, Simple was holding up a copy of the Chicago Defender and reading about how a man who looks white had just been declared officially colored by an Alabama court.
>
> "It's powerful," he said
>
> "What?"
>
> "That one drop of Negro blood-- because just one drop of black blood makes a man colored. One drop-- you are a Negro! Now, why is that? Why is Negro blood so much more powerful than any other kind of blood in the world? If a man has Irish blood in him, people will say, 'He's part Irish.' If he has a little Jewish blood, they'll say, 'He's half Jewish.' But if he has just a small bit of colored blood in him, BAM! - 'He's a Negro!' Not, 'He's part Negro.' No, be it ever so little, if that blood is black, 'He's a Negro!' Now, this is what I do not understand-- why our one drop is so powerful. Take paint-- white will not make black white. But black will make white black. One drop of black in white paint-- and the white ain't white no more! Black is powerful. You can have 99 drops of white blood in your veins down South-- but if that other one drop is black, shame on you! Even if you look white, you're black. That drop is really powerful. Explain it to me. You're collaged."
>
> "It has no basis in science," I said, "so there's no logical explanation..."

This rule still applies to other mixed-race children. The one-drop rule, grounded in legal and historical traditions, still operates informally to support racial discrimination. Because it is still popular among Americans to believe that there are only four races, being multiracial threatens this view. The desire to categorize individuals into rigid racial categories is not universal. In Brazil, individuals are classified by the color of their skin. As a result of this categorization, there are six or more racial categories. In *Race in Another America*, Edward Telles (2006) explains how the meanings of race are not fixed but relational. In preferring the notion of color, Telles found that 95% of non-Asian and non-Indigenous Brazilian respondents used six color terms. These included Branco (white), Moreno (brown), Pardo (brown), Moreno Claro (light brown), Preto (black), and Negro (black).

Contrary to the American hypodescent rule, Brazil exercises a flexible classification. In earlier history, people with dark skin, the Moors, had dominated the Portuguese. As a result, the Portuguese did not see Africans as inferior but as dominants who conquered and colonized Brazil. Consequently, there were no problems regarding miscegenation. In Brazil racial boundaries are easily crossed. In 2006, 23% of marriages were among persons of different color (Telles). Racial segregation and anti-miscegenation laws practiced in the United States affected the lower rates of intermarriage and resulted in the different race relations compared to Brazil. Before 1967, less than 1% of Black men and women were married to Whites, 25 years later it changed to 4.4% of Black men and 2.3% of Black women married to Whites. The effect of interracial marriage is smaller in the larger White population, where only 0.3% of Whites are married to Blacks. The number of biracial and multiracial Americans is 6.8 million or about 2.4% of our population. These numbers are growing rapidly as Americans begin to accept the idea of interracial marriage. The popularity of well-known public figures will probably help increase the acceptance of biracial and multiracial individuals:

Vin Diesel (1967-). Actor. Italian American & African American
Soledad O'Brien (1966-). TV news caster. Black Cuban & White
Barack Obama (1961-). President of the United States. African American & White
Zadie Smith (1975-). English novelist. Jamaican & White
Booker T. Washington (1856-1915). Educator. Mulatto & White
Adam Clayton Powell Jr. (1908-1972). Congressman. Mulatto & Black
Bob Marley (1945-1981). Singer-songwriter. White English & Black Jamaican
Sade (1959-). Singer, composer, producer. Nigerian & English
Mariah Carey (1970-). Singer-songwriter. White mother & Black father
Lisa Bonet (1967-). Actress. Black & Jewish
Alicia Keys (1981-). Musician, actress. White & Black
Rashida and Kidada Jones (1975- and 1974-). Actors White & Black
Maya Rudolph (1974-). Actress, singer. White & Black
Etta James (1938-). Singer, songwriter. Black & White
Lenny Kravitz (1964-). Singer-songwriter, producer. Black & White
Derek Jeter (1974-). Professional baseball player. Black & White
August Wilson (1945-2005). Playwright. Black & White

This list of individuals, including Tiger Woods and Halle Berry, represent millions of other multiracial and biracial people. Despite the growing numbers of multiracial Americans, people's response to them often remains a mixture of ignorance, judgment, ridicule, and cruelty. What binds biracial, multiracial, and multicultural individuals together is their placement and position as a marginalized group of individuals.

Over the years, dominants have created racial categories in order for them to clarify their confusion about, or toward, multiracial people. Multiracial people are then forced to respond to these oversimplified categorizations. The rigid system of classification in the United States contributes to the unique responses of multiracial individuals. The persistent questioning of the origins of an individual's physical features and background helps perpetuate the social and institutional racism of the marginalization that multiracial individuals experience. In turn, social institutions also force multiracial people to separate their racial identities within them and to choose only one.

For students interested in other biracial and multiracial individuals, go to www.mixed-folks.com, to discover politicians, businesspeople, actors, singers, athletes, writers, and poets who have a biracial or multiracial background.

I WILL PAINT YOU BY QUESTIONS

Multiracial students frequently mention their experiences of being questioned. Questions such as, "What are you?" often create discomfort and unease. A biracial student describes her own uneasiness when asked to identify her ethnicity:

> It wasn't until high school that I really started to feel the impact of what being "half" of something really means. It didn't really matter what I was half of. My friends didn't really care but encounters with strangers were a whole other story. Sometimes I would get a question such as "What are you?" before I would even get a "Hello." The facts that these people were assessing me for what and not a who troubled me. I didn't know what to do about it. Sometimes I would play games with them. My answer to that infamous question would be, "I'm a girl." To me, it was amusing to see people squirm. I enjoyed their uneasiness. It was my way of dealing, of turning the tables on them. The only problem was that each time this happened, it reaffirmed the fact that most people are not willing to see my value for anything more than what my skin looks like. (Biracial, Chinese-White, female)

This student copes with the continual questioning of "What are you?" by giving unexpected responses and by withholding the information that the questioner desperately desires to know. When the multiracial person does not comfort the questioner with an expected answer, the questioner remains uncomfortable and uneasy. Angela Nissel (2006), author of *Mixed: My Life in Black and White*, and a writer and consulting producer on the television show Scrubs, reveals her technique when asked this question:

> As a biracial person whose facial features could come from any number of countries or races, she is frequently asked the question "What are you?" She responds: "It used to upset me. I'd use it as an opportunity to practice my fiction skills. When a businessman with argyle socks asked what I was, I replied, Argylian. I ended up having a long conversation about how unspoiled the Isle of Argyle was, and how there was even undiscovered gold in the rainforest. While it was fun imagining that man trying to cash in his frequent flyer miles to a land that didn't exist, the more mature part of me wondered if I was the only person who thought the question "What are you?" was rude. Now that I'm older, I think that many Americans become tongue-tied when it comes to race, and that uneasiness is multiplied when talking to someone whose race they can't discern.

When one is trying to racially classify an ambiguous-looking person, there are questions one can ask that are less offensive and general than "What are you?" Nissel uses humor to illustrate that the ignorant question "What are you?" should only be asked "if you're approached by green men who floated to your doorstep in a hovercraft."

In the following example, a multiracial student writes about her discomfort when faced with such questions. She describes how she is unable to truly identify with any of her three ethnicities:

> I have always been uncomfortable and unsure about discussing the issue of race and ethnicity. I am at a point now where I am comfortable enough to want to understand and confront myself and others . . . to extend myself and recognize that, indeed, my experiences as a Japanese/Mexican/Filipino gal growing up in Southern Orange County are significant. That the prodding and condescending questions of "where were you born?" and "where are you from?" and "you're not truly a Mexican because you're only 25% and you don't speak Spanish and you're really not Filipino either!" and the constant shock expressed on the faces of many that such a strange mix could occur . . . the possibility of my existence is shocking to most people. (Multiracial, Japanese-Mexican-Filipina, female)

Multiracial individuals are continually required to provide information about their background and to justify their existence in the world. Because of dominants' reliance on defining people purely based on their physical characteristics, multiracial individuals feel that they are sometimes not accepted as legitimate members of their own ethnic or racial group.

A biracial female describes people's insistence on "figuring her out" so that they can categorize her:

> I can tell when I first meet someone that they look uncomfortable because they don't know how to classify me. "What's your ethnicity?" and they give an explanation, "I'm just curious." And with no care to match their political correctness I reply, "I'm Black and White." And I can sense that they feel relieved because they can place me in a category. Somehow, then, they feel they know where I'm coming from. I think it's ridiculous that we can't relate to someone if we don't know his or her race. (biracial, African American-White, female)

The questioning comments and looks multiracial students receive are ongoing and seem to never stop. As long as their multiple realities challenge and confuse dominants' ideals, multiracial students will have to continue to explain and justify their existence. In the next example, a tri-racial female student describes her overwhelming struggles of explaining her multiple identities to dominants and monoracial people of color:

> For the millionth time, I am half Filipino, a quarter White (Irish to be exact), and a quarter Mexican.
>
> Now you look at me, what do you see? All my life, I have ALWAYS ALWAYS ALWAYS had to explain myself. How can you be so mixed? OMG how weird! Well what do you most identify with? Are you going to marry someone outside your races? What ethnicity box do you pick? What kind of friends do you have? Are you trilingual? WHY AREN'T YOU TRILIGUAL? Why don't you speak Spanish? Why don't you speak Tagalog?
>
> Why didn't your mother teach you Tagalog? Why didn't your father teach you Spanish? How come you know how to cook Filipino food, but not Mexican food? How come your sister has blonde hair, but you have brown hair? How come you don't have freckles, but your sister has freckles? How come you listen to reggaeton music, do you even know what they're saying? WOAH, you know how to dance Bachata? I thought you were whitewashed!

I am stating just a FEW of the sarcastic, ignorant, stupid questions that I face all the time and, to me, don't all these questions end up being in some form MY FAULT or MY PARENTS' FAULT for not being enough of whatever they want me to be? (multiracial, Mexican-White-Filipina, female)

I WILL PAINT YOU BY CATEGORIZING YOU

To deal with the ambiguity that arises from multiracial appearances, dominants press biracial and multiracial persons into categories.

One student explains how she is treated as a non-Mexican person because of her White features. She is often angry because she wants to be identified as Hispanic, but instead goes unnoticed. In Mexico, she is always addressed in English, while her darker, olive-skinned siblings are spoken to in Spanish:

> I am a part of two cultures; one being the obvious White man's world and the other the hidden Hispanic cultures. For one, I am half Hispanic and I look White. So when my family used to go to Mexico every summer, I felt like an outcast. On our family vacations, I was treated very differently than both my sister and brother. I was always asked questions in English. Now mind you—my sister and brother who both have olive skin, dark hair and dark eyes—could not speak Spanish. Yet they were always greeted and spoken to in Spanish upon being greeted. This used to piss me off . . . I wanted to be treated like I was part of the Mexican culture not as if I was a White girl there to shop and get bargains. These vacations as a child made me realize that I was different. (biracial, Mexican-White, female)

In this next example, a student describes how she was excited about a forthcoming project on ethnic pride that all members of her sixth-grade class participated in. She is forced to realize that the ethnicity that she wishes to celebrate will not be recognized by her teacher. Being from El Salvador was not going to be favored by the teacher as much as being from Italy:

> In the sixth grade we had these class projects called "Ethnic Pride." Everyone in class had to do a presentation about their ethnic background. It involved a written report, a speech to the class, and bringing food from your country of origin.

I got excited, particularly about the food preparations. My mom is from El Salvador, which meant that I could bring pupusas and horchata, and my dad was born and raised in Argentina, which meant that I could bring *empanadas* and alfajores, and his parents (my paternal grandparents) were Italian, so I could make some pasta too. I seriously wanted to cook and bring all of these different foods to class—I took pride in the fact that I would contribute something very unique in comparison to everyone else in the class. I was the only Salvadoran student in my whole school, which was mostly comprised of rich white or Jewish students. I just couldn't keep it to myself—I had to tell my teacher about the fabulous buffet of ME that I was about to prepare. I thought maybe she could give me some ideas on how to present it.

But I didn't get the response I was hoping for. "Did you read the assignment completely?" she asked me. "I specifically asked for you to choose only one country of origin, not three. If I let you use all these countries in your report, I would have to let everyone in class do that, and we just don't have the class time for it."

The news disappointed me, but I wasn't that discouraged. I wanted to do El Salvador more than anything. Nobody knew what pupusas were, which ensured me an original presentation. But when I told my teacher, she gave me a perplexed look. "Isn't your last name DiVito? That's an Italian surname. And doesn't your father own an Italian restaurant? What if you bring in a pizza from there?" I still wasn't catching her drift completely. Wasn't it MY choice for the assignment? "El Salvador will be a little difficult for the students to understand, especially if they know that your last name is Italian," she said.

I eventually chose Italy, mainly because my teacher was so excited about the whole idea. On the day of the presentation I made fettuccine alfredo for everyone in the class. I knew that in the scheme of things, I didn't stand out like I wanted to. Everyone in the class had tried pasta before. (bi-ethnic, female)

Another biracial student tells of constant attempts made to place her into a particular category without any regard to her own identity:

I get so angry when people tell me, "You're not really Black" or "But you're not like them." It's so amazing that people still believe that they can construct someone else's identity and then treat them accordingly. In my life I can't remember the number of times I've heard, "But you're not like them." I can't sit down with everyone and discuss my identity, nor should I be forced to. (biracial, African American-White, female)

In the following example, a Filipino female describes how she was unaware of the unique struggles of biracial individuals to have a legitimized identity. She learns from her roommate how biracial students are always forced to choose sides:

> I never really understood the dilemma that so many biracial students go through when they fill out a simple application. I know that I am Filipino and that I can identify with my culture, but my roommate who is half-German and half-Korean has to face a daily reminder that she must choose her identity. You shouldn't have to choose, but our society places such an emphasis it causes problems for the people who are biracial. It makes you have to pick, do you love your mother or your father more? You want to say that you love them the same but it really is hard to choose. You are not able to be yourself. (Filipina, female)

The personal interactions that our biracial and multiracial students have to contend with are supported by institutions that also use classification schemas that exclude them. In this first example, a biracial male struggles with the categorical system used by bureaucratic institutions. He describes his ongoing confusion over the forms he has to complete, which force him to choose one race with which to identify:

> I am always confused as to what to put down for my ethnicity. All applications have basically the same choices: White, Hispanic, African American, Japanese, Chinese, etc. But what about those of us who are mixed? Since I am half Japanese and half White, what am I supposed to do—fill out half of each box? (biracial, Japanese-White, male)

The pressure to conform to one racial category extends beyond the walls of the university campus. In the following excerpt, a biracial female student struggles with society's preoccupation with racial classifications and its unilateral vision:

> I struggle with the fact that "biracial" is not identified as a group. Society has formed a mentality where people identify groups to be one way or another but never in between. For example, people look at me and identify me as Latino or White . . . I wasn't conceived by a mother and father so that I would have to choose between the two. I was conceived by two people that loved each other and wanted to make a child to share both of their cultures. (biracial, Mexican Portuguese, female)

A multiracial student discusses her anger about the personal and institutional neglect regarding ethnicities in the college environment:

> It's been difficult for me, since attending [this university], to appreciate my biraciality, and in this sense, lack of a single racial identity. In an institution where so many put so much emphasis on such, it's been difficult to deal. I don't feel comfortable with ethnic/cultural identity groups. It thoroughly pisses me off that I don't see [this university] offering me a niche where I am allowed to assess both my Japanese and Jewish heritages. It's as if the student body at UCLA and virtually everywhere else, has imposed on me and people like myself, to find a label. What happens if the options they give do not apply, such as college applications where there was no place for me to pencil in that I am of two ethnicities. I'm so sick and tired of trying to assert that I am of two cultures and value each of them equally. (biracial Japanese-White, female)

Sometimes, the barriers drawn between monoracial and multiracial extend even further into language, culture, and customs. In this next example, a multiracial female student (Filipina, White, and Mexican) discusses the pain, anguish, and frustration that come along with being considered an outsider amongst her three racial communities:

> My grandfather, the only Mexican family I had, died 5 years ago. I had no idea who he was, and at his funeral I met at least 50 people coming from Texas and Tennessee (all Mexicans) whom all spoke Spanish, made the best BBQ ranchera ever, listened to tex-mex and ranchero music, all danced together, laughed together, cried, it was beautiful. After this awakening, I knew I rejected my Mexican heritage up to that point only because, well, I did not identify myself as Mexican. I didn't speak the language, didn't have many Mexican friends or family (that I knew of), and so, I knew I was Mexican, but I didn't feel Mexican. I knew the blood ran through my veins, but it didn't show on the outside.
>
> So when I was a freshman in college, I joined a Latina-based sorority. Here I found home. My sisters all treated me equally, loved me like their sister, and I am thankful for that. But even so, my Latina sisters speak Spanish. The only Spanish I know is the 4 years of Spanish in high school, other than that, it is really hard for me to communicate. As someone said in class yesterday, "there are words in Spanish that is impossible to communicate in English, so therefore, you are missing a common understanding that WE SPANISH-speaking people know and if one doesn't know the language, one will never know that common

understanding." I completely agree, which makes me sad. Because then, no matter how many Mexican friends I got, no matter how Mexican I try to be, not speaking Spanish will always set me apart from my Mexican counterparts. Thus, I WILL ALWAYS BE SEEN AS AN OUTSIDER IN SOME FORM. If you say it's my fault, then fine. Blame the victim.

I don't understand. See, what I have felt growing up was that even if I tried to speak the Spanish that I knew, joined a sorority full of Mexican-Americans, I was always seen as the "different one." For instance, in high school, I was singing a song by Don Omar (reggaeton Spanish music for those who do not know) in the hallways when someone (who was Salvadorean) said, "What? You know that song? You don't even know Spanish. Don't embarrass me."

DON'T EMBARRASS YOU? As if I didn't have a right to like that music because I didn't speak Spanish? Not only do I get this on the regular, but also with my sorority as well. Yes, you might think it's all in good humor to call me lola Ms. Chinky but NO, you can't disregard a half of me because its different from YOU. Or even my white side, when my white friend asked me if I would ever accept a job from her mother to clean their house as a part time job. ARE YOU KIDDING ME? **So I'm Mexican enough to clean houses, but I'm not Mexican enough to sing a Spanish song. Oh, but I can be Filipino only when you want to call me a chink. Makes perfect sense.**

So those of you who say it so easily that "it's your fault your building those barriers" and "we accept you even if you don't know the language"...I think you guys are missing our point. And mine is, it's not that easy. If it was, then I wouldn't be complaining about my multi-racial background. We are ridiculed every day. When A… said that she didn't have any friends because she wasn't white enough for white people and she wasn't black enough for black people, I completely identify myself with her. I never had any Filipino friends growing up, nor any Mexican friends either. My only best friend that I grew up with was half white and half Portuguese, and even so her family always saw me differently because I looked white, but I wasn't white enough. (multiracial, Mexican-White-Filipina, female)

The barriers multiracial students face often seem insurmountable when dominants and monoracial persons of color continue to place rigid restrictions on racial categories. In classes, multiracial students of different racial backgrounds can validate each others' experiences. In the following, a multiracial student responds to the previous students' post with words of understanding and encouragement:

You gave an account of a white friend asking you to take a job cleaning her mother's house, a Latino telling you not to "embarrass" him by singing a Spanish song, and your sorority sisters recognizing your Filipino identity when they want to make jokes about Asian people. These are powerful stories because it depicts how society chooses our racial identity for us. Your white friend chose for you to be Mexican, because "only a Mexican" could clean her house, the Latino gentleman choose for you NOT to be Latina, because "real Latinas" speak Spanish, and your sorority sisters chose for you to be Filipino to amuse themselves. We can never be all of our races at once, society picks which one is convenient for them. By doing so they are able to discriminate against us based on the stereotypes and racist ideologies they hold against the minority groups we belong to. The class did not see that THEY were choosing for some of us. Though some of the confusion has been cleared up through *some* of the post, at the time they were making us prove ourselves. We had to prove that our experiences are just as legitimate as theirs. They didn't realize that we have to think about what we are everyday and they can wake up and know, "I'm Latina/o" "I'm African-American" "I'm White" etc. We don't have that luxury because we are questioned everyday about "what we are." (biracial, African American and White, female)

I WILL PAINT YOU BY NAMING YOU

Because the physical appearance of multiracial individuals confuses dominants, they tend to feel a loss of control. Instead of waiting to find out about the identities of biracial individuals, or insisting upon their choosing one particular identity, dominants prematurely label multiracial people. Just as names have been used to degrade people of color, they are also used to humiliate biracial individuals. These names indicate to the multiracial person that they are something less than human.

A White male describes the experiences of his female friend and her child in a food market:

> This weekend a friend of mine witnessed some explicit racism. I just wanted to pass this story on because it has been bugging me for the past two days. I am still disgusted . . .
>
> My friend is a White female. She had a relationship for two years with an African American male, who became the father of her child. Susan is

now a single mother in a mostly White community with a one-year-old daughter of mixed ethnicity. She was in a supermarket checkout line Friday when an elderly woman behind her pointed out some kids outside. The five or six kids who were playing in the parking lot were either African American or White (about half of each ethnicity), and of both genders. The elderly woman said that she "couldn't believe that those kids would play together." She expressed disgust for kids of different ethnicities simply running around together. She then said, "Before you know it, they will grow up and there will be zebra babies running around." Susan turned to the woman and said "I think the friendship between those children is a beautiful thing." She then exposed her baby in the cart and said, "By the way, my daughter is M, not a zebra baby."

I was very proud of the way she stood up for herself. When she told me the story I could see how pissed off she was. I don't remember ever having personally experienced any such blatant expressions of racism. I was completely disgusted that this woman lived in a nearby community of mine. (White, female)

This student develops his own metaphor about what happened to his friend as he ponders the racism that affronted her. He similarly analyzes the name "zebra" inquiring into its origin as a prejudicial slur. His comments on the class website provoke a number of other students to respond to his experiences and his question:

I was thinking of a parallel between this lady and a cockroach. They say that for every cockroach you actually see in your home, there are hundreds around that are living outside of your vision. I think this lady was kind of like the cockroach. The fact that I know one is out there provides some evidence that hundreds more are lurking around. Although in my experience racism does not overtly present itself all the time, accounts such as these pop up in my life periodically and provide evidence to confirm that racism is alive and well.

I'm still thinking about that lady and her thoughts. Sometimes I think I am lulled into a false sense of Utopian bliss, a world in which her and her ideas do not exist. Then something comes along and gives me a reality check. Recently this class and my friend's story have given me that check. This weekend, reality made me nervous.

I wanted to add a quick question . . . has anyone ever heard the term "zebra" or "zebra baby" to describe someone of both African American and

White descent? I had never heard the term and wonder if the lady was creating her own derogatory phrases. (White, male)

When this question was asked in class a biracial male responded:

> I think that the analogy that you gave was right on the money. Personally, I think that far too many people believe that racism is a thing of the past or isn't prevalent in today's society. Unfortunately, many people, like the old lady in your story, are also in positions of power such as teachers, bankers, police officers, judges, and members of Congress. To answer your question, yes I have heard the term "zebra" many times throughout my life. My mother is White and my father is Black. I have felt the "stares" from people when I am in public with my mother. I have also witnessed people act "differently" towards my mother once they found out that I was their son. (biracial, African American-White, male)

A biracial female also responded to the question:

> I just wanted to say that I have heard and used the term "zebra" when referring to people of that specific "mixture" of ethnicities. It sucks to acknowledge that I used that term. My ex-boyfriend (he was ½ white and ½ Mexican) and I (½ black and ½ Philipina) would say that if we had kids they would be zebras—although that isn't really accurate. Luckily, I have learned to really think about what I said and I've figured out why it is that I said certain things. It is kind of like the groups that we were split into on Wednesday. I have referred to myself as a mutt or half-breed. So, yes, although it is wrong, I have used zebra before. (biracial, African American-Filipina, female)

In the next excerpt, a monoracial student recognizes the unique implications of racial stereotypes for multiracial people. She reevaluates her own use of derogatory names to label multiethnic individuals because of her frustrations as a person of color. She attributes her name calling to curiosity:

> I realize that at times I would be curious about a person's ethnicity. I sometimes called people half-breed. I never thought the comment that I was making was derogatory. I never meant it to be a statement that was demeaning, but I now know that it is. I am able to appreciate that there are people that are a mixture of everything and that I am not helping by calling some people "half-breeds." I know that I have to be sensitive to the feelings of biracial people because I am just as sensitive [when I am] identified as something other than Filipino. (Filipina, female)

As a monoracial student of color, she realizes the pain of being racially stereotyped and recognizes that the multiracial individual faces further complications as a person without a single ethnic identity. In the following example, another monoracial female admits to her use of derogatory labels targeting multiracial people and realizes it is another tool of dominance. She had never imagined that she was prejudiced against biracial individuals.

> Sometimes on campus I will see people and say to myself, "oh, she must be a 'mutt' or 'half-breed.'" I have come to realize how derogatory these labels are. Saying such things is just as bad as saying Jap, nigger, bitch, or wetback. I have learned that each group is given a belittling stamp, even biracial individuals. I never really thought I could be prejudiced against biracial individuals, especially with Chicanos or Latinos. (Latina, female)

In the next excerpt, a student who was interested in the multiethnic background of her high school peer describes her lack of awareness of the derogatory nature of labels associated with multiracial individuals. These labels, she states, were tools to help her understand the concept of mixed ethnicities. Now, she realizes how "half-breed" is another derogatory term used to simplify or destroy the humanity in all of us:

> I distinctly recall the first time I heard the term "half-breed." This derogatory term was used in reference to a biracial student in my high school. I remember asking this individual, "What are you?" I was interested in knowing what her ethnic background was. She told me she was biracial, half Mexican, and half White. I had never met anyone with dual ethnic backgrounds so I questioned, "What do you mean you're half and half?" A friend of mine attempted to explain biraciality by stating, "She's a half-breed, kind of like dogs . . . they call dogs with a combination of different breeds 'mutts' . . . those with two breeds are . . . half breeds." It was then that I adopted the term "half-breed" to refer to biracial individuals. I am ashamed to admit that I used this term out of ignorance and lack of interaction with biracial individuals. As a result of my interaction and familiarity with biracial individuals, I am now aware of how derogatory the term "half-breed" is in reference to biracial individuals. (Chicana, female)

In his first press conference as president-elect, Barack Obama referred to himself as a mutt. Although we don't encourage students to disparage themselves, the fact that such a high-level person could be self-depreciating may allow biracial children who are teased with the microaggression of "mutt," "zebra," or "mulatto," to say, "Yeah, I guess I'm just like the president of the United States."

Subordinates' Demands for One Identity

Dominants create the categories for multiracial people and patrol the borders of the classification schema to force multiracial persons to select an identity. Most people would like to believe that close friends and family would never measure an individual's worth based on how one identifies racially. Our students' voices, however, illuminate that even close peers paint each other.

In the following example a student describes the salience of race on her university campus. Her peers express anger toward her for identifying as multiethnic and not Mexican. She discovers that people on campus, and even her own friends, rely heavily on assessing her worth based on her ethnic identity. To be accepted she must prove her allegiance by identifying with only one group:

> During my stay at UCLA, I have felt alone and somewhat of a "drifter" always looking for the "right road" (by that I mean what is comfortable to me as an individual), yet never stumbled upon that road. It all started my first year. Everyone asked me what my nationality was and this not only angered me but confused me. Why did it matter? Couldn't they be my friends based on my personality, beliefs, or interests? I soon found out that my ethnic background did matter as well as my physical characteristics. I was proud to be of multiethnic blood. However, my peers, mainly the Mexican/Latinos, believed that my sense of pride was inappropriate and I was subjected to their antagonism and hostility on many occasions. (biracial, Mexican-Native American, female)

Another student describes how even her own friends do not give her the support and freedom to identify the way she pleases. She turns to her parents for consolation:

> But never once have I come across a peer or even a friend who will truly allow for me to be the Japanese, Filipino, Mexican individual I am—comprised of all the things that I value, all the experiences and characteristics that make me feel proud, comfortable, and safe. I've always received this space and a great deal of support, throughout all of my changes, from my parents. So it isn't a surprise when I mention that I've frequently called my mother from pay phones on campus just to be assured that I can face everyone. (multiracial, Japanese-Filipina-Mexican, female)

A biracial student describes the profound effect his father had in contributing to his identity crisis. At a young age, his father shows remorse toward his son's Mexican heritage. Only later does this student challenge his father in order to assert his own identity:

Being half Mexican and Iranian, I feel that I have the best of both worlds. At times I feel like I am caught in between. Being biracial opens new doors of opportunities, but since my father [who is Iranian] never taught me about my Iranian culture, I never had a strong connection with my Iranian roots. To make matters worse, I never had a strong connection with my mother's Mexican heritage because my father would always put her down and say negative things about Mexicans. These negative reinforcements by my father to my mother made me very confused when I was a child. If he put down my mother for being Mexican, then I must be a half bad person because I am half Mexican. Only later on as a teenager did I go against my father to stand up for my mother and for myself, and I am proud of my mother and myself. (biracial, Persian-Mexican, male)

While multiracial people are challenged, questioned, and named by Whites, the hurt and betrayal from members of their own ethnicity can be just as distressing, if not more so. In this next excerpt, a tri-racial women describes the hurt and betrayal she feels when people of her "own kind" prevent her from asserting her identity:

I think the thing that is most frustrating is to constantly have to legitimize and validate my experiences to all people, including those who are of the same ethnicity. It always seems that others see me for their own ease and benefit. In doing so, they disregard my experiences and reality altogether. Whereas I used to believe that a greater understanding would result from other ethnic minorities, I am now beginning to feel as though I am subtly being displaced by members of my own ethnicity, not solely by Whites. It hurts so much that I'm not Japanese, Mexican, nor Filipino enough for my own peers and that this is assessed for me. I expect this abrupt displacement from dominants, but not my "own kind." I feel even more hurt and less safe when viewed in such ways by other group members because I expect it from Whites and the differences are incredibly obvious. With other people I always hope that the solidarity exists . . . that other ethnic minorities can relate to centering their lives around and making compromises for the White majority. But I guess things have changed and solidarity is defined in pureness . . . by conditions . . . and mostly by appearance and somehow, my mindset and experiences are not valid. (tri-racial, Japanese-Filipina-Mexican, female)

This tri-racial student describes her frustrations when persons of color do not accept her into their community. As a person of mixed ethnicity, she describes how her "own kind" have betrayed her, and that she feels incapable of belonging or feeling in solidarity with any group.

In this next example, a woman with three identities expresses her hurt because she doesn't speak Spanish. The pressure and ridicule she receives creates a feeling within her of having been "robbed." It is not enough for her to just say to her peers, "My entire family speaks Spanish":

> I was coined as "White-washed" or "coconut" (Brown on the outside, White in the middle). When they would make fun of me it was always in the form of a joke (they would all laugh afterwards, including me), or they would speak Spanish at times and then a few minutes into the conversation someone would look at me and say, "Oh! You don't speak Spanish, do you?" This would infuriate me more (although I wouldn't let them see) than the name-calling because both my mom's and dad's entire family speaks Spanish. I feel like I have been robbed of my Spanish culture and have to endure the pressure from my peers. (multiracial, Spanish-Native American-Irish, female)

These students illustrate how multiracial people are painted by dominants. Subordinates who have internalized oppression in turn apply rigid rules of belonging to multiracial and multicultural individuals in order to establish a "legitimate" membership into one identity (Root, 1996).

BIRACIAL AND MULTIRACIAL STUDENTS RESPOND

Passing

So far, we have illustrated how the need to classify and evaluate multiracial individuals is based on a physical appearance which is not easily categorized and how frustrating and painful it can be. A multiracial person can also respond to the dominants' reliance on physical characteristics by turning the tables on the dominant via "passing":

> Passing is the word used to describe an attempt to achieve acceptability by claiming membership in some desired group while denying other racial elements in one's self thought to be undesirable. The concept of passing uses the imagery of camouflage, of concealing true identity or group membership and gaining false access.

Bradshaw (1992) notes that the phenomenon of passing is associated with marginality, in which particular racial groups are stigmatized. Passing is one way multiracial people respond to their stigmatized role as a result of their physical ambiguity. Thus, the multi-cultural individual is aware of racial privilege in certain contexts as he or she "passes" to feel more comfortable.

Some individuals describe their ability to "pass" as a benefit because it allows them to identify differently in various situations. Others see the ability to "pass" as a double-edge sword because often individuals who choose to pass find themselves shunned by their own racial groups. "Passing" is an extremely complex, personal, and social choice. Even though some multiracial students choose to use this method, it could ultimately hurt them in the end because they have to be something they are not just to gain acceptance. The fact that "passing" is a phenomenon that is occurring further exemplifies the op-pressive and restrictive nature of racial categories as well as the presence of White privi-lege. The complexity of this choice is illustrated by Kich (1992) who describes herself as a "chameleon," whose racial ambiguity allows her to temporarily benefit from White privilege in certain situations. This complexity is further illustrated by a student who is White, Asian, and Native American and can "pass" as Mexican among her friends. Thus, she can benefit from White privilege while not wanting to be White (which she is), and wanting to be Mexican (which she is not):

> When I think about it though, I realize that in some ways I benefit from being able to pass as White. I think that my ability to "pass" depends a lot on the people I am with. When I was in high school, most of my friends were Mexican, so when we would go out I would always be assumed to be Mexican and in this situation it was beneficial for me to be perceived this way. My friends even gave me the nickname Jenita, so that my name would sound Mexican. I would even do my bangs high so that I would fit in better with my friends. My friends were by no means "cholas." I think that in this period of my life, I actually wished that I was Mexican. I did not feel like I fit in with the White people at my high school. At the same time I also think that I benefited by being racially ambiguous. I felt almost like a racial chameleon. Like I could pass for almost anything just depending on the ethnic make-up of the group I was with. (multicultural, White-Sioux-Korean, female)

Another biracial student describes her ability to gain access to White privilege as she "passes" because of her "ambiguous looks":

> I have come to realize just how prevalent white privilege is in our society, and how, though I'm half Thai and half Eastern European, my neutral/ambiguous looks allow me to profit from those White privileges. I can catch a cab the first time I try to hail one, unlike some African Americans,

and I can receive prompt and cordial service unlike some Latina women. Such simple, everyday "conveniences" are granted to me through White privilege. . . . Being denied service, being watched while shopping, or being ignored at a restaurant have never been my realities, and I know that most of it is due to my mixed looks that nobody can place. (biracial, Thai-Eastern European, female)

This student describes the very source of the dominant's frustrations because ambiguous physical features make it difficult to know whom to oppress. The student realizes that she "benefits" from her racial ambiguity because the painters identify her as a "normal" White. Kich (1992, p. 312) describes this as the "chameleon ability" which fosters temporary privilege and a sense of freedom and relief from the restrictions of being "both" and "neither." This chameleon ability makes occasional "passing" possible for the multiracial individual but is confusing for some dominants that insist on distinct racial categories. It is difficult for multiracial people to please any one group because White dominants and monoracial people of color are painters who prevent multiracial people from asserting their own identities.

The next student who details the complexities of his multiracial experiences illustrates this difficulty of acceptance. The Mexican community disregards his Hispanic identity and the White community categorizes him as Mexican because of his physical appearance:

> It has been very difficult for me to understand my race and my place, ethnically. Although I am half White, have grown up in a White town, gone to White schools, and prayed in a White church, I am automatically seen as a Mexican by all people who don't know me because of my physical features. Because of this, and my anger towards the prejudices, which I have seen in my hometown by Whites, I have claimed and will claim Mexican American as my ethnicity. Naturally, because part of me is being discriminated against, I will protectively side with that half. My problem (if it is one) is my inability to relate with "real" Hispanics. The White community sees me as Mexican because of my physical appearance, yet the Mexican community sees me as White because of my White upbringing. Because I have been raised in a White society I feel deprived of my Mexican background. (biracial, Mexican American, male)

While emphasis on having to prove one's ethnic legitimacy for the comfort of the dominant group can lead to "passing," this is not without consequences. In the following excerpt, a biracial and multicultural student describes how justifying her ethnic legitimacy has plagued her and caused her to feel distanced from both races:

I have always felt a void in my life when it comes to racial issues because I could never truly identify with one party, and hence, felt my "allegiance" and cultural pride lacked for both ethnicities. Though I've been told my features tend to look more "White" and I have, consequently, reaped the benefits of White privilege, I can also identify with issues involving Asian Americans. Yet, because of this dichotomy, I seem to have been disregarded and gone unrecognized by both groups. (biracial, Japanese-White, female)

The students' testimonies illustrate how painters, both White and non-White, make it difficult for multiracial people to assert their identities.

Other Choices

The challenge for people of mixed race and ethnicity is to differentiate between the pictures that painters paint for them and who they believe themselves to be. These students' voices portray some of the unique struggles that face multiracial individuals as they recognize that they are different from others. Facing one's struggles, challenges, and the reality of the multiethnic experience lays the foundation for exploring one's ethnic identity development.

Racial categorizing, questioning, naming, and insisting upon choosing are the responses that biracial and multiracial persons face. As a challenge to racial oppression, people of mixed race and ethnicity can choose to embrace any and all parts of their ethnic background. Some students recognize that one has the right to identify the way he or she desires rather than conforming to dominant ideas of how one should be. Spickard (1992) states, ". . . these days people of mixed parentage are often choosing for themselves something other than a single racial identity."

In the following example, a multiracial student asserts her own identity as she realizes that the pressure to choose only one identity reinforces the power exerted from the dominant perspective. This student illustrates the way she wants to be treated rather than submitting to fixed racial categories:

When you are multiracial in this country, a choice of race is preferred so that now everyone can stop trying to figure out what you are and have you nicely labeled. But having to choose creates a dilemma, because no one side fully embraces your identity . . . . One of the most important things I have learned is that my struggle to choose was not a struggle I entered in of my free will. It's a struggle that society has wanted to place me in. Instead of running all over the ethnic spectrum, I have at this point decided to sit smack dab in the middle and define myself as mixed/multiracial. If anyone still wants to ask what I am, they better be prepared for the list. Because the truth about my identity is that I am a mix of a variety of rich and full cultures that have all been part of the traditions and values that have given fullness to my life and the lives of my family. And this mixture has occurred within the realm of American culture, which has further shaped me. Therefore, I cannot check any one box these days. So, I mark "other" and when the surveyor tries to figure out what to do with that answer, they can struggle for a solution, for it is becoming less and less my problem. I am finally entering a stage of embracing my identity, though I still face issues concerning race on an everyday basis. I am realizing that I am a taste of the future of this country. As we come closer and closer together and as intermarriages increase, as well as mixed children marrying other mixed children, the nice little boxes suddenly won't apply. Embracing the difference will become the only choice we have left. It's either that or living in self-denial. (multiracial, Italian-Cuban, female)

This student embraces her multiracial identity as she realizes that being multiracial is legitimate. Another student who is of mixed race chooses to identify herself as African American. She maintains that she can assert her own ethnic identity despite the dissatisfaction of dominants:

> The dominant is normally the group that actually has the problem with multiracial or multicultural people but that problem in turn makes their inability to understand who I am, my problem. I feel that my situation is unique because I wouldn't consider myself bi- or multiracial. I would consider myself African American, and when I fill out a survey I check the African American/Black box, but I feel as if I've had the experience of a bi- or multiracial person based solely on my appearance. (African American, female)

This student explores her own ethnic identity and contends that the dominants' discomfort with people of mixed ethnic and racial backgrounds is the source of her struggle. She understands that racial identification is her choice, and that it should not be about pleasing dominants. The need to question one's origins, categorize one's racial identity, and use derogatory names to label multiracial people are examples of the painters' tools of dominance. Spickard (1989) states:

> As long as "outsiders" presume to label and define the experience of biracial individuals, and as long as biracial people fail to speak out and advo-

cate for determining self-identification, externally imposed marginality will continue. Prerequisite to embracing the right to self determination is an understanding of race as a social and political construct, primarily a tool of dominance.

Indeed, we have also found that speaking out about experiences has helped our multiracial students validate their multiple realities and assert their own racial identification. A Mexican and White class facilitator was impacted by a biracial student with very different biracial identities. The facilitator addresses the student in the classroom at CSUN:

> I just wanted to personally thank you for being so open about sharing your experiences with the class. I cannot express how much I relate to you on almost everything you have said about your experiences of being bi-racial. I love that even though our racial backgrounds are different on one side, I can still completely and fully align myself with you and your pain. For example, when you spoke about feeling not completely comfortable talking with other African-American women about being black because they have invalidated you as a bi-racial African-American woman. I have had similar experiences with friends and family who are full Mexican or Latino who express that I can't completely understand their pain because I'm not "brown." All of my life I have wanted to be as "brown" as my cousins from my Mexican side, and have felt not completely accepted because I am half-White.

> Another thing you mentioned during one of the first class sessions was how you felt ashamed of your White side but also felt extremely proud of being Bi-racial. This statement really taught me something about myself and about multi-racial experiences in general. Although many may be confused by this seemingly contradictory statement, I completely understood what you meant and have felt the same way. Even though I am ashamed of the privilege, stigma, and history of oppression that comes with my White side, I am completely and utterly proud of being bi-racial because it is those experiences that come with being bi-racial that have made me the person that I am today. Being half White and half Mexican or half White and half Black is completely different than just being of one race. It is because we have been pushed away from both sides of our cultures and not fully accepted that we have created this third identity that people don't understand because they want to categorize us as one or the other.

> I am not sure where you are in terms of your racial identity and self-esteem, but it is my hope that you come to fully appreciate the beauty

and complexity of being both White and Black. I know that I was once in a state of self-hatred because I wanted to be something I wasn't but couldn't because I didn't feel accepted. But, I now see the beauty in the painful experiences I have had in being bi-racial because it has molded me into the person that I am today.

Today in class I also wanted to further elaborate on your experiences and about multi-racial experiences in general but I didn't want the class to feel as if I was only trying to push forward my own agenda about multi-racial experiences. And then it hit me that I felt inhibited from sharing more because multi-racial people do not usually get a space to express their pain and thus I am not used to having a voice in expressing the pain that comes along with being bi-racial.

I just wanted to emphasize my thanks to you and the other multi-racial students for creating the space for this issue to be addressed. Your experiences validate my own and I feel good knowing that our class is now aware that the multi-racial experience does come with pain but also beauty. (biracial, Mexican-White, female)

In this next example, a student reviews her history with being categorized and being forced to choose one racial category. She is angry and upset that painters used this tool of dominance against her in the fifth grade and through high school. She asserts her belief that she is not "one race":

I remember a time when I was in the fifth grade and I was taking an elementary standardized test. While filling out the front page of the exam I came across a question that asked my ethnicity. At the time, I was not confused about why I was being asked for my race, but instead confused because of the long list of instructions that told me to mark only one box. I raised my hand and asked my teacher, Mrs. Wolf, what box I was supposed to check. Mrs. Wolf asked me what nationality I am and when I answered "African American and White," she chuckled and looked puzzled. I was not quite sure why she had this funny look on her face; maybe because she found it funny that a ten year old called herself African American and not simply Black, maybe she assumed that I was white or maybe because she felt that the obvious box for me to check was White, I still do not know. But I will never forget when she walked over to my desk and whispered in my ear "Just mark one." I was definitely a stubborn and intelligent child because I marked both.

This incident had a big impact on my racial identity because this was when I first realized that I was multi-racial in terms of how society would see me. All my life I could see that my mother was physically pale skinned and that my father was a darker shade and I knew that I was African American and White; but it was almost like I did not realize that this was important information until I saw that awkward question on the test. After marking both boxes something changed inside me. I had never stopped wondering about my teacher's reasons for telling me to just mark one box or why the other students found it easy to mark just one. As a teenager in high school it always frustrated me when I had to mark the box that corresponded with my ethnicity before taking a standardized test or filling out an application. I could not understand why I was being limited in my choices and why I could only mark one box. I am not ONE race! (biracial, female)

Multiethnic individuals will continue to struggle for recognition and acceptance for ethnic legitimacy as long as our categories of racial classification remain rigid. Through open and honest classroom discussions we may begin to diminish the rigid categories and barriers that exist between monoracial and multiracial people, so that multiracial individuals might find acceptance within our society. In an email to the professor, a tri-racial female student discusses some of the barriers created within the class due to language, culture, and misunderstanding. She suggests solutions for how these barriers might be overcome:

The only thing that I would want the class to recognize is that although this recognizable barrier exists, the fault or blame of this barrier cannot come just from within those who are multi-racial, and this is the concept that I am struggling with. If it was my fault that I do not know these languages, well, I blame being an American. And if I'm going to blame being an American for the ignorance of my cultures, then, well everyone came blame themselves for the same thing. I grew up with a multi-racial family where English was the common language of the three cultures, and I grew up accustomed to the transformed mixed cultures along with the playable factor of the acculturation of the American culture. I felt like the class was putting blame on the victim and the victim's family for missing out on that part of the culture, not personally, but systematically. Is the class looking for an excuse as to why we are just different, and we are always going to be different?

And I think now what needs to happen is a further discussion on recognizing how this barrier, and other barriers such as skin color or other

viewable cultural differences, affects the relationships between multi-racial people and the people of just one race, especially in the relationship
between the multi-racial and the persons corresponding race. (multiracial, Mexican-White-Filipina, female)

THE IDEALS AND NEW BILL OF RIGHTS

The biracial and multiracial students you have heard from are struggling to recover and
assert lost identities. The following excerpt illustrates the struggle to deal with the other
and the self:

> I was raised White and no one told me the consequences of being a mi-
> nority. My mom had White privilege so she didn't know the importance
> of acknowledging race and what it means. As I uncovered my prejudices,
> I realized the fear and misunderstanding of the other (and my unknown
> self) was really a fear of not knowing or wanting to accept who I was.
> (biracial, African American-White, female)

Another student has come to understand that her parent's instructions were not in her
best interest:

> All throughout my life my dad has always told me that I should identify
> with being only White and not to worry about the other part of me be-
> cause my Whiteness and the fact that I look White would take me the
> farthest and give me the best advantages. I now see he was wrong and
> that it was harmful. (biracial, Native American-White, female)

The ongoing difficult but similar struggles of biracial and multiracial persons have led
Maria Root (1996) to create a Bill of Rights for such individuals. This bill has a set of
truths, which are not self-evident. We believe that all those who have questioned, name
called, and sought to classify biracial and multiracial individuals should read this document carefully. Biracial and multiracial individuals have been part of American history
and have been involved in all our wars, and in the struggle to end slavery and to bring
about civil rights. Their history is a neglected history and needs to be restored to the
awareness of Americans.

Bill of Rights for Biracial and Multiracial Individuals

1. I have the right
   a. Not to justify my existence in this world
   b. Not to keep the races separate within me
   c. Not to be responsible for people's discomfort with my physical ambiguity
   d. Not to justify my ethnic legitimacy
2. I have the right
   a. To identify myself differently than strangers might expect me to identify
   b. To identify myself differently than how my parents identify me
   c. To identify myself differently than my brothers and sisters
   d. To identify myself differently in different situations
3. I have the right
   a. To create a vocabulary to communicate about being multicultural
   b. To change my identity over my lifetime—and more than once
   c. To have loyalties and identify with more than one group of people
   d. To freely choose whom I befriend and love

The voices from these student journals indicate that biracial and multiracial individuals cannot easily escape from the continuous scrutiny and attacks upon their identities. Painters insist and demand that the multiracial person in the United States adopt the dominants' own perceived reality; a reality that is in stark contrast to the actual identities of biracial and multiracial people.

We do not want to end this chapter with the Bill of Rights for Biracial and Multiracial Individuals to fall into the dust bin of empty rhetoric, which occurred when schoolchildren were forced to memorize the U.S. Bill of Rights. We prefer to leave you with the eloquent and forceful words of a student who sees a beautiful future for biracial and multiracial people:

> I'm proud that we are multi-racial. I'm proud that our parents thought "outside" the box. I'm proud that I've met all the other multiracial students in this class, WHO ARE ALL BRAVE ENOUGH TO CHALLENGE THE STATUS QUO BY BREATHING. OUR EXISTENCE CHALLENGES SOCIETY. OUR EXISTENCE IS BEAUTIFUL. WE ARE THE FUTURE.
>
> I have no idea what's going to happen after this class has ended, but I know I will remember the 6 of you for the rest of my life. I will remember this class for the rest of life, heck I might even write about it one day. (biracial, African-American and White, female)

PINK TRIANGLE EXPERIMENT EXERCISE

For the Instructor:

Used by Nazis to identify homosexuals in concentration camps during the Holocaust, the pink triangle has since been appropriated and embraced by gay men and lesbians. The display of the symbol now demonstrates alliance with lesbian and gay communities. In the exercise described below, your students are being asked to don the pink triangle. This exercise was first used by Chesler and Zuniga (1991) in a classroom as a way of teaching students how to resolve conflict by wearing the pin for a period of 24 hours. Rabow, Stein, and Conley (1999) asked students to volunteer wearing the pin for 1 week. Milman and Rabow (2006) extended the period to 5 weeks of pin-wearing. The longer the person wears the pin, the greater the impact on the "self" and on the understanding of gays and lesbians.

The purpose of this classroom experiment is to have your students identify with a stigmatized "other" to experience a reality that is mostly unknown to heterosexuals and to discover what their own deeper attitudes and feelings might be toward the gay and lesbian community. The experiment challenges the self-perception of students who consider themselves "liberal" and supporters of gay rights. It is important that students not be required to do this experiment. Reading any of the articles will also help students think about whether they want to volunteer or not.

Possible outcomes of this exercise include:
1) Heterosexual students becoming aware of their privilege of unawareness.
2) Students indicating a greater consciousness of the ways in which they may be complicit with discrimination.
3) Students displaying "attitudinal and behavioral shifts" toward the LGBT community and themselves.
4) Students maintaining their positions of "outright condemnation and rejection" of gay rights.

Methods

For this exercise, you can ask students to make their own pink triangles or you can make them for students out of thick, pink construction paper. They should be of sufficient size as to be visible. One alternative to the pink triangle is the symbol of gay pride, the rainbow. We have also used a rainbow ribbon that is glued to a pink triangle. This ensures the likelihood of recognition of the symbol. For those students who do not wish to participate, it is important that they not be stigmatized. We have made an assignment for the non-wearers which involves partnering up with someone who is wearing the symbols and speaking to them about their experiences. They should speak with their partner once a day, every day for the length of the 1-week experiment. It is also suggested that students all put on the pink in class together at the same time and remove them at the same time. Different types of written assignments can be developed. We have found it useful to have all pin-wearers talk about the most critical, the most awkward, the most difficult, and the most satisfying experience during their pin-wearing. It is also important to have students talk about the impact that the pin-wearing might have had on the "self."

Writing assignments for pin-wearers and non-wearers could include the following:

For Pin-Wearers
1. Describe the most powerful moment/incident in your week of wearing the pink. Explain who, what, when, where, and most importantly, how you were feeling.
2. What was most difficult for you while wearing the pink?
3. What was most rewarding for you during this time?
4. What was the impact that this entire experience had on you?

For NON-Pin Wearers
1. What did you learn about the other (your pin-wearing partner)?
2. What did you learn about yourself?
3. What was most challenging in talking to the other?
4. What was most rewarding in talking to the other?

If you as the instructor are going to have students write about the experiences it would be important to collect all the papers and have the class describe what they learned, what their biggest fears were, and how they feel as a result of their experiences.

CHAPTER

Getting Rid of the Paintbrush

"The concept of race 'evolved as a world view, a body of prejudgments that distorts our ideas about human differences and group behavior…' It fuses myth about human behavior and physical features together in the public mind. Such myths bear no relationship to the reality of human capabilities or behavior."

—American Anthropological Association, Statement on Race, 1998

Our students have established that racism is an omnipresent reality in their lives. They have expressed their feelings and described experiences with race, racism, privilege, and oppression. Students of color and multiracial students have documented the multiple ways they are dishonored by Whites, and denigrated by other subordinates, even those of their own background. This wounding is the legacy given to children of color born and raised in this country. Their voices reveal that racism is part of their daily life. White students have shown that they are often unaware of their privileges, ignorant about the reality of the lives of their classmates of color and how they perpetuate racism. You have heard student voices describing prejudicial and racist treatment in classrooms, playgrounds, retail stores, and public spaces by parents, peers, friends, teachers, police, retail clerks, strangers, and university professors.

You have read the ways in which children of color are treated as less. You have learned that statements like "I don't see color" and "You're being too sensitive" invalidate the speakers' experience. You have discovered how the legacy of racism leads to self-oppression and self-hatred. You have realized how biracial individuals are pushed and pulled to the point where they become chameleons in order to get along while denying their key identities. You have become aware that the questioning of "others" is often intrusive and implies that the other is "alien," "foreign," or "strange." When Whites point out the racism that exists between subordinates, it is often accompanied by a refusal to examine their own racial practices. Is it enough to know that all of these comments and arguments reside in a deeper belief of the racial inferiority of people of color?

In this text, we have not emphasized the institutional discrimination that occurs in housing, college admissions, renting, loan lending, and public accommodations. The cost of all of this discrimination is enormous: lost talent, anger, bitterness, fear, and self-segregation. Most importantly, there is an increasing distrust in our institutions of law, education, the police, and America as a democracy.

The students you have heard from confronted racial oppression in a forthright and honest manner. They did not reside in the comfort of their anger and denial, or the safety of their hurt and guilt. They were "ordinary people doing extraordinary things out of simple decency."[1] Their decency is reflected in their willingness to listen, to acknowledge, and to accept their fellow classmates' reality and experiences. There is a process that students engaged in as they confronted their prejudice and racism. Did our students change? In research that evaluated the way this class is taught, significant movements in identities where found when compared to a control group of six other traditionally taught classes (Rabow & Yeghnazar, 2009). This quantitative study did not capture the struggles and issues that students confronted. The work on identity shifts in racial attitudes and behavior by Helms (1990) and Jackson (1974) documents the ways in which the self is implicated with the beliefs and activities of individuals toward racism. We wish to simplify these shifts into a number of dimensions that we identified from an examination of students' journals and web-posts.

This chapter documents the ways in which students were transformed by their experiences. Not all students were transformed and ready to speak out against racist jokes,

---

1 Camus cited in Judt (1994). "The lost world of Albert Camus," *New York Review of Books*, VXL VIII, No. 9.

prejudicial statements of belief, or racist actions. Indeed, a few students were not able to move forward. In the following excerpt, a Korean woman describes why she is stuck. She is unable to go beyond her years of pain, anguish, and hiding. She is not in denial about racist reality, but she feels unable to change:

> I used to wish so many times that I was back in Korea when I never had to think about myself in a category as an Asian. I was just me. I was free to explore and define myself with the offers that my surroundings gave me. I want to be free. I'm all tangled up inside right now. I know I can't redo time and go back to when I was in Korea, but it's too hard to deal with the past. I can't let go. Every day, everything I do and say is reminiscent of people hurting me, treating me a certain way, seeing me in a boxed way, and I have become that. I didn't know how to fight back. I just let them define who I was and in the process I have become that. Now there is a hidden part of me that longs to come out and just be but there are too many fears and too many years of habit to cover me up and it's easier to act as if nothing hurts. Yet inside, I don't like myself for being that way. (Korean American, female)

Although this student was stuck in her fear, others were able to move beyond hurt, anger, and fear. How did this occur?

OVERCOMING DENIAL

Denial is something all human beings do when reality becomes too painful. It is a defense mechanism that humans employ at various times in their lives. Denial comes in many forms. There can be denial of responsibility, denial of knowledge or truth, denial of actions as hurtful, and denial of the possibilities of changing racist practices. Fear seems to be an underlying component of denial. One of the major steps taken by White students occurs when they begin to see society differently than they had prior to the class.

A White male writes about his former beliefs and his sense that the United States was a society that is open to all individuals who want to succeed. He realized the inaccuracies of his former beliefs:

> Before taking this class I honestly thought that everybody in this society, no matter what race or gender, had the same chance to do and achieve whatever they wanted in their lives if they only applied themselves. Sure, the socioeconomic background of one's family played a major role, but it could be overcome through hard work.

What I did not take into account was that first of all, everything happens according to and within the White culture's rules and limitations. Secondly, even if someone from a racial or ethnic minority "makes it" in most cases there are restrictions on how far he/she will be allowed to climb up the ladder. And even if someone is compliant all the way, skin color and gender will, in the vast majority of cases, continue to set limitations no matter what one's qualifications. (White, male)

Fundamental beliefs about society are hard to modify. White students found it difficult to believe that racism is alive, rampant, and strong.

Until he was faced with class readings on racial identities, a 21-year-old White male had never thought about racism. Gradually he becomes cognizant of some of the perks he receives as a White person:

When entering this class six weeks ago, the idea of "racial identity" never even really entered my mind. I can now attribute that to the fact that as a White individual and a member of the dominant group, I never needed to be aware of race. My day-to-day actions and relationships with others has never been highly influenced by what others may think about the color of my skin. But in sitting in this class and listening to the stories and how race highly affected my fellow students (and I can now say, my friends), I realized that I have been extremely naive.

I come from a middle-upper-class background and have always "got what I wanted" from society in general. I have no problems with getting jobs, no problems with making friends, and no problems being understood by other people. I used to feel embarrassed if my friends and family ever saw a Mexican woman walk down the hallway and into the door next to mine. Throughout my whole life, I have taken this kind of attitude and made them a part of who I am. I have never had reason to question them . . . until now. (White, male)

In another example, a White student transitions from recognition of White privilege to guilt to helplessness. She struggles with the idea that racism is her problem:

I look at my life, my experiences, and realize how privileged I've been on account of my paleness. That is when feelings of guilt turn to helplessness and frustration. I know I'm White, but there's nothing I can do about that. I can't help it that there are only peach colored band-aids at the store. It's not my fault that cops pull over minorities, and not me. It would be so easy if I could say with conviction that it's not my problem. I believe it more often than I should, and one of the things I'm trying to work on is not settling into a seat of privilege. What if I start to think that it isn't my problem, and that I can't do anything about prejudice or racism? Then I won't do anything about it. That's one of my biggest problems, and it is evident in what I've written about in my journals so far. I have a hard time recognizing that it is my problem, or rather what it is about ME that I can fix. I see it in my family, my history, my schooling, and in other people, but seeing prejudice in me is something I'm struggling with. AND IT IS SO FRUSTRATING. (White, female)

In this final example of White denial, a student reviews her process in the class and her prior approach to racists as idiots. This allowed her to dismiss her recognition of privilege and her contribution to racism:

I didn't get why people were being so "sensitive" in class, why people were getting so offended by the stereotype board; I kept thinking to myself, "stereotypes exist and yes, there are some terrible, idiotic, racist people but everyone has an equal opportunity to college, to jobs—people just need to work harder and stop complaining." But as I read McIntosh's article I began to understand that even if at an individual level I never behaved explicitly racist, (which I now understand that I have done, and am especially guilty of many, many, subtle microaggressions) that racism was not just about individual acts of hatred but more importantly it is about the dominance and subordinance of groups as a whole. I am now starting to understand why people are upset in class; they have had to deal with years of being racially profiled by dominants and had to watch people like me and other members of the "white identity" be given privilege, encouragement, and affirmation while we are completely oblivious to our dominance and oppression. I am now grasping this with the embarrassment and shame that I could have been so ignorant of my own racism and privilege for that last 20 years. (White, female)

Whites are not the only students who find comfort in their denial and privilege. A Chicana discovered her own racism and stereotypes towards Blacks. Initially, she was unable to understand her prejudices and the ways in which Latinos and Blacks have a common enemy. It was through reading Malcolm X that she became aware of her own stereotypes. While it was obvious to her that a lack of access for Latinos was the cause of poverty and lack of achievement, she had not considered this same reality for most Black communities:

I used to think that Blacks themselves created their conditions of hopelessness and poverty by being lazy, immoral, drug-addicted, and violent people. These are heavy statements to make, but racism itself is very heavy. I have never actually been in an all-Black urban community, but I envisioned it to look like the images and stereotypes I have learned from the mass media and among people I have met who painted a very racist picture. I noticed that none of these images reveals the institutional factors that have a tangible role in "keeping Blacks in their place." Because I never had a broad-based knowledge of how inequality works in perpetuating disempowerment among Blacks, I made racist assumptions on why they are always, collectively, as a group, at the bottom rung of the economic, political, and social ladder. It is because the top rungs have been removed and prevents them from climbing to higher positions.

Many of the issues that Blacks face, Latinos face as well. My own racism was confronted when I justified Latino poverty to be caused by lack of access to what Whites have and Blacks because of racist notions that they are too lazy to work. These same stereotypes can easily be turned around at Latinos too, but I refused to see it that way. Reading Malcolm X helped me see that Blacks are very determined to overcome their struggles. These barriers that we put up for them strip them of power and dignity. (Chicana)

Another student of color also lived in denial. As an African American woman, she was continually being told about racism from her family and friends, but she adamantly refused to believe them. It was only after 3 weeks of class discussions that she began to realize the painful events that she had denied:

My parents, their friends, and relatives would tell me stories of blatant, extreme racism. Yet, I wouldn't believe them. When they told me the recruiting representative at this firm was racist and didn't take African Americans as seriously as other candidates, I didn't believe them. I wouldn't believe them when they told me it was a racist act for my White friend's parents to look intrusively around our house and that because we were African American they felt obligated to check that our house was nice enough or safe enough for their child. When I heard the stories of police pulling African Americans over because they were "driving while Black" or even worse, taunting them at gunpoint, I barely believed it.

Up until a couple of years ago, I couldn't fathom these dramatic expressions of racism. I thought my parents and other such storytellers were unusually and detrimentally sensitive when it came to race. I related to many of the white students and the less conscious students in the class when they said the storyteller must be exaggerating or making a big deal out of nothing. It reminded me of myself in the past. I thought that things weren't really that bad, and I had my own experiences to prove it. I had never encountered any dramatic acts of racism.

When I started speaking up in class, the memories of the stories came back to me quickly. The ones that were too close not to be true flashed through my mind. That time when I was at a party on campus and my Black male friend ran up to me shaking and scared. He told me that the police had just jumped him, beaten him to the ground, and accused him of some crime. I couldn't deny that that story was true. And still every dramatic act of racism aroused feelings of disbelief in me.

Remembering all the stories I have heard in my life, and suddenly remembering those things possibly blocked by a selective memory, I realize that incidents such as these have sprung up often in my life. Although they happened to friends and loved ones, they still happened to people who were just like me—and that they were true. They weren't isolated incidents, and I had formerly believed them to be, but they were a constant reality that was always manifesting itself. (African American, female)

CONFRONTING SELF-HATRED

For many students of color, overcoming their self-hatred was an important step in their movement toward liberation. The students, who were targets of prejudice as children, continued to face racism as a daily aspect of their existence. As such, all have experienced difficulty with their self-worth.

Many subordinates develop this double-consciousness at a young age. From the moment children wish their skin was lighter, they begin to evaluate themselves against the dominant ideal—an ideal that destines them to fall short. For most of these children, this double-consciousness only deepens with age. Identities are established in the shadow of a White model. The self-doubt created by the White paintbrush can last a lifetime.

A Latina reveals the shame she feels about speaking Spanish, her parents, and physical being. Her shame is so profound that it leads her towards assimilation:

I remember not wanting to go shopping with my mom, just because I had to translate. I didn't want others to see me as an "immigrant." I would tell my mom that I would rather go by myself. This was in high school. I would shop by myself. I was ashamed of my language. I was ashamed of my physical characteristics. I was ashamed of myself. Just like my classmates, I would use silence as a method of survival. In doing so, I wanted to blend into the mainstream society. I wanted to become someone I wasn't. I saw total assimilation as my only way of accomplishing this goal. (Latina, female)

As these young adults struggle with self-examination, their self-perceived "inadequacies" sustain their belief that they are not "good enough." The struggle to accept oneself as equal to Whites is difficult to overcome. In the next excerpt, a Chicano describes his feelings toward White women. He describes them as beyond his reach:

I find women of all colors to be attractive. But I have this feeling inside of me that I am not good enough for a White girl. It's not that I think they're prettier or anything like that, it's just that I don't see them as something within reach. I maybe think they prefer to stick to their own or that I'm not good enough. I can't explain it. I believe I could approach a Latina, Asian, and Black, anything but a White. Why is that? Internalized oppression? Maybe seeing all of these Anglos in magazines and on TV makes it seem as if they were some special untouchable. (Chicano, male)

In the following, a Mexican American male discusses the difficulties involved in trying to strike a balance between loving oneself and one's culture and being able to be comfortable with Whites. The student felt that he must become different depending on the group he was with. He struggles with being himself:

I feel ashamed of being Mexican American. I feel like depending on who I am with, I have to deny some part of me. When I am with White people, I feel as though I have to assimilate, and deny my Mexican heritage. On the other hand, when I am with Mexican Americans, I sometimes feel like I have to be something I'm not. Mexican Americans constantly tell me that I am White-washed, that I'm selling out, and that I'm a coconut (Brown on the outside and White on the inside). The biggest thing is that I don't speak Spanish. My father speaks Spanish, but my mother does not, and so it was never taught in my home. One individual in this class actually told me that I am not Mexican. She was not the first person to tell me that. I have no response to that. What do I say? I know I am, but she makes me feel like I'm really not, or at least she makes me question it.

Either way, I feel like I can't win. If I'm with one group I feel like I have to act a certain way, and if I'm with the other I have to act another way. It leaves me with a feeling of giving up. I'm just me, and why is it not right to be who I am, listen to the music I want to listen to, and do the things I want to do? (Mexican American, female)

Overcoming the self-hatred bred by raw racism is a difficult goal for our students of color. DuBois described double-consciousness at the turn of the century and more than 100 years later our students still struggle with this conflict.

AWARENESS OF PRIVILEGE

Recognition that one's experience limits an understanding of America, racism, and privilege comes about when we can trust the experiences and reality of the "other." Because students had honest dialogues about their radically different experiences, these "others" became the messengers of truth and allowed for the increased understanding of privilege by White students. The class allows students to analyze their own identities, with an emphasis on the internalized racial and ethnic stereotypes of themselves and others. "Self-awareness" and "other" awareness was a major step in the transformation of identities.

A student writes about the process of awareness he went though in the class. In his own words, his "blindfold" has been removed:

This class helped me become aware of the ignorance that is out there, whether it's from Whites or from other people of color. I remember the struggle between someone in the class and another female student in trying to get her to recognize her privilege. I don't know if she has come to terms with it, but it seemed to me as if she was unable and unwilling to recognize it. I believe that this is the first step in getting rid of the racist attitudes and stereotypes that we have formed, and she will not be able to do this until she accepts and recognizes her privilege and uses it positively. Another example, which I remember clearly, was when another female student told the class that she didn't think racism was that big a deal and that it seemed to her that most of the female students' stories were exaggerations. This upset me because I don't imagine a person of color not being exposed to racism in their life, and in turn stating that Whites were more exposed to racism than people of color. I explained to her that she has probably been the victim of racism many times; she just didn't know it because it is too "normal" and it is so covert.

Earlier this week in class, a male student said that the people of color see all Whites as the same, and therefore he now feels like he has to show others that he is an individual, and prove that he is not like the rest of the group. I feel like this has been our (people of color) struggle since day one—trying to show Whites that we are not who they think we are, we are all different. Every day we struggle to prove to them that their stereotypes were wrong. Now it is up to Whites to show us that, and become allies.

It wasn't until I took this class for the first time that I realized that this whole time I had been living with a blindfold on. An example of this was when I looked up the meaning of the word "mutt," which is what I've been referring to myself as because I am multiracial. I wrote, "I knew that it meant a dog that was mixed with various breeds, but never a stupid person. Now I feel stupid for calling myself that." I am mad at myself for adopting such a negative word, and assuming that it was good, and calling myself that on a regular basis, this just shows the power of language, and how it affects everyone, whether it is positively or negatively, on a regular basis. My blindfold has finally been removed. (biracial, Japanese-White, male)

In order to become aware of our own racist tendencies, we must also acknowledge the privilege that our race engenders. In our society, being White allows one to enjoy privileges that others do not have. White people are usually provided with superior education, higher job placements, and are rarely hassled by law enforcement. In the following, a female realizes that her color is like a passport or a blank check. It is always given credit and is accepted everywhere:

I am White and I have never tried to be another color and/or race. That can be explained, though, by the fact that by being White, I don't feel the need to change. White is accepted at more places. I feel like a VISA credit card, "Accepted almost everywhere." (White, female)

Another White student acknowledges how her parents' lives and her own are much easier because of their race:

My fellow students taught me that there are so many things that I do not have to worry about because I am White. There are places I don't even have to think about walking into. I realized how lucky I was that even though my parents were divorced and my mother supported us three kids, she didn't have to worry about losing her job because her children's skin is White. I did not have to worry about my father being killed because of the color of his skin. (White, female)

Similarly, a White female learns about her privileged journey, which has led her to realize that she had not escaped the influence of racism. She points out the contradictory beliefs she once held. She is no longer able to believe in the fabrication that she was a non-racist:

> Ever since coming to UCLA, I have been on a continuing journey of learning about my "White privilege" that I have and have grown up with, and I am always discovering ways that I benefit from it in my everyday life. I grew up in a White, middle/upper class neighborhood, and was never really conscious of race issues until I got to UCLA. It was in a Women's Studies class during my freshman year that I began to learn about people of color. This was a new term for me, although I had grown-up thinking that I was a very non-racist [sic] individual (a non-racist individual with no race consciousness . . . go figure). As my professor lectured about the ways in which women of color have been oppressed in our society, and how, in many cases, the way in which their voices have been left out of White feminist discourse. I began to look at myself, and I began to realize that I too was a racist. (White, female)

A White male discusses his awareness of racism and how he can personally relate to the class. He begins to see that treating all people equally is just the beginning step on a long road to an anti-racist identity:

> I look at people of racial/ethnic minorities as well as women and gays differently now. I am acutely aware of the fact that they may come from and perceive a reality completely different from mine. That theirs is just as legitimate, and that I should be careful with my assumptions and how I, most of the time unknowingly, impose and perpetuate cultural and institutional racism while thinking that I am not racist at all. After all, my girlfriend is Black and I treat everybody in my life the same regardless of ethnicity, color, gender, or sexual orientation. This is only a tiny part of the equation, though. Actually, it doesn't mean much at all; racism has taken on a completely different, much, much further reaching meaning, and I feel rather powerless and uncomfortable about it.

> Although I think that the entire process of participating in this class—the discussions, student's comments, and the readings—caused the shift in my awareness, my thinking and hopefully my future actions, I can give a few specific examples of what were real eye-openers for me:

It started with one of the student's analogy in regard to women's constant fear of sexual harassment or rape. She suggested to the men in the class to simply being locked up in a prison cell with one or more other bigger guys, who in no uncertain terms had let you know that they would, sooner or later, sexually take advantage of you. I have been arrested and briefly locked up, fortunately without such experiences, and was, for a moment, able to really feel what it may be like for a woman to walk home at night from the bus stop, down a not-so-well-lit street, and suddenly hear footsteps behind you. I will never make a comment like "What was she doing in that area at that time?" or "Why was she wearing a mini-skirt?" again because it ought to be completely irrelevant.

Another important contribution for me was when another student described in detail how he was humiliated and threatened to be shot during a routine traffic stop, and how afraid he was and generally how submissive he has to be, as a Black man, when having contact with the police. It brought back memories of how I have interacted with police officers in an arrogant and demanding manner, in a way that would have gotten me injured or killed had it not been for my White skin. I got away with it, though, together with some friends of mine. I even went on the offensive once, forcing a local police chief and two deputies on to a live radio talk show where we continued our attack on two particular officers for their excessive use of force. I do not regret my attitude at all, but I realize now that not everybody can act like that without putting one's self into serious danger.

The third real eye-opener came in the form of an article in our textbook, where Studs Terkel describes a 40-year-old man of Mexican descent's struggles with the contradictions of his understanding of himself and the American dream. He had been a "good boy" all his life, chased that American dream, and little by little come to find out that there really exists no such thing for him, that the American dream means not losing for those who are already privileged. Education, opportunity, and hard work do not govern it, but power and fear. He ends up quitting corporate America and now teaches at a university.

I especially related to this article because I am of the same age and have also tried, for well over a decade now in this country, to "make it." Although I am from a privileged background, as a White male from Europe, the way I feel about my experience is very similar. I can feel the power, I experience the fear, the constant need to compromise, because, after all, I need to put food on the table for my kids, so better not make too many waves. . . . To hell with this kind of thinking! I feel so much better and affirmed in my decision now to go back to school and to slowly move away from a career in business, where no accomplishment is ever big enough anyway. (White, male)

A female student discusses how she has taken her privileged status for granted, including immunity from the daily strife of racism:

The book by Lois Stalvey[2] did teach me about White privilege. It taught me that because I am White and have always been that I have taken many things for granted. I have never had any problems trying to rent an apartment. I have never been denied access to a restaurant, a club, a grocery store, a department store, or anywhere else because of the color of my skin. I have access to the best schools, the higher paying jobs (although I am still a woman, which limits the pay); I can be whatever I want. I received only support from my teachers throughout the year. I was never told I was stupid, but when I needed help with math, I was immediately given a tutor to assist me in developing the needed skills. I never had to worry about being in a neighborhood past dark. When I had encounters with the police for speeding, I did not have to worry that they would beat the shit out of me, or shoot me. I am, and always was, able to sit anywhere on the bus that I wanted to. I had the privilege of not having to deal with any of this racism on a daily basis. (White, female)

In this final excerpt, a White woman shows her understanding of her process in becoming aware of privilege. She develops a distinction between being a non-racist person and an anti-racist person:

A non-racist person is how I would define myself before I took your class. I had no race consciousness but I had no problem with people of another race. I was conscious of the underprivileged status of people of color, but I was not conscious of my privileges as a White person. I was very conscious of the racism that divides the American society, but felt that as a foreigner I was not part of the American racism.

An anti-racist person is much more proactive. An anti-racist person is aware of the existence of the underprivileged and is also conscious of the people who have privileges. An anti-racist is aware that the society is designed by and for the privileged and dominant group. An anti-racist,

---

2 Stalvey, Lois. (1989). *The education of a WASP.* Madison, WI: University of Wisconsin Press.

after understanding the mechanism of the society, is willing to destroy the system and change it. (White, female)

AWARENESS OF SELF-INVOLVEMENT

Another step toward eradicating racism is recognizing that it exists in each of us. None of us have escaped the painting or the painters. This recognition is expressed in the following excerpt:

> Slowly, I've been coming to see where my prejudices lie. Unfortunately, I haven't found a methodical, easy to replicate manner in which to accomplish this. It's more like accidentally bumping into a light switch in a pitch-black room, or like Wylie Coyote running off a cliff. He looks down, realizes that the ground has suddenly dropped several hundred feet below him, and he thinks, "I can't have run off a cliff, I would have seen it coming." In my case, I look down and think, "I can't have done something prejudiced; I'm not a prejudiced person." Sometimes, that eerily effective human ability to rationalize lands me back on solid ground. However, all too infrequently, I find myself falling, and recognizing some small piece of what it is that makes me prejudiced. (White, female)

In this next excerpt, a White female faced her stereotypes about Latinos and realized that she painted them as somehow inferior:

> In the film "500 Years of Chicano History," I was able to identify with the White American majority saying, "You don't belong here. You can stay as long as we need you but then get out." The realization hurt me deeply. I have worked in restaurants where the kitchen crews were all Mexican. I laughed with them, enjoyed their company, tried to speak Spanish with them, and tried to understand their English. And all the while, I unknowingly saw them as inferior. I simply do not understand my own duplicity. I genuinely enjoyed their company and liked them, but I never respected their culture. I feel like I should go back and apologize to them. (White, female)

In the next example, a White female describes how she was always able to maintain her "White perspective." Her own version of a privileged reality maintained because she dismissed the stories of racism that students and friends had shared with her:

I've been learning to be more introspective, and the results are less than desirable. To date, my biggest discovery is that I didn't really believe that people were being discriminated against because of their race. I could hear them say it, but in my head, I kept running a parallel reason from the White perspective. A Chinese lady says that her party had to wait longer while Whites kept getting seated in front of them. I say, other people had made reservations. A Black man says that the receptionist was rude, and made him wait longer because he's Black. I say she had a bad day, and the person he was there to see was busy. A Puerto Rican couple says that the second they drove into Modesto (I think that's the town) a cop started tailing them, and continued to do so until they reached their hotel, which they opted to drive right on by because they didn't feel safe. I say, there's nothing to be afraid of in Modesto. It's a nice little town. And surely the cop wasn't following you because you're Puerto Rican. I bet your hotel was on his way to the station. I know that for every story in which something bad happens to someone because of their race, I can counter it with a White interpretation. And while I was listening with a sympathetic ear, I silently continued to offer up alternative explanations, benign explanations that kept my world in equilibrium. (White, female)

Another White student examined her assumption that an African American man wanted money when he addressed her. She was forced to ask herself if this assumption was based solely on his skin color:

Last weekend I was walking in Westwood when an African American man approached me. The first thing that entered my mind was that he was going to ask me for money when he really just wanted to know what time it was. My assumption really disturbed me and so I asked a friend who was with me if she had the same assumption, and she said she did. Ever since this incident, I have been wondering why I made the assumption that I made. Was it because I was in Westwood and had already been approached several times for money? Or maybe it was because of what he was wearing. But then again, maybe, just maybe, it was because of his skin color, and that is wrong? (White, female)

One of the most difficult challenges for many of the students was overcoming the positive stereotypes of Asian students. In this first example, a student began to recognize her "illusions." Naming something as false is a big step for moving toward an anti-racist identity:

I realize I have labeled Asians in a certain way. I saw them as all model minorities, very studious, competitive, stoic, cheap, and passive.. I really feel I have come a long way in the last seven weeks to get beyond this labeling and stereotyping. I think this is because I have seen and interacted with a number of Asians in our class and my LTD[3] group They have all failed to live up to my stereotypes, none of them fit this image, and I see tremendous diversity among them as human beings. I feel very grateful for this opportunity to look at my labeling of this group because it really bothered me. I think the interacting that I've done with the number of Asians in the class has been the most important, but also writing in (the journal) and exploring the issue has helped as well as the class readings. I think specific articles that had to do with Asian issues were very enlightening. I think the sheer irrationality I've witnessed throughout our readings, films, discussions, etc., has really helped me to question and be aware of my unconscious stereotypes which are really based on nothing when I deconstruct them, so I am better at seeing them for what they are . . . ILLUSIONS. . . . (White, female)

In this next example, a student described how contacts with other students in the class transformed her views of Asians as the "model minority":

Although I have Asian American friends, I have to admit that I have found myself buying into the myth of the model minority. I'd nod my head when I would look at the front row of my classes and see three rows predominantly full of Asian students, assuming that Asian students in my classes were better students than me. It really does take personal experience to rid myself of my belief in this myth. It has taken this class, in which I have had the opportunity to read articles, and actual students saying, "No, it is not that way for me, and I feel pressured to conform to it," for me to be able to begin to challenge this myth in my head. So I would imagine that at some point, the fact that I did harbor those stereotypes could have affected people and perhaps perpetuated their feeling of "less-than" or as model minority "study nerds." (White, female)

CONFRONTING GUILT, FEAR, AND ANGER

Self-awareness can be frightening. This is particularly true when it is the first time we are examining an issue about ourselves. Few individuals would want to look deeply within and find that they have been harboring racist ideals, beliefs, and practices. But the sooner

---

3 Rabow, J., & Yeghnazar, P. (2009). *A Guide to Learning Through Discussion: For Students*. San Diego: University Readers, Inc.

that we collectively face this dilemma, the sooner we might begin to do the work that will eventually help alleviate our need to oppress. For our students, this was the first time many of them had come face-to-face with their own internalized racism.

In the next passage, a White female addresses the issue of ignorance and the stand she has decided to take against it:

> Ignorance is truly bliss. At least, it was. To go day-by-day denying racism and oppression, to live each day refusing to watch or read the news in anxiety that I would learn even more negativity about society and the world, to be ignorant of my surrounding and environment was blissful. Although I am aware of certain stereotypes that I still currently hold, awareness is the first step to eradication. Life is harder once one becomes aware and conscious. Like the naive child, the unknowing and blinded individual sees no evil and hears no evil, yet evil is abounded. I know now that with my knowledge, with my awareness, I have a responsibility to act accordingly. I have to spread this seed planted within me. If I opt not to, I am no better than the racist. Being anti-racist means taking an active stance against racism. (White, female)

This process of soul searching provokes the natural reaction of fear. However, it may do much more than that. It may inspire movement beyond fear, which can generate change within oneself and interactions with others.

After realizing his own racism, a White male comes to believe that he must take responsibility for his racism:

> Awareness also brings responsibility. It is my responsibility, as well as others', to tell family, friends, relatives, and strangers about confronting racism and prejudice, instead of running away from them the way I did for quite awhile. I feel that I have a responsibility to tell these people, it is a part of my job, now that I know what lies ahead of them; I would have to spread the awareness about how racism and prejudice may be harmful to oneself if it is not faced. It will consume you from the inside out as it did me when I avoided the confrontation. I was unhappy and unsatisfied with always trying to hide behind a wall nonchalantly. (White, male)

In the following example, a White student questions what he would have done back in the days of Jim Crow laws. Though he is concerned that he would have been apathetic, he also begins to examine what active role he can play presently to fight racism:

I am pretty upset right now from the reading. I feel so horrible from the persecution that Richard Wright felt, described, lived through, and how he was forced into submission into Jim Crow ways. I read without any awareness of time or page numbers. I was immersed in his terrifying world. About half way through I felt that I couldn't take anymore. I wasn't able to cry and I wasn't able to pretend that it was not true. I felt like I didn't know how to be. I was numb, ashamed, guilty, and scared. I endured reading the rest, as Wright had to endure his struggle his whole life. I can't believe the suffering of so many people in this world. It is so painful. It breaks me up and destroys my spirit and faith in the human race. What would I have done if I were alive and White back then (or even today in the Deep South or any place for that matter where deep, overt racism occurs)? Would I have helped Blacks even though I would have faced ostracism, and probably violence or death myself? Would I have been as racist and violent as the rest? How do I live my life awake from here on in? How can I live my life with the courage to be willing to die? How can I live my life so that I never tolerate being so inhuman or allowing others to be inhuman as well and to not allow such forms of overt racism to exist? As Freire says, how can I get it that I am not nor ever will be free if one of my brothers is suffering on the planet? What do I do? (White, male)

Another student explicitly states that awareness is scary. Still, she begins to face the harsh reality that racism is commonplace for many students who have expressed their pain in class:

I have a fear of speaking as a member of the dominant group, being 3/4 White. My feelings of fear stem from not wanting to be labeled as being a racist. I think that fear also stems from the inner fear that I do not want to know what happens to people of color every day. I may not directly be a racist, but not reacting or speaking up to try to change things is a result of my guilt. By doing this journal we are asked to look inside ourselves. This is a frightening prospect because I do not want to see the possibility that I have been a racist. Awareness is scary. I take for granted my Whiteness, not wanting to accept that racism is commonplace, but it must be so because the others [in the class] have shown examples and [shared] anecdotes. (biracial, White-Mexican, female)

A White student questions his passivity toward racism and realizes that his laissez-faire stance is now unacceptable. He will now actively address racism:

I used to feel that if I just do my thing, don't discriminate, that I've done my part and nothing more is needed. I used to think that I am only responsible for myself and for no one else. How could I be part of the problem? It's not my fight. After thinking about it, I am realizing it is my fight. I am responsible.... that's why if I'm not part of the solution, I am like all those who have gone before me and done nothing [about racism]. (Irish American, male)

On a poignant note, one student ponders about friendships that never developed. He described how he was always waiting for the "other" to approach him. He was afraid to make a mistake, so he never attempted to reach out in order to understand other races and cultures:

I feel like I have lost so many possible friendships because I was never able to look past those labels before . . . Like the Black man said in the "Color of Fear," I was always waiting for the "other" to come to me. Afraid to make a mistake, not willing to take a step, I have lost many potential friends. I do not expect others to emulate me; rather I realize that it is time I made the first step. (White, male)

In the next statement, a White student's newfound awareness helps him realize that he can no longer ignore racism:

In the movie "The Color of Fear" I found myself watching David [a White male] and cringing. What he was saying were things I have said. His beliefs were beliefs that I have held. That is who I was before I took this class. I was ignorant to what was going on around me, just like David. I was blind to the pain. I did not want to accept the truth. Now I can never be blind to it; it will always be with me. (White, female)

In this final example of guilt, denial, and anger, a student reviews a friendship that she had with a Korean American for over 20 years:

C was my best friend in high school and is a first generation Korean immigrant who moved from South Korea to California when she was five. I believed that most Asians that had not been born in America had accents, only played musical instruments, spent all day studying, and did not play sports. C did not fit my racial mold; yes C played the bass and is now at Harvard but C had no accent, was on ASB, and went to school dances. I would describe C by saying "Well she is from Korea but she is completely whitewashed, you would never known she was born somewhere else. She isn't a fob...." I only now realize the meaning behind my words, I was saying that it was wrong that she was from Korea, that it was "less than," but that she made up for because she was like "us," that she fit in with me because she did not fit my racial profile of Asian immigrants that I considered "different" and "inferior." I was putting down C's identity and denying her ethnicity so that I could make her whiter because I now understand that I thought these traits were better. I am now both embarrassed and ashamed of having done this to someone I love, and feel so guilty that at times I must have made her feel inferior because she is Korean or that she had to try to become more white in order to fit in. (White, female)

CHANGE

"The struggle is inner: Chicano, indio, American Indian, mojado, mexicano, immigrant Latino, Anglo in power, working class Anglo, Black, Asian—our psyches resemble the bordertowns and are populated by the same people. The struggle has always been inner, and is played out in outer terrains. Awareness of our situation must come before inner changes, which in turn come before changes in society. Nothing happens in the 'real' world unless it first happens in the images in our heads."

—Gloria E. Anzaldua (1942–2004, Chicana/o culture and queer theorist)

The following is a link for the lyrics of a song called "Changes" by Tupac Shakur. Although he exams the harsh truths of racism, he also hints at the possibility of change that comes with awareness that racism is a reality that we must actively work against in order to change.

http://www.azlyrics.com/lyrics/2pac/changes.html

Transforming identities, changing beliefs, dropping assumptions and stereotypes, and intervening to stop oppression are challenging and difficult tasks. Recognizing that we are all racist and that we are all implicated in racism is a fundamental step in the process of attaining an anti-racist identity. We all have had moments when we wanted to say something, stand up for someone, do something, and, yet, we did nothing. No one is clean. We have been taught to paint and we all have painted. When White people hear about the sins of the past and present and discover that many Whites have acted as oppressors, they often feel ashamed of their lack of awareness. The students' indicated that listening to their fellow classmates' experiences provided them with some ammunition and tools necessary to examine and question their painting instructors. In the following, a student confronts her anxiety about a dental assistant:

> I had gone to the dentist's office for a checkup and I was filling out my paperwork, I saw an African American lady with a white doctor's coat come into the reception area and call out my name. She was the new dental assistant the office had hired. For a second I panicked. I thought to myself, 'I have never seen her before . . . she's new . . . what if she is not capable of doing her job right . . . what if she doesn't have enough experience. Maybe I should ask for the doctor?' Then, right in the middle of my thought process I stopped and asked myself, "Is there any reason why you're doubting her capabilities?" the answer was NO. Then I asked myself, "Would you be this apprehensive if she was White?" the answer was no, again. At that moment I realized I was undermining the value of this very intelligent and sophisticated lady based on the color of her skin. I was reacting based on my racist, socialized beliefs. Right there and then I stopped myself. I closed my eyes for a second. When I opened them again, I looked into her face and truly saw this beautiful African American lady for who she is rather than the color of her skin. (White, female)

In the following, a woman refutes the idea that it is a compliment to be called a good White person:

> But I do not like the way White is defined as a non-ethnic group just because it is main stream or has been dominant. It is not any better than any other group nor is it any worse. Every ethnicity has importance and worthy ideals. Each group has something great that it can contribute to American culture. I also want to change the perception of White people. I don't want people to call me a good White person. I should not have to be praised for not having racial prejudices and for being open-minded and tolerant. (White, female)

In the next example, a student understands that the job of dismantling racism falls more heavily upon her own racial group than people of color:

> I believe myself to be a strong individual, and the more I learn about myself, the stronger I become. Because I am White, I feel that it is my duty to fight the hardest because it is White people who have the most history of oppressing others. For reasons such as these, and because I am a woman who knows what it is like to be sexually oppressed, I pledge to continue in

this process of learning and understanding so as to help raise my own consciousness, as well as the consciousness of society. (White, female)

Many of our students have begun to put down their paintbrushes and are letting their canvas dictate their art instead of the other way around. Speaking out is a way of promoting anti-racist behavior. In the following example, a woman of color describes her new "voice":

My voice became more prominent, as I would be sure to make myself heard whenever I felt an injustice was being done. I went to a club one night, and a light-skinned Black young lady was in the restroom making a fuss over how dark skinned the men were, calling them such atrocities as "crispy" and "burnt," and wondering aloud why they didn't "just go back to Africa where they came from." I shook my head at her and told her "shame on you," and asked her how she would feel if someone said that about her parents; two other girls similarly chided in. She dismissed my comment and said she was just drunk, and not to mind her. As she bounced out of the bathroom, several of the females looked at each other in awe and made comments about how they couldn't believe people like that. I was proud of myself. I was proud that I initiated such a debate. I was proud that I (unlike the other females in the restroom) spoke my mind in the face of a conflict. I was proud that I incorporated the concepts I was exposed to in the classroom. (Asian, female)

A Latino describes the isolation that he felt prior to the class and the struggles he made toward achieving an anti-racist identity:

As I review the way I've changed as a result of this class, I have realized that the hardest parts for me dealt with many of my own demons. I had grown up in a predominantly White neighborhood, so talking with dominants was not something I found terribly difficult. As one can imagine, though, I didn't often pass the time discussing racial issues with many of my White friends. However, at times I felt more at ease with them than with "my own." Because of where I grew up, how I spoke, and how I acted, I have always been considered the sell-out, the White-washed Mexican. Consequently, I grew up in a state of racial confusion. Other Latinos did not accept me, yet as I unconsciously internalized the dominant view of myself as a person of color, I still could not completely embrace my White neighbors either.

Before this class I had no idea that others thought or felt the same way I did. When I first heard someone in class echo a thought or belief or even express confusion like my own, I felt I had found a new family. I thought that I had finally found people that I might be able to relate to, to talk with, to help me through all of the tough questions I was beginning to ask about myself. Most importantly, I had found others I could simply dialogue with and help muddle through our racial identification process together. Finding just one class like this at UCLA has made my academic career more fulfilling than I had ever possibly imagined.

This course has helped me to find a voice. But before I can have a meaningful dialogue with others, I first have to deal with my own inner turmoil. I never realized all that I take for granted. I have learned so much that I have never questioned—things about myself, as well as about other groups. I look at the labels that I use, the way I view myself; I try to question everything now. I see that no one is free from this racial internalization. (Latino, male)

In this final excerpt a White female describes how she was educated to believe that great progress has been made in race relations in America. Her shock and surprise is that for many people of color, racism is still a major factor in their lives. At the age of 20, she has become aware of the salience of racism and the significance of privilege for many White Americans:

When an event of racial or social inequality was mentioned, it was taught in a very cut-and-dry, absolutely historical sense. Good thing Harriet Tubman led some slaves to freedom; good thing Lincoln fixed the South of its morally misguided affinity for slavery; good thing that's all behind us now. With that in the past, we can finally live as equals as just humans. Race is taught as a nonissue. Imagine my surprise when it was made clear to me that for some people, namely non-Whites, race is an issue. And now I'm starting to learn why, 20 years too late. (White, female)

This chapter described the understandings students developed about their own and others' racism as well as some steps that students made in combating racism. Can these well-trained painters who were so accustomed to painting be expected to change? What happens to students who no longer have the support of peers who have gone through a process of identity transformation after they leave class? Can the experience of one class change students to the point that they can continue to speak out, challenge, and fight against the racism that surrounds them? Our final chapter addresses these issues.

Instructors:

We offer three exercises that will help bring your students to a deeper understanding of themselves and of each other. In this first exercise, each person can understand the four common experiences that they all share. While these previous exercises can trigger disengagement and resistance, it is necessary to counter any such tendency by uniting and bonding the class.

OPPRESSION AND INTERVENTION EXERCISE

The first exercise involves putting all students into groups of three to five. Each member of the small group is asked to share a time when they have:

1. Seen oppression and done nothing
2. Seen oppression and done something
3. Experienced oppression and done nothing
4. Experienced oppression and done something

This exercise is processed by having students focus on the feelings associated with each of these circumstances. The feelings for each are written on the board so that students can see the differences between feeling proud, empowered, and strong versus feeling violated, hurt, and shameful. A benefit of this exercise comes from understanding that none of us are pure. We have all participated in each of these actions. Hearing how people have stood up for themselves and others models intervening against injustice and often inspires students.

AWARENESS OF PRIVILEGE EXERCISE

All students are asked to stand up and move to one side of the room. All students start in the same place. When a statement is read and applies to a student, he or she takes on step forward. Some statements include:

- If your parents owned their own home
- If you had your own room
- If you had your own cell phone in high school
- If you participated in an SAT/ACT prep course
- If you ever went on a vacation cruise with your family
- If your parents took you to museums and art galleries
- If you are unaware of how much heating bills were for your families
- If you didn't have to work while in high school
- If you don't have to work now
- If one of your parents were born in this country
- If both of your parents were born in this country
- If you were born in this country
- If you are not the first person to go to college in your family

This experience creates a physical awareness of privilege. Having privilege does not necessarily imply that you worked less hard. It does mean that you had a head start. Everyone in the class seems to be equal. Differences in GPA and clothing are not important. This exercise uncovers the veneer of "we are all equal." This exercise helps students see the invisibility of privilege.

WALK-ACROSS-THE-ROOM EXERCISE

The third exercise that can help students bond and understand each other is a physical one. After helping students understand that their basis for responding to the race, gender, and sexual orientation is in fact superficial, this exercise allows students to discover that there are a number of key experiences and background factors that can be of much deeper and genuine connection.

- First person in your family to go to college
- Lost a loved one to violence
- Grew up poor or on welfare
- Had a member of your family die of cancer
- Had a member of your family die prematurely
- Have been forced to go bed because there was no money for food
- Has experienced parental divorce
- Has experienced alcoholism in the family
- Has experienced drug addiction in the family
- Has grown up with physical violence in the family
- Has grown up with psychological and emotional abuse
- Has grown up with a disabled sibling
- Has been forced to drop out of school to support your family
- Has seen or been a witness to police brutality

While the students are standing there, we furnish words that probably describe some of the experiences and feelings associated with each of these statements. For the poor, we might say, "having to wear hand-me-downs," "using food stamps," and "feeling ashamed of your family." This exercise ends with the understanding of how little we know about someone and their experiences, their background, and their struggles when we know someone's race, gender, or sexual orientation. After weeks of dealing with tears, grief, empowerment, sadness, hurt, anger, and frustration about their own identities, students can now look at the world as a place where pain has not only existed and been pervasive, but has been overcome, possibly fostering a feeling of hope. Moreover, students who have not been able to see eye-to-eye may be able to unite over a shared experience or a greater understanding of the multiple dimensions of the other and that we all have.

CHAPTER

Beyond the Class

"Each time we stand up for an ideal, or act to improve the lot of others, or strike out against injustice, we send forth a tiny ripple of hope, and crossing each other from a million different centers of energy and daring, those ripples build a current that can sweep down the mightiest walls of oppression and resistance."

—Robert F. Kennedy

"Whatever career you may choose for yourself —doctor, lawyer, teacher—let me propose an avocation to be pursued along with it. Become a dedicated fighter for civil rights. Make it a central part of your life. It will make you a better doctor, a better lawyer, a better teacher. It will enrich your spirit as nothing else possibly can. It will give you that rare sense of nobility that can only spring from love and selflessly helping your fellow man. Make a career of humanity. Commit yourself to the noble struggle for human rights. You will make a greater person of yourself, a greater nation of your country, and a finer world to live in."

—Martin Luther King Jr. (1959)

It is difficult to assess whether the changes students make during the course of the class endure beyond the duration of the teaching experience. Racist attitudes in your family may still be the same and peer groups may still be telling jokes about minorities, women, and gays. Public places and your workplace could still be arenas for the expression of racism. There are pressures in the classroom to conform to other students who are changing their racist attitudes and behavior. Students can instigate change during the class without being able to maintain these changes once the class is over. I sent an email to my current and former students in an attempt to gauge behavior that was anti-racist as a result of taking my classes. I told students that they did not have to report change if none had occurred. Many students described general changes in attitudes and specific behavior. The first excerpt, by an African American woman, reflects the general shift that was expressed for many of the email respondents. One, she has developed a voice; two, she sees that the responsibility for ending racism is hers'; and three, she is unconcerned with the reactions of others, but with fulfilling a personal responsibility for changing racism:

> I grew up in a small suburban town in Northern California and was one of the few black students in my class of 300 plus students. Racism for me was a black/white issue. I had experienced racism throughout my life, but never really saw myself as a racist; at that point I hardly knew that I, who was black, could be racist.

> After I took your class, it opened up my eyes to a lot of new things. Race is not a black/white issue. Race is a people issue. We all—Black, White, Asian, Latino, Iranian—have the capacity to be racist. The class allowed me to see the world in different shades besides black and white. I was able to listen and learn from other people, from different races, and learn about their experiences and see how at times in my life I may or may not have aided in the spread of racism.

> I also learned not to resent the fact that it was my responsibility to help others and part of that responsibility was being willing to dialogue, share my experiences and myself, and be open. It was very difficult at times because you think, "All I'm doing in this class is teaching other people. Why is it my responsibility?" But I soon recognized that if I want the world to change and the others in this room want to learn and want the world to change, it has to start somewhere and that somewhere is me.

> Now that I have been removed from the class I know that I carry around many of the concepts, people, and stories with me in my daily life. I have learned that I do have a voice and a right, and more importantly, a responsibility to speak up and speak out when I see something that I do not

believe in or don't want to be a part of. Before the class I would let jokes slide or derogatory comments go. Why, because everyone says them, including myself. But after the class I become much more aware of myself and the people I wanted to have in my life. I learned that it was okay to speak up and if a person disagreed with me that was okay too. I could only hope that maybe my comment would have some sort of effect on them and maybe make them think about how they treated others. (African American, female)

In the following excerpts, students are specific about who, what, when, where, and how they felt about their actual behavior that they attribute to their class experiences.

A UCLA student, who up until the class, had never noticed her father's attitudes toward non-Whites is exposed to the racist attitudes of her father during a Hawaiian family vacation. The class helped her become sensitive to comments she had never paid attention to before. She uses her voice by challenging her father even when he is reluctant to examine himself:

My dad and I have never been particularly close, but I never really noticed his approach to race and racism until after taking your class in the Honors College on Dominates and Subordinates in Public Education.

We were on a family vacation in Hawaii, staying in a high-rise in Waikiki. Hawaii is a popular tourist destination for residents of the whole Pacific Rim, so there were many Asian tourists. After a long afternoon out on the beach and navigating the crowded streets, we returned to our hotel to make dinner and relax a bit.

"Man, those Orientals just don't stop bumping into you, do they?" my dad said.

"Dad!" I glared at him. We've had conflicts over his use of the word "Oriental" before.

"Sorry. Those Asians are everywhere though!"

"So are those 'haoles'" I told him with a frown.

"Well, no, it's just . . . they're all so used to living in crowded cities that they don't even notice you there."

"Dad, the same could be said for white people from New York or London."

He spluttered and made up some excuse, and I dropped the issue because I didn't want to cause tensions on our vacation. It bothered me, though, and whenever he made comments like that I made sure to express my unhappiness with them.

Later in the month, while watching the halftime show of a football game between two historically black universities, my dad and I got into a discussion about whether is was hypocritical to have black universities and not have white universities.

"It just seems kind of contradictory to me," my dad said. "If I started an all-white university, people would burn me in effigy."

"Well, Dad, academia has kind of been traditionally white anyway, so if you wanted to go to an all-white school, just pick some small liberal arts college in the Midwest," I responded.

"That's just an old argument used by liberals for years to justify affirmative action," he said.

"But it's true! How many students of color do you think attended Harvard in 1650, or 1950 for that matter? Higher education has had an overwhelmingly white-dominated history!"

Dad looked at me with the same face he always makes when he's humoring me. "Well anyway, look at those awesome marching bands!"

I bring these stories up not so much because I said anything particularly special or was able to really change his mind, but because I said anything at all. A year ago, I wouldn't have noticed his comments. They simply wouldn't have registered as anything out of the ordinary. Today, I find myself frequently pointing out racist, homophobic, and sexist remarks and behavior when, a year ago, I would have just stayed quiet (if I had even noticed at all).

The changes created within me by this class are by no means temporary, nor are they easily dismissed. I've gone from being a highly non-confrontational person to one who has found herself in multiple arguments stemming from racist, sexist, or homophobic remarks/behavior. Does it make life a little bumpier? Sure, but I feel better about myself as well. (White, female)

A student makes a life-changing decision about whom she wants to teach and work with. Without knowing the quote at the beginning of this chapter by Martin Luther King Jr., she is making a career choice that will "enrich her spirit":

> Before I took your class I never understood what my white skin gave me. The class did that for me. I didn't like looking at that but eventually I saw that it was true. Being white gave me privilege. I had worked hard to get where I was so I never thought that I had privilege, but it was true. Once I could see that, I began to understand how I consciously and subconsciously judged others. I began to see that these judgments were a whole bunch of learned stereotypes and how I was hurting others as well as myself. I made a decision to dedicate the majority of my teaching to children of color because I believed that for the most part white children would benefit from public education. Minority children needed teachers who could provide them with a quality education. Up until the class, I had no desire to work with the students that I am currently working with. (White, female)

This next example recounts a dinner party where a Turkish-born woman and her husband are exposed to anti-Latino statements. The impact she expresses herself, by making a sarcastic comment which probably did very little to change the attitudes of the dinner guests. However, her comments spark a conversation that strengthens the bond between them to the point that he changes his behavior with his friend:

> At a recent dinner party that my husband and I attended, everyone was talking about real estate. One of my husband's friends, N..., stated that property values were being lowered by "Latinos with lots of tattoos." I responded sarcastically to this racist remark, "How dare they spoil a prestigious neighborhood like Porter Ranch!" Following my comment, there was a very tense silence.
>
> On the drive home from the party, my husband and I had a very deep conversation. I mentioned to him how your class has made me more vocal about racism. I told him that I did not care that I might upset people whenever I defended what was right and expressed disgust for what I believed was wrong and hurtful. He reported that when N... made the racist comment, he felt uncomfortable but helpless. I replied that he should not fear stating what is on his mind, even though he could lose a friend

over it. I told him that being frank about his beliefs could give him the opportunity to change other people's ignorance. I continued saying that although correcting others does not necessarily have to be argumentative, sometimes emotions get involved and that is OK. My husband does not befriend N… in the same way that he used to. (Turkish, female)

The next five examples come from everyday interactions that many of us encounter. The examples are taken from the institutions that were the learning centers for racism described in Chapters Two and Three. Each of the stories reflects the voice that students found to fight injustice and reflects their anti-racist identity.

PUBLIC

The first public example comes from a Chinese American woman who overhears two White ladies mimicking a Chinese accent. She is horrified and upset and takes some time before she speaks up. When she finally speaks, her calmly spoken words have an immediate and profound impact:

Last Thanksgiving my family and I took a bus tour in Montreal, Canada. A specific incident sticks out in my mind. The bus made a quick restroom stop, and two Caucasian women and I proceeded to get off of the bus. One of the women asked the other how long the stop was going to be. I was mortified when I heard the other respond in a stereotypical Chinese accent, "10 minah 10 minah." My shock continued as they both laughed. The comment wasn't directed towards me, but I couldn't believe that these two innocent and kind looking women could say such a thing. I always liked to believe that racist people would have "skinned heads" or "scary looking features" but the fact that these two people were so normal looking and resembled people whom I have contact with everyday, was a harsh reality check for me. Even after everyone got back on the bus, I couldn't stop thinking about what the woman had said.

I mustered enough courage to say something: "Excuse me." "Yes dear," the woman responded. Though I had the urge to act hostile and mean to her, I calmly proceeded to tell her that I had been sitting behind her at the last bus stop when she faked the Chinese accent. I told her that the comment really upset me. A look of sheer horror and terror crossed her face. Before I could say anything more, the woman put her hand on my shoulder and stopped me. She apologized profusely and said she had no right to say what she had. She promised never to say something like that again. Relieved, I thanked her politely. Your class helped me see that there are instances where people need to just be told, with the right approach, what they have done wrong. (Chinese-American, female)

The next excerpt of speaking up occurs in an upscale restaurant in San Francisco. It is written by a White woman born in Germany who notices the differential treatment given to a White couple compared to that given to her and her Peruvian friend. She develops a sick feeling throughout her dining experience, but is able to use her voice and confront the manager about the discriminatory behavior of the hostess:

I have always considered myself sensitive and embracing of differences and I would never have belittled, put down or dismissed anyone based on the color of their skin. However, I did not speak up very often when I witnessed discriminatory behavior by others. After taking the class, I have been much more inclined to confront injustice. Last year, I spent a couple of days in San Francisco where I met up with a good friend who is Peruvian. We decided to go out on the town and live it up a little. We chose to have dinner at the Hyatt Regency, Embarcadero, which is quite upscale and very expensive, but offers a fabulous view of the bay.

Several people were waiting to be seated, and we started talking to the white couple behind us. Like us, they were visiting the city and had not made reservations. Finally, the hostess called our name and took us to a small table near the door where the waiters go in and out to bring the food. I spotted another empty table near the window and asked if we could be seated there instead, but the hostess explained that those tables were only for guests who had made reservations and had specifically asked for those tables. That explanation seemed fair enough until. Just seconds later, I saw the hostess seat the white couple we had been talking to, which, as you might remember, also had no reservation, at that very same table. My radar went off and throughout the dinner, I could not shake this sick feeling which had settled like a brick in the pit of my stomach. When we got ready to leave, I asked to speak to the manager and I explained to her that I wanted to make her aware, if she wasn't aware already, that this hostess discriminated against patrons of color and that she, as a manager of one of San Francisco's finest restaurants surely did not want to be party to such practices. With that, we left. Has anything changed? I don't know, but I know that I lost that brick in my stomach. (White, female)

An Iranian male indicates his unwillingness to treat subordinates in a manner that he witnesses every day when he picks up his food:

> Three times a week, I walk to Whole Foods Supermarket in Santa Monica for lunch. Every time I get the same turkey sandwich with provolone cheese, tomatoes, cucumbers, alfalfa sprouts, and olive tapenade dressing. I could not understand why after even one month of my regular visits, the same employee would be so rude to me. She never smiled and many times ignored my request to turn around and occupied herself with something just to make me wait. Looking around, I realized the discrepancy between the customers and the employees. The Santa Monica-Brentwood area is a very affluent and well-to-do neighborhood and locals mingle among the organic fruit and tofu delicacies. More times than not I heard the huff and puff of a lady over the delay of her specially ordered sushi. Of course at least one customer fails to make the simple gesture of eye contact with the employee at the register because their cell phone conversation precedes any other priority at any one time. In contrast to their customers, none of the employees that I spoke to lived in the local area but rather traveled far distances away from their family for work.
>
> The course taught me to not only recognize where racism occurs and paintbrushes are used but also how to improve the situation. I have often found that rich people act with disregard to others. I thought back to our course and how a dangerous form of racism is the inability to recognize one's oppressive actions. Previously I would see that employee and think of her as lazy and rude. I simply assumed that her personality was a simple reflection of her low socioeconomic status. I never thought that her behavior towards me could possibly be a direct reflection of my actions. How could I expect her to respect me as a customer if I come in and throw my order at her without stopping to say hello?
>
> The following day I walked to the counter but made sure not to place my order right away. Rather with a quick glance at her name tag, I greeted Rudy by her name with a big smile. I told her it was a beautiful day and how great it is to see her every day. I expected a mutual greeting but her usual rudeness continued. I continued my efforts for five consecutive days despite her disregard. I was discouraged but persisted in my friendly greetings. One day as I was leaving the store with sandwich in hand, I felt a tap on my shoulder. Rudy had tears in her eyes and apologized for being rude to me for so long. Apparently neither she nor any of her coworkers expect nor received the respect and friendliness that I gave her. I smiled

and just asked her to keep being wonderful because it makes my day that much better.

My smile persisted for the rest of the day and everyday that I walked into Whole Foods looking for her. She started asking me about my work and I asked her about her husband and two young children. She moved shortly after I befriended her. I wanted to believe that her move was because she found a better job but she told me that as an African-American she felt uncomfortable working outside of her own community. I told her how I would miss her not for the sandwiches but that I knew there was a friendly face waiting for me every day. She started laughing because apparently I had stolen the words right out of her mouth. (Iranian-American, male)

In the following, a Korean American student was handing out flyers for a health fair and was approached by a White woman who was "so admiring of those people." The student is able to overcome her ambivalence and voices her discomfort upon hearing the phrase "those people":

I was at work at OCKAHIEC, the Orange County Korean American Health Information and Education Center. I had to go hand out flyers (about an upcoming health fair) to people in front of a Korean market. A lady (White) from the American Cancer Society had come to our center for a meeting about an upcoming Relay for Life event, and on her way out, she volunteered to help me pass out the flyers because she knew I was going alone.

Of course, passing out flyers was rather tedious, because some people ignore you; some people throw it away on their way to their cars or just leave the flyers in the shopping carts. We just began to make small talk. Then, I noticed something and mentioned that the Asians (mostly Korean) coming out from the market seemed to be happier to receive the flyer from her. I didn't know if it was because they're just so tired of students (especially from churches) handing out flyers or what, but they seemed to smile more at the lady I was with. Then, she started talking about her work and how she got to meet many Asians, as Orange County has many groups of Asians. Then, she said "I love to work with people like that," referring to Asians. I was shocked. I've met her a couple of times before, and I know she's very sweet and she loves the work she does. I know she didn't mean it, but I felt upset, not at her, but at how such things are just so engrained and that even a person as she would say such a thing.

At first, I thought maybe I should just let it go since I knew she didn't mean it. But then, after she spoke a few more sentences, I stopped her, and told her that just now, she used the phrase "people like that" and that I wasn't comfortable with it. When she realized what she had said, her shocked expression let me know that she had offended me. I explained to her that I understood and that I knew that some of us say some things that we don't mean simply out of habit and it's something the person who says doesn't notice but that it still affects the person who hears it. She told me she couldn't believe she just said that and she thanked me for pointing it out to her. We discussed how some things we say, especially when we are referring to other ethnicities, can be offensive to others and that it is important for people to be constantly reminded.

I'm glad I said something although I hesitated at first, and I'm very happy that she seemed to sincerely take in what I said. I'm usually hesitant because I'm afraid the other person will react defensively or negatively. (Korean American, female)

As we have stated throughout this book, racism is an ongoing fact of American life. In the following, a student observes the discriminatory behavior of a cashier in a fast-food restaurant. This male college graduate would have ignored such behavior prior to the class. He speaks up and finds out that making a difference, "no matter how small," can add up:

As I was waiting in line in a Panda Express Chinese fast food restaurant there was a Latino male between the ages of 30 to 35 sitting in one of the tables waiting for his food. He had ordered meals for himself and about three other co-workers who were waiting for him in a truck full of gardening tools. Giving the fact that it was between 2:00 or 3:00 pm, I figured they were taking a quick lunch break. As soon as I placed my order it seemed like the man had been waiting for his food for a long time because he keep looking at the cashier to see if any of the three cashiers would give him his food. After a few minutes, they asked him to pick up his food. Being right behind him in line to pay for my order I noticed how careless and rude the cashier was to the Latino when providing him with his food. She gave the man his food without any napkins or utensils. The man was trying to ask for utensils in Spanish. The young cashier's facial expression reflected a feeling that he did not belong in the restaurant. The man proceeded to show the cashier his bag, so she could notice that he had not received utensils or napkins. The cashier continued to ignore him even after he showed her his bag asking for napkins and utensils. The cashier knew exactly what the man wanted yet they continued to ignore his questions and his existence in this world. The cashier told him to move aside. At this point, I felt anger towards the cashier and felt very sad for that man. Here is a man who probably works his ass off and gets ignored. I saw sadness in his face and my stomach felt sick. When the man turned around with his face full of shame and an empty stomach, I stepped in and asked the cashier whether he was expecting the man to eat with his hands. The cashier did not say a word, she knew exactly what I meant and proceeded to help the Latino man. The Latino man said "thank you" to both the cashier and me. This surprised the cashier. As the man said "Thank you" I felt a sense of pride for standing up and speaking out for what is right, something I probably would have not done before. However, when I got home, I felt that it really was up to me to make a difference, no matter how small. Eventually, it will add up. (Mexican American, male)

Dealing with strangers is a bit easier than dealing with friends and family—strangers may never cross your path again and you have very little invested in the relationship. In the next section, the interventions are a bit more complicated and challenging.

FRIENDS AND FAMILY

In this first example, a young Armenian woman is exposed to stereotypical statements about Asians. She challenges her aunt and in doing so, fractures their relationship. She comments that it was about a year ago that she was racist like her aunt:

At a family gathering at my parents' house, I was sitting in the kitchen talking with my sister and two aunts. The casual question, "How's work?" directed at one of my aunts became a story, full of anecdotes and details about the problems she was facing with her clients. She suddenly began talking about how she could not stand having Asian clients because they were "so cheap." To my surprise, she used the word "all" in reference to Asians, which led me to believe that she was talking about that minority in general terms. I began to laugh at her audacity and the errors in her statements, not realizing how sensitive and intolerant I had become to racial and ethnic discrimination since fall 2004 when I first took one of Professor Rabow's classes. I began to argue, saying that since she had not met every single Asian she could not make generalizations about them. The discussion escalated and she said, "You're speaking from textbook experience, I'm speaking from real-life experience. This isn't something you learn in textbooks." I responded: "But that's the difference between you and me. You didn't go to college. I did. Whereas I'm lacking in real life experience, you're lacking in education." I think I proved something to her that day. She was shocked to see how much her comments bothered me. To this day, even after a few months later, she won't treat me the same way she used to and I feel uncomfortable talking to her. It's upsetting, but I'm glad I found the courage to voice what I felt and believed in. Just one year ago, I was just like her. Now, I am glad I have a voice that can speak out against stereotypes and hurtful comments. (Armenian, female)

Speaking out to peers is one of the more challenging struggles that students had during the class. Males who use joke telling as a way of bonding and competing are quite resistant when challenged. A White male driving in Santa Barbara does in fact confront a female peer, with no support from other peers. He knows that he did the right thing even if it may have been offensive towards his "host":

> The biggest change in my behavior that I have noticed as result of your course probably has to do with my use of language. Before your course I thought that racism was only the clearly defined action of treating certain people differently based off of some racial quality, i.e. physical feature or a cultural practice. I learned through this course and book that any thought or idea, not just physical action, which subverts one person or group of people on the basis of racial qualities, is racism. Before this class I never would have admitted to acting in any racist way whatsoever. However, with the understanding gleaned from this class that the things we say, not just do, can be racist I will plainly admit that I have committed racist actions.
>
> While growing up my friends and I would tell jokes of a racial nature that either put down or stereotyped certain ethnic groups, and one time when I was visiting some friends that I had not seen in a few years, they began to tell these racist jokes. Having just completed your course, I had a heightened sensibility towards those types of comments and I felt that I had to say something.
>
> The situation was as follows: We were driving around downtown Santa Barbara and my friend made a comment about a person on the corner, and I spoke up and said that it was not right for her to say those things. Although my other friends (who were also in the car) later told me that they agreed with me, they, at the time, told me that I was being rude to

her since she was our host. I felt somewhat embarrassed at the time for possibly having offended our "host," but I thought about it and realized that I did the right thing and that she should have been embarrassed for her negative and racist language. Instances like these help me to see how people like myself who have the privilege of being free from racism don't necessarily see the still existent forms of it. These instances also strengthen within me a will to control my language towards positive ends, as well as influence and change those around me that use negative, racist language. (White, male)

Other stories in which students confronted peers often ended up with deep changes in the nature of the friendship. Occasionally, friendships were permanently ruptured, and in other cases they were considerably diminished in intensity and frequency.

In the following example a future member of a student's family felt free to express her racist views on Facebook. This description occurred 2 years after this biracial student took the class and graduated from CSUN. Her example alerts us to the ways in which Facebook and the Internet can be used to perpetuate racism. He is biracial (Latino and White) and at first is hesitant about speaking up to his brother's fiancé. Her comments cut through him like a knife and so he does speak up. As a result, she removes him from her Facebook. A family gathering proved to be awkward as neither she nor he talked about her behavior. Despite the awkwardness created by his challenge to her, he is glad that he spoke up:

> I know that some sites, like Facebook, feel like an open forum to say whatever is on your mind (no matter how inane). But be forewarned that we all make ripples in the universe and sometimes we don't know just how close or how far those ripples go. This last July my brother's fiancé made a comment on her Facebook about almost running over some "stupid Mexicans" by a nearby Target. I was taken aback by her comment because I had never known her to make comments (at least online) about race. Then I became offended and actually quite resentful; I knew she had no way of knowing that the pedestrians were Mexicans. Dr. Rabow's class taught me many things about myself and about what I am willing to stand up for. However, I still often feel conflicted. Being half Latina and half Caucasian often means I'm put in situations where I feel forced to downplay one part of my heritage for another. But when I read her callous comment it was as if a knife had cut right through me. Here was a woman I had opened my heart to, a woman I had tried to make feel welcome because I was once in her shoes, and her comment was as if she didn't know me at all.

I had to say something, that much was clear, but what do you say to a sort-of family member where the situation is delicate? I finally decided that I would take a "play dumb" approach. I commented on her status with, "How do you know they were Mexicans?" Harmless, so I thought. The playing dumb approach totally blew up in my face. She then came back at me with a tirade about how "everyone knows" that "those people" are Mexicans. By now I was really ticked off. I had to stop and take a breath because this was definitely not going in a direction that I was expecting. She and I were going back and forth and my point was not getting across. I wrote back to her and point-blank said that I am half Latina and take offense to her comments and that she sounds racist and ignorant to me. She removed me as a friend from her Facebook that very same day. A family event came up shortly after the Facebook incident. We were both there and it felt awkward because we gave each other a quick hello and then she avoided me the remainder of the night. Ultimately I learned that as great as the internet is, it still is a tool that can be used to spread knowledge or ignorance when it comes to race. Although the confrontation was not face to face, it still had the same social affect as if it had been. Sometimes we just don't know how far our actions go, or who our words will hurt. I'm glad I spoke up. Hopefully she'll think twice about what she posts online, and I won't think twice about being straight-forward from the get go. (Biracial, male)

POLITICAL

A white male recognizes his own lack of financial privilege but the benefits of his Whiteness. Two years after the class, he uses an offhand remark made by his professor to create scholarships for needy students. The scholarships were funded and judged by students. What better way to give voice to subordinates?

> Along with this book, another resource from your course that was very influential to me was "Domination and Subordination," by Jean Baker Miller. The examples in that book helped to bring the ideas that the other students in the class were discussing to a level that was real for me. I am a white male and have had little to no experience being discriminated against for being either of these things, but these two books helped show me how my privileged traits helped me avoid such discrimination. Although I have been free from racial and gender discrimination I have been subject to other forms of discrimination such as: economical and

age discrimination. My parents had a difficult time paying for college (not that uncommon these days) and I had to take out student loans to be able to afford it.

One day when I happened to run into you (Professor Rabow) on the way to our class, you were just leaving the parking lot designated for faculty only. You off-handedly mentioned how the fact that the faculty have their own conveniently placed, rarely filled-to-capacity parking lot was a visible example of the privileges that accompany dominants. I know you were trying to remind me of the article that we had read on "domination and subordination." Although it was an extemporaneous comment, it stuck with me and after that I further saw how the academic system perpetuates a sort of economical domination over its students. During my senior year in college I was lucky enough to serve as the president of a student organization. I had many ideas as how to help the students we were designed to serve; in the end I decided to create a scholarship that was funded by students' efforts, judged by students, and, of course, available specifically for students with a particular need. This action was partly motivated by your comments coupled with the materials and classroom discussions of your course. (White, male)

WORKPLACE

In this story, a young woman tells her boss why she must leave her job. After making some "badgering comments" about her ethnicity as a Latina, he then probes whether she is sure about wanting to have a child. She is capable of not condemning all Whites as "another White racist male" but individualizes her feelings toward the racist and sexist comments of her boss:

One of the major impacts of your class has been in giving me a sense of confidence in myself and in academics. Being a low income, minority female with immigrant parents, and also the first person in my family to graduate from college, that belief in myself was invaluable. Another impact of your class, especially in speaking candidly about racism and how it is fueled, has helped me in many situations involving covert racism. After graduation I worked for a law firm for a short while. When I told my boss that I would have to quit because of my pregnancy, he became upset. During this meeting he made badgering statements about my ethnicity as a Latina. He also asked if, "I was sure that I didn't want to have an abortion." I clearly saw the sexism and racism in this statement. I refused to see him as just another "white, racist male" and believe, as I would have before, that "all these types of people are like that." I would not categorize him in the way he had categorized me. Your class has helped me to recognize and correct my mistakes in judging others. (Latina, female)

In the following, an African American woman discusses her early belief that being Christian was right and "the only way to go." She is able to discover that respect for another religion does not mean betrayal to her own. She feels that such respect and understanding make her a better Christian:

Before I took Professor Rabow's class, I never had any friends who were Muslim. Well, I dated one guy who was Muslim but we broke up due to our religious differences. I didn't want to have discussions about religion with him because I knew mine was the right choice. It's not that I hated people who were Muslims; I just knew being Christian was the only way to go. While taking Dr. Rabow's class, I had the opportunity to facilitate with a student who was Muslim. We became friends fast, and at that point, her religion didn't matter to me. I was curious about her religious practices, but I never really asked her any questions. I know she would have answered them but at that moment, I didn't feel comfortable. So I told myself if I ever meet another person who is Muslim and we have some type of relationship, I would take the time to learn about their religion.

About six months ago, I took a position at a residential treatment center for pregnant teens. I met a really cool girl named R. I knew from our first meeting that we would hit off as friends. R and I had the same schedule (working overnight) and so we were able to learn a lot about each other. One day around the second month of working together, we began to discuss religion. Well of course I am Christian and we work for a Catholic treatment center, but R began to tell me she was Muslim. Now I have never had any issues with any other religion, but I have definitely been a pro-Christian. As we began to discuss religion, I wondered would this be the dividing factor in our friendship, but then I remembered the missed opportunity I had in class and that motivated me to learn more. Once we started interviewing each other about certain practices and beliefs, we came to the realization that there were more similarities than differences. Obviously she prays to someone different than me, but her prayer was about the same concerns I had. For example she and I both pray about peace, guidance, love, grace and mercy.

Over the past four months we have been able to have mature discussions about both of our religions without disrespecting or stereotyping each other. With so much friction going on between Muslims and Christians, I am glad that we are able to have this unlikely bond. The greatest thing about our friendship is that we pray for each other and continue to break the negative cycle of religious hatred. Before I took this class, I was close-minded to other religions because I didn't want to betray my own, but now I feel liberated and free to accept and love all because that is what being a Christian is about. God is Love and I am love. (African-American, female)[1]

SCHOOL

Earlier in this chapter, an example of anti-racist behavior in public was made by a Korean American female who confronted an older White woman. In the example below, she challenges two Asian American high school students about their behavior. Although she regrets not having said more, she is hopeful that her act will have some enduring effect:

I was at the annual "Relay for Life" held by the American Cancer Society (ACS). Two high school students were helping out at the event at our OCKAHIEC table/booth as volunteer service. We were helping to go around and have the participants at the event to fill out a short survey for ACS. Afterwards, we had little to do, so we just sat at our table, handing out pamphlets when people came by. The two high school students, the boy being 16 and his younger sister a year or two younger, and I started talking about random things. We didn't know each other too well, but we had met at another previous health event and got to know each other a little bit. But they seemed to be comfortable with me, and asked me questions about college life and I asked them about their future plans. Then, the brother decided to tell some jokes. I actually cannot remember the first one . . . The second one was the classic one about Chinese. "Do you know how the Chinese name their kids? . . . By throwing pots and pans down the stairs!" Then he made weird supposedly Chinese-sounding gibberish. He seemed like a smart guy, and I was rather disappointed with what he said. He was laughing and so was his sister. I was definitely not laughing, and actually, I was trying to think what I could say to them. The sister saw that I wasn't laughing and caught me shaking my head at his joke. Then, she immediately stopped laughing and told her brother

---

1 As a footnote to the idea that Kennedy proposes about ripples creating currents, I (Jerry Rabow) cannot resist pointing out that the African American women in this excerpt had a mother who was one of the Black students who integrated the high school in Little Rock. Just as her mother created ripples, her daughter continues to move into a new arena where many more ripples are needed.

to stop. I can't remember exactly what she said, but it was along the lines of "That's so wrong! It's racist." The brother was just quiet. It probably made him uncomfortable.

Afterwards, I knew that I could have said more, but unfortunately, I didn't. I suppose I felt good that it seemed like the sister sort of looked up to me, that I may have been a role model for her. Maybe that's why I didn't say anything, because I didn't want to be the lecturing type. I wanted to be the "cool" role model. I was happy that she spoke up to her brother like that.

I haven't seen them since, but I would like to have encouraged her to stand up to her friends as well if she knew whatever they were doing was racist. And the brother . . . I would have liked to have him admit to the fact that it can hurt other people (because it's not like Koreans have easily pronounced names either). (Korean American, female)

In the following example, a former student describes how she advocates against racism for her daughter:

I always knew that because my daughter was African-American she would be faced with racism but, being a white person who never had to deal with that in my life directly, I was very reluctant to use that label for negative behavior towards my daughter. I was afraid of being accused of playing 'the race card' and in all honesty afraid that I might be less than objective simply because I naturally want to protect my child.

After about two years of listening to all of Dr. Rabow's students share their experiences in life and more specifically in school I felt more than capable of handling a disturbing situation that occurred last year when my daughter was in the 5th grade. My daughter was placed in a class with a White teacher and as usual in the school my daughter attends, she was one of the few African-American students in her class. Every year in the beginning of the school year the class is split up into different math groups. All students study the same concepts but some groups move more quickly than the others. My daughter came home very upset and discouraged when she was automatically placed in the lowest math group. I was immediately upset by this placement because my daughter's standardized test scores (which are so prized by her school district) showed her to be in the 80th percentile statewide in math. I considered this a pretty good score and while I did not expect her to be placed in the highest math group, I also certainly did not expect her to be placed in the lowest. Because of all the stories I had heard from the African-American and Latino/Latina students I had been exposed to over the previous couple of years, I was very aware of the low expectations that are placed on these students by teachers, counselors, and others in the school system. I suspected that this was probably what was happening to my daughter but because it was a new school year with a new teacher my daughter and I decided to use her goal setting conference with her teacher as a way to express interest in moving to a different math group.

My daughter made it very clear to her teacher that she desired to be challenged in math and that she did not want to be in the low math group. I also made it clear that this was my intention as well. After her first report card came and she received an A in math we were certain that the teacher would move her up. But this is not what happened. Instead my daughter started coming home complaining that she was never being called on in class when she raised her hand and also that when treats were being passed around the class room, she would often times get left out of receiving seconds. One thing that amazed me was that not only was she recognizing these things but she also was sharing these experiences and her feelings that arose because of them with another African-American girl in class. It turned out that the other girl was also feeling that she was not being called on in class and that she also was sometimes passed over when things were passed around the classroom.

Shortly after another report card came home with another high grade and again she was kept in the lowest math group I was really starting to get upset. I was still a little reluctant to do anything, not wanting to have my child labeled as the one with problem parents and certainly not wanting her to be known as the one who "cried racism." Then one day in the spring my daughter came home and told me about how she had started crying silently in class because she was raising her hand and jumping out of her seat and still could not get the teacher to call on her. When my daughter shared with me just how much this treatment was hurting her, all the stories from the students in Dr. Rabow's class and from the book Voices of Pain and Voices of Hope flooded my memory. I thought of all the students and how they all shared their pain and all wished that someone had done something. This gave me the strength to make sure that my daughter knew that someone would do something for her.

I contacted the principal and my daughter and I both shared with them our feelings. It amazed me that I was not only able to make them see our point of view, but I was also able to counter the couple of patronizing remarks that they gave me as false reassurance. When they told me "we treat all children the same" I was very clearly able to convey how much that is impossible to do and how all children are not the same and therefore each needs to be treated as a person who is a sum of their individual traits and their experiences. I was able to recommend literature that I had been exposed to in Dr. Rabow's classes to help them understand my point of view and to see things from a side that was lacking in their school district.

Another thing I was able to do because of all the things I had learned from Dr. Rabow's white students over the years was to understand that this white teacher was not doing these things on purpose. She was a caring person, a parent, a teacher, and a friend who simply had been brought up in this culture of racism in America. I understood that bringing these behaviors to her attention was going to be very traumatic for her and I made it very clear to the principal and to the teacher that I was not going to blame her or hold a grudge, but that I did need to bring this to everyone's attention so that my daughter could have a more positive experience in school. Even now with my daughter having moved up to a different grade, I look back on this experience and I feel so good about it. I know that I did for my daughter what so many of Dr. Rabow's students wish they could have done for them. I was her advocate even when it came to the tough issue of racism. (White, female)

In this next example, an Armenian woman reflects on her experiences in a class that she took 5 years ago. She has gone on and earned a Ph.D. This young woman describes the recognition of her own racism and the benefits that she receives from asserting her privilege. This recognition led her to a deeper understanding of what it is like to be a man or woman of color in our country. Her discernment of what happens to people of color allowed her to see that she herself was not a member of the "all-White club." Whereas before she was blind to the racism of Whites toward non-Whites, she now believes and feels that she is also a target. When the racism is directed at her, she seems more tentative and less sure about what to do and feels helpless. Despite her hesitation, she makes a choice to fight racism, whether it's directed toward her or others. Her choice is not always accompanied by a belief that it will change the "other." Her choice is mingled with feelings of sadness and an occasional sense of futility, and leads to isolation from friends and family. She works to empower those who have received, and will continue to receive, prejudicial statements, uninformed questions, "boundary-less" stares, and the insensitivity and cruelty that comes from dominants who continue to be blind to what is going on in America and to what they themselves do. Even so, her choice to help others is done with great resolve:

> I came into your class without realizing that I was like many white people, blind to Blacks, Asians, Latinos, and pretty much anyone who wasn't white. Ironically because I am Armenian, I too am sometimes disqualified; I am not white enough. I had enough "whiteness" to use my privilege as a benefit and would have probably continued had I not taken your class.

> Here is an example of how I used my privilege. I was working at a very prestigious Ballet School and the owner told me that she hired me because "Armenians are hard working people and that Mexicans are lazy and Blacks are thieves." As I continued working there and she felt comfortable that I would not stand up to her, she told me the following, "Only take checks from the white people. Do not accept checks from Mexicans or Blacks. They can't be trusted." She was from Holland and felt that she was superior to everyone. She was so full of anger and rage all the time. I hated working there and I can see now, after I became aware of my white supremacy, that I was racist and that I was not immune. I am sensitive to it now; I can see. I can hear. My blindfold has been taken off.

> Removing the blindfold has allowed me to see what is going on with people of color in America, has made me aware of the privileges I still receive, as well as my lack of privilege because of my almost "whiteness." Every day, I get walked over by white people. It is difficult for me to communicate how this happens but here is an example: I walk into a public restroom and there is a white woman standing at the sink. Clearly, I am waiting to wash my hands but she makes no eye contact with me; she doesn't move and almost brushes my shoulder as she moves away. I am invisible yet my very existence seems to bother her. When she does look at me, she stares at me with no boundaries. This is the type of racism that I experience all the time and is the reason why I don't like being around white people. I feel invisible and when I am visible, I am violated. Do you understand? This is all a very non-verbal experience and putting it into words is quite difficult. By writing these words, I feel like I am giving you some of my armor and that leaves me somewhat vulnerable. What is the point of my "standing up to the oppressor"? Do you really think they would really care by my one act? I am not sure. Even if the white person turns around and says, "I am so sorry," I don't believe that they actually go home and change.

White people are very educated in whom to say what to. They wouldn't dare overtly say anything to me, but I really wish that they would. That way I could really express myself. I am sure that there have been many incidents when I have said something, but I don't see a lot of significance in my "standing up" and am having a difficult time recalling those moments. I feel defeated every day, especially when watching the way our government responded to the men and women of color in New Orleans, and to the recent beatings of a black male that was just like the Rodney King affair all over again. What I do now is reach out and talk to people and seek to empower them. I work with people who may be feeling what I am feeling. Unfortunately, I feel isolated a lot of the time because my friends and family are not aware of the subtle injuries and assume that I am just paranoid. They feel very comfortable with their status and are not interested in changing from their views or behavior. They don't want to give up their privilege. (Armenian, female)

INTERNATIONAL

The following two excerpts demonstrate that what was learned in the class on a personal level can translate into efforts aimed at challenging ongoing institutions and developing new ones. It further argues for the value of personal learning that can be translated into other cultures. The first example comes from a UCLA student who is working for the Peace Corps in Ecuador:

My first class with Professor Rabow was in 2007, interested in his teaching style, I enrolled in a second class and later worked with him as his assistant. Personally, the most important lesson that I learned during this time was how I was unknowingly taught to keep silence when faced with sexist or racist microaggressions. I would like to say that I now speak up every time I hear such things, but it has been difficult to unlearn something that has been ingrained in me since I was a little girl. I'm definitely not as silent as I was before and I'm trying to, little by little, become the person I want to be and work towards equality. I'm currently a Peace Corps volunteer in Ecuador and I naively believed that being a Salvadoran-American serving in a Latin-American country I wouldn't face discrimination, but I do. The idea that everyone from the United States is white, blonde, and has blue eyes is extremely prevalent here. Being the complete opposite of those three features I've received a lot of comments such as, "but you're not from the U.S., where are you from?" or "I was expecting a real American," comments that never seize to hurt me. In discussing my experiences with other volunteers of color, I was amazed at the different comments that they've received and how unprepared we were to deal with it in a culturally sensitive manner. Thus we decided to create a diversity support group that would deal with these situations in Peace Corps Ecuador and address diversity issues with fellow Peace Corps Volunteers, staff and in the communities we serve. Fortunately we have an amazing Country Director who is supporting us in this process of establishing such group. I really believe that if I hadn't worked with professor Rabow and had realized my silence, I wouldn't be able to do the work I'm currently doing. (Salvadoran American, Female)

The second example comes from a California State University–Northridge student who lives in Canada, but does a lot of work with South Asian and Arab communities in addition to the work she does in her country of origin, Bangladesh:

When I was at Cal State University Northridge, I came across a class in the Department of Sociology taught by Dr. Jerome Rabow. The classroom was an exercise in learning and "un-learning" the intersectionality of oppressions…gender, class, race, and sexual orientation—all topics explored deeply on a personal level.

As a young woman from Bangladesh, I was deeply impacted by an incidence of woman abuse. I witnessed the impact of the dynamics of power and control within the lives of distant relatives and understood the impact it had on their children. Stories of "eve-teasing," a form of sexual harassment that makes women responsible for the harassment they receive, were ever present in the news. The notions of safety and risk became common themes in day to day activities. As well, Bangladesh was a country with an ever widening income gap between the rich and the poor, I was raised with a distinct understanding of privilege. This context became further crystallized through our class discussions where it became evident that the expectations that we shall overcome to succeed as is the American Dream is not entirely possible when our socio-economic levels are separate and unequal. Additionally, having been raised Muslim in a country deeply affected by the event of 9/11 and the subsequent marginalization of immigrants of South Asian and Arab communities, I understood constructs such as race that serve to disempower and criminalize individuals and "other" their experiences. Lastly, the notions of heterosexual privilege was introduced into my vocabulary and it became important to analyze the institution of marriage, access to healthcare, and parenthood and who exactly is allowed to observe these rights.

Ten years after my introduction to anti-racist and anti-oppressive practices, I am now working at a women's shelter working towards violence prevention and intervention in the lives of countless women and children. Having worked on legislation on the rights of immigrant women, organized migrant workers, and fought to end discrimination and hate against people of color, I have been in the trenches challenging power politics and being accountable to my community. I am a volunteer for various women's organization and have worked to found a girls school in Bangladesh. I know another world is possible and I strive to create that reality with my community every day. (Bangladesh American, female)

It is our hope that the students' voices that you have read can inspire you. Though you may not know them personally, you certainly can understand the things they stood up for and struggled against. You need not be inspired by great historical or contemporary figures or poets to stand up against racial injustice. In fact, it is probably easier to be inspired by people who are closer to you in age and experience than historical figures.

We close the book with an example of the inspiration felt by a Beatle. Paul McCartney wrote a song about the civil rights struggle for Blacks after seeing the integration efforts in Little Rock, Arkansas, on television.[2] He did not know who these students were but he saw the hatred, spitting, and name calling that the children received. He was inspired by children, just as we hope you will be inspired by these students. Years later, in 2008, in *Mojo Magazine*, McCartney explained the significance of the song: "We were totally immersed in the whole saga which was unfolding. So I got the idea of using a blackbird as a symbol for a black person. It wasn't necessarily a black 'bird,' but it works that way, as much as then you called girls 'birds'; the Everlys had Bird Dog, so the word 'bird' was around. 'Take these broken wings' was very much in my mind, but it wasn't exactly an ornithological ditty; it was purposely symbolic."

Please take the time to review the lyrics in the link below.

(http://www.metrolyrics.com/blackbird-lyrics-beatles.html)

---

2 In 1957, Governor Orval Faubus mobilized the Arkansas National Guard to prevent nine African American students from integrating the high school. President Dwight D. Eisenhower took action against the defiant governor by removing the Guard from Faubus's control, and ordering 1,000 troops from the United States Army 101st Airborne Division in Ft. Campbell, Kentucky, to oversee the integration. The nine students entered Central High School, a school with an enrollment of approximately 2,000 White students. There are a number of books that describe the integration efforts at Central High School in Arkansas.

Conclusion

Some readers may feel that we have been selective in picking journals or web-posts or that these experiences are only those of young people in California. Racism is pervasive, omnipresent, and abides in all our institutions in all our 50 states. The incidents described throughout our book are similar to those that Elijah Anderson (2011) describes in his book, *Cosmopolitan Canopy: Race and Civility in Everyday Life*. He refers to these incidents as "nigger moments." Anderson's "nigger moments" occurred to our Latino, Asian, Middle Eastern, and Native American students.

Our students were heroic. They exposed themselves to pain and committed themselves to learn about others. In learning from others, they learned about themselves. It would be a mistake on the part of parents, politicians, and educators to consider this accomplishment. Students at UCLA, Cal State Northridge, Cal State Channel Islands, and USC were eager and indeed hungry to talk and write about racism. No one had ever encouraged them. No one had ever showed them how to listen. No one had ever let them believe that it was possible for dialogue and understanding to occur. The classes illustrates that it is possible to change well-meaning people from being non-racist to anti-racist. It is also profoundly necessary.

I hope the reader recognizes that the voices in this book are gifts. They are the gifts of openness to the pain. They are gifts of our young who, despite being raised in a racist society and are still inundated on a daily basis with racism, have hope for themselves, their families, and our country. Their voices gave each other the hope that America can change. May their voices earn your respect and give you hope.

References

Anderson, E. (2011). *Cosmopolitan canopy: Race and civility in everyday life.* New York: W. W. Norton & Co.

Blumenthal, S. (1994). The Christian soldiers. *The New Yorker,* July 7, 31.

Bobo, L. D. (1997). *Civil rights and social wrongs: Black-White relations since World War II.* In J. Higham (Ed.), Pennsylvania: Pennsylvania State University Press.

Bobo, L. D., & Hutchings, V. L. (1996, December). Perceptions of racial group competition: Extending Blumer's theory of group position to a multiracial social context. *American Sociological Review, 61*(6), 951–972.

Bonilla-Silva, E. (2006). *Racism without racists.* Lanham, MD: Rowman & Littlefield Publishing Group.

Bradshaw, C. K. (1992). Beauty and the beast: On racial ambiguity. In M. P. P. Root (Ed.), *Racially mixed people in America* (pp. 77–90). Thousand Oaks, CA: Sage Publications.

Chesler, M. (1981). Creating and maintaining interracial coalitions. In B. P. Bowser and R. G. Hunt (Eds.), *The impact of racism on white Americans.* Thousand Oaks, CA: Sage Publications.

Chesler, M., & Peet, M. (2002). White student views of affirmative action on campus. *The Diversity Factor, 10*(2), 21–27.

Chesler, M., & Zuniga, X. (1991). Dealing with prejudice in the classroom: The pink triangle exercise. *Teaching Sociology, 19*, 19-22.

Clark, K. B., & Clark, M. P. (1947). Racial identification and preference in Negro Children. In T. Newcomb and E. L. Hartley (Eds.), Readings in social psychology (pp. 169-178). New York: Holt.

CNN Staff. (1998a, July 6). 3 whites indicted in dragging death of black man in Texas. Retrieved from http://edition.cnn.com/US/9807/06/dragging.death.02/

CNN Staff. (1998b, October 12). Beaten gay student dies; murder charges planned. Retrieved from http://web.archive.org/web/20051206171043/www.cnn.com/US/9810/12/wyoming.attack.02/index.html

Conley, T. D., Rabinowitz, J. L., & Rabow, J. (2010, December). Gordon Gekkos, frat boys and nice guys: The content, dimensions, and structural determinants of multiple ethnic minority groups' stereotypes about white men. *Analyses of Social Issues and Public Policy, 10*(1). doi: 10.1111/j.1530-2415.2010.01209

Cose, E. (1993). *The rage of a privileged class*. New York: Harper Collins.

Crosnoe, R. (2009). Low-income students and the socioeconomic composition of public high schools. *American Sociological Review, 74*(5), 709-730.

Desmond, M., & Emirbayer, M. (2010). *Racial domination, racial progress: The sociology of race in America*. New York: McGraw-Hill.

Diamond, J. (1999). *Guns, germs, and steel: The fates of human societies*. New York: W. W. Norton & Company.

DuBois, W. E. B. (1903/1995). *The souls of black folk*. New York: Signet.

Duster, T. (1992). *The diversity project*. Berkeley, CA: Institute for the Study of Social Change, University of California, Berkeley.

Duster, T. (1993). The diversity of California at Berkeley: An emerging reformulation of "competence" in an increasingly multicultural world. In R. Thompson & S. Tyagi (Eds.), *Beyond a dream deferred: Multicultural education and the politics of excellence*. Minnesota: University of Minnesota Press.

Dyson, M. (2005). *Come hell or high water: Hurricane Katrina and the color of disaster*. New York: Basic Civitas.

Essed, P. (1991). *Understanding everyday racism: An interdisciplinary theory*. Thousand Oaks, CA: Sage Publications.

Ezekiel, R. S. (1995). *The racist mind: Portraits of Neo-Nazis and Klansmen*. New York: Viking Books.

Feagin, J. R. (1991). The continuing significance of race: Antiblack discrimination in public places. *American Sociological Review, 56*(1), 101–116.

Feagin, J. R. (2000). *Racist America: Roots, current realities, and future reparations*. New York: Routledge.

Feagin, J. R., & McKinney, K. D. (2003). *The many costs of racism*. Lanham, MD: Rowman & Littlefield Publishers.

Feagin, J. R., Vera, H., & Imani, N. (1996). *The agony of education: Black students at a white university*. New York: Routledge.

Ferguson, A. (2010, December 27). *The boy from Yazoo City.* Retrieved from http://www. weeklystandard.com/articles/boy-yazoo-city_523551.html

Fisher, C., Hout, M., Jankowski, M. S., Lucas, S., Swidler, A., & Voss, K. (1996). *Inequality by design: Cracking the bell curve myth.* Princeton, NJ: Princeton University Press.

Freire, P. (1973). *Education for critical consciousness.* New York: Seabury Press.

Freire, P. (1994). *Pedagogy of the oppressed.* New York: Continuum.

Gerschick, T. J. (1995). Should and can a White, heterosexual, middle-class man teach students about social inequality and oppression? One person's experience and reflections. In *Multicultural teaching in the university* (p. 200). Westport, CT: Prager.

Hacker, A. (1992). *Two nations: Black and white, separate, hostile, unequal.* New York: Simon and Schuster.

Hacker, A. (1998). Grand illusion. *New York Review of Books,* June 11.

Helms, J. E. (1990). *Black and white racial identity: Theory, research, and practice.* Westport, CT: Greenwood Press.

Helms, J. E. (1992). *A race is a nice thing to have: A guide to being a white person or understanding the white persons in your life.* Kansas City, Kansas: Content Communications.

Herrnstein, R., & Murray, C. (1994). *The bell curve: Intelligence and class structure in American life.* New York: The Free Press.

Hirschfeld, L. A. (1996). *Race in the making: Cognition, culture, and the child's construction of human kinds.* Cambridge, MA: MIT Press.

Holden, J. (2010, August 12). FULL AUDIO: Dr. Laura Schlessinger's N-word rant. Retrieved from http://mediamatters.org/blog/201008120045

Howard, R. G. (1999). *We can't teach what we don't know: White teachers, multiracial schools.* New York: Columbia University Teachers College Press.

Hughes, L. (1953). That powerful drop. In *The Production of Reality.*Edited by Jodi O'Brien. Pg. 84 2005. Sage Publications. Thousand Oaks, CA.

Hughey, M. (2010). A paradox of participation: Non-whites in sororities and fraternities. *Social Problems,* 57(4), 653-679.

Hurtado, S., Milem, J., Clayton-Pedersen, A., & Allen, W. R. (1999). *Enacting diverse learning environments: Improving the climate for racial/ethnic diversity in higher education.* ASHE-ERIC Higher Education Report, Washington, DC: The George Washington University, Graduate School of Education and Human Development, Volume 26(8), 133.

Illich, I. D. (1971). *Celebration of awareness: A call for institutional revolution.* New York: Doubleday.

Iwata, E. (1994, May). Race without face. *San Francisco Focus,* 50–57.

Jablonski, N. (2006). *Skin: A natural history.* London: University of California Press.

Jackson, B. W. (1974). Black identity development. In L. Golubschick & B. Persky (Eds.), *Urban social and educational issues.* Dubuque, IA: Kendall/Hunt.

Jacoby, R., & Glauberman, N. (1995). *The bell curve debate: History, documents, opinions.* New York: Times Books.

Johnson, E. (2007, April 12). *Nightline classic: Al Campanis*. Retrieved from http://abc-news.go.com/Nightline/ESPNSports/story?id=3034914

Judt, T. (1994). The lost world of Albert Camus. *New York Review of Books*, June 23, VXL VIII, No. 9, 6.

Kich, G. K. (1992). The developmental process of asserting a biracial, bicultural identity. In M. P. P. Root (Ed.), *Racially mixed people in America* (pp. 304–317). Thousand Oaks, CA: Sage Publications.

Kinder, D. R., & Sanders, L. M. (1996). *Divided by color: Racial politics and democratic ideals*. Chicago: University of Chicago Press.

Kinder, D. R., & Sears, D. O. (1981). Prejudice and politics: Symbolic racism versus racial threats to the good life. *Journal of Personality and Social Psychology, 40*, 414–431.

King Jr, M. L. (1989). *The trumpet of conscience*. New York: HarperCollins Publishers.

Lee, A. M. (1955). *Fraternities without brotherhood: A study of prejudice on the American campus*. Boston, MA: Beacon Press.

Lee, S. J. (1996). *Unraveling the "model minority" stereotype: Listening to Asian American youth*. New York: Teacher's College Press.

Loewen, J. (2007) *Lies My Teacher Told Me*: Everything your American history textbook got wrong. Touchstone Publishing. New York, NY.

Lynd, R. S. (1939). *Knowledge for what? The place of social science in American culture*. Cambridge, NJ: Princeton University Press.

McIntosh, P. (1998). White privilege. In P. S. Rothenberg (Ed.), *Race, class and gender in the United States*. New York: St. Martin's Press.

McLaren, P. (1998). *Life in schools: An introduction to critical pedagogy in the foundations of education*. New York: Longman Publishers.

Miller, J. B. (1998). Domination and subordination. In P. S. Rothenberg (Ed.), *Race, class and gender in the United States*. New York: St. Martin's Press.

Milman, N., & Rabow, J. (2006). Identifying with the role of 'other': The pink triangle experiment revisited. *Qualitative Sociology Review, 2*(2), 1-10.

Morrison, T. (1970). *The bluest eye*. New York: Vintage International.

Most, A. (2000). You've got to be carefully taught: The politics of race in Rodgers and Hammerstein's South Pacific. *Theater Journal, 52*(3).

Nieto, S. L. (1996). *Affirming diversity: The sociopolitical context of multicultural education*. New York: Longman Publishers.

Nissel, A. (2006). *Mixed: My life in Black and White*. Villard.

O'Brien, J., & Kollock, P. (2001). *The production of reality*. Thousand Oaks, CA: Pine Forge Press.

Orcutt, J. D. (1996, August). Teaching in the social laboratory and the mission of SSSP—Some lessons from the Chicago School. *Social Problems, 43*(3), 235–245.

Pershing, Ben. (2009, October 23). Senate passes measure that would protect gays. Retrieved from http://www.washingtonpost.com/wp-dyn/content/article/2009/10/22/AR2009102204689.html

Pierce, C., Carew, J., Pierce-Gonzalez, D., & Willis, D. (1978). An experiment in racism: TV commercials. In C. Pierce (Ed.), *Television and education* (pp. 62–88). Beverly Hills, CA: Sage.

Pyke, K., & Tran Dang. (2003). "FOB" and "whitewashed": Identity and internalized racism among second generation Asian Americans. Qualitative Sociology, 26(2), 147-172.

Rabow, J., & Yeghnazar, P. (2009). Transformative teaching in the university: Uncovering and confronting racism, sexism and homophobia. In *Teaching Race and Ethnicity in Higher Education: Perspectives from North America*. The Center for the Study of Sociology, Anthropology, and Politics, The Higher Education Academy Network, University of Birmingham, UK.

Rabow, J. R., Radcliff-Vasile, S., Charness, M. A., & Kipperman, J. (1999). *Learning through discussion*. Long Grove, IL: Waveland Press.

Rabow, J. R., Stein, J. M., & Conley, T. D. (1999). Teaching social justice and encountering society: The pink triangle experiment. *Youth & Society, 30*(4), 483–514.

Richardson, T., Reyes, N., & Rabow, J. (1998). Homophobia and the denial of human rights. *Transformations, 9*(1), 68–82.

Rockquemore, K. A., & Brunsma, D. L. (2002). *Beyond black: Biracial identity in America*. Thousand Oaks, CA: Sage Publications.

Root, M. P. P. (1996). A bill of rights for racially mixed people. In *The multicultural experience: Racial borders as the new frontier*. Thousand Oaks, CA: Sage Publications.

Rosenthal, R., & Jacobson L. (1992). *Pygmalion in the classroom: Teacher expectation and pupils' intellectual development*. Norwalk, CT: Crown House Publishing.

Rothenberg, P. S. (1998a). *White privilege: Essential readings on the other side of racism*. New York: Worth Publishers.

Rothenberg, P. S. (1998b). *Race, class and gender in the United States*. New York: St. Martin's Press.

Said, E. W. (1978). *Orientalism*. New York: Vintage Books.

Sampson, E. E. (1999). *Dealing with differences: An introduction to the social psychology of prejudice*. Orlando, FL: Harcourt College Publishers.

Schuman, H., Steeh, C., Bobo, L., & Krysan, M. (1997). *Racial attitudes in America: Trends and interpretations*. Cambridge, MA: Harvard University Press.

Searle, J. R. (1993). Is there a crisis in American higher education? *Bulletin of the American Academy of Arts and Sciences, 1*, 24–27.

Sears, D. O., & Kinder, D. R. (1985). On conceptualizing and operationalizing "group conflict." *Journal of Personality and Social Psychology, 48*, 1141–1147.

Sears, D. O., Hensler, C. P., & Speer, L. K. (1979). White's opposition to "busing": Self-interest or symbolic politics? *American Political Science Review, 73*, 369–384.

Seltzer, R., & Johnson, N. (2009). *Experiencing racism*. Lanham, MD: Rowman & Littlefield Publishers.

Sleek, S. (1997, October). People's racist attitudes can be unlearned. *APA Monitor*, 38.

Smelser, N. J., Wilson, W. J., & Mitchell, F. (2001). *America becoming: Racial trends and their consequences. Volume I.* Washington, DC: National Academy Press.

Smith, P. (1990). *Killing the spirit: Higher education in America.* New York: Viking Penguin.

Sniderman, P. M., & Carmines, E. G. (1997). *Reaching beyond race.* Cambridge, MA: Harvard University Press.

Solorzano, D. (1998). Critical race theory, racial and gender micro-aggressions, and the experiences of Chicana and Chicano scholars. *International Journal of Qualitative Studies in Education, 11*(1), 121–136.

Solorzano, D., Ceja, M., & Yosso, T. (2000). Critical race theory, racial microaggresions, and campus racial climate: The experience of African American students. *Journal of Negro Education, 69*(1/2).

Spickard, P. R. (1989). *Mixed blood: Intermarriage and ethnic identity in twentieth-century America.* Madison, WI: University of Wisconsin Press.

Spickard, P. R. (1992). The illogic of American racial categories. In M. P. P. Root (Ed.), *Racially mixed people in America* (pp. 12–23). Thousand Oaks, CA: Sage Publications.

Staples, B. (1995) *Parallel time: Growing up in Black and White.* Harper Perennial. New York, NY.

Steele, C. M. (1997). A threat in the air: How stereotypes shape intellectual identity and performance. *American Psychologist, 52*(6), 613-629.

Steele, C. M., & Aronson, J. (1995). Stereotype threat and the intellectual test performance of African Americans. *Journal of Personality and Social Psychology, 69*, 797-811.

Steinem, G. (2008). My debate with Gloria Steinem continues: Race, gender & the election. *Huffington Post*, January 14.

Stewart, J. B. (1997). Coming out a Chrysler. *The New Yorker*, July 21, 38–50.

Sue, D.W. (2010). *Microaggressions in everyday life.* New Jersey: John Wiley and Sons, Inc.

Takaki, R. (1993). *A different mirror: A history of multicultural America.* Boston: Little Brown & Co.

Takaki, R. (1998). *A larger memory: A history of our diversity with voices.* Boston: Little Brown & Co.

Tatum, B. D. (1997). *Why are all the black kids sitting together in the cafeteria? And other conversations about race.* New York: Basic Books.

Telles, E. (2006). *Race in another America: The significant of skin color in Brazil.* Princeton Univ, PR, NJ.

TMZ Staff. (2006, November 20). Kramer's racist tirade—caught on tape. Retrieved from http://www.tmz.com/2006/11/20/kramers-racist-tirade-caught-on-tape/

TMZ Staff. (2010, July 27). Gibson's racist rant triggers immigration complaint. Retrieved from http://www.tmz.com/2010/07/27/mel-gibson-racist-rant-minutemen-immigration-customs-enforcement/

Thernstrom, S., & Thernstrom, A. (1997). *America in black and white: One nation, indivisible.* New York: Simon and Schuster.

Tolerance.org. (2001). Tolerance in the news, bias 101. Retrieved November 21, 2001 from http://www.tolerance.org/news/article

Van Ausdale, D., & Feagin, J. R. (2001). *The first R: How children learn race and racism.* Lanham, MD: Rowman & Littlefield Publishers, Inc.

Wise, T. (2004). *White like me: Reflections on race from a privileged son.* Brooklyn, NY: Soft Skull Press.

Wise, T. (2009). *Between Barack and a hard place: Racism and white denial in the age of Obama.* San Francisco: City Lights Books.

Wolfe, A. (1998). *One nation, after all: What middle-class Americans really think about: God, country, family, racism, welfare, immigration, homosexuality, work, the right, the left, and each other.* New York: Viking Press.

Wright, R. (2001). The ethics of living Jim Crow: An autobiographical sketch. In P. S. Rothenberg (Ed.), *Race, class, and gender in the United States* (pp. 21–30). New York: Worth Publishers.

Zinn, H. (1999). A people's history of the United States. New York: Harper Collins Publishers Inc.

CPSIA information can be obtained
at www.ICGtesting.com
Printed in the USA
FSOW04n0038180216
17047FS